Catholicism and Scripture

Rev. Msgr. Paul J. Hayes
James J. Drummey

"The Ad Hoc Committee to Oversee the Use of the Catechism, United States Conference of Catholic Bishops, has found this catechetical text, copyright 2006, to be in conformity with the Catechism of the Catholic Church.*"*

C.R. PUBLICATIONS INC.
345 PROSPECT STREET
NORWOOD, MASSACHUSETTS 02062

C.R. Publications Inc.
345 Prospect St.
Norwood, MA 02062

NIHIL OBSTAT
Reverend Joseph N. Rosie
Censor Librorum

IMPRIMATUR
+ Most Reverend John M. Smith
Bishop of Trenton
January 6, 2006

The *Nihil Obstat* and *Imprimatur* are official declarations that a book or pamphlet is free of doctrinal or moral error. No implication is contained therein that those who have granted the Nihil *Obstat* or *Imprimatur* agree with the contents, opinions, or statements expressed.

First Printing

Cover by Ariel Design
Printed in the United States of America

ISBN 0-9776099-0-1

Contents

Preface 7

1. Bible Questions and Answers 11

2. The Big Picture: From Adam to Christ 21

3. Creation, Fall and Flood 39

4. The Patriarchs: Abraham and Isaac 51

5. Jacob (Israel) and Joseph 61

6. Angels in the Bible 71

7. Out of Egypt: Moses and the Exodus 83

8. In the Wilderness: Ark and Golden Calf 95

9. The Promised Land: Joshua and the Judges 105

10. Bible Heroes and Heroines 115

11. A Unified Kingdom: Saul and David 129

12. A Divided Kingdom: Solomon and Others 139

13. Enter the Prophets 149

14. Prophets of the Exile: Jeremiah and Ezekiel 161

15. Return from Exile and the Maccabees 171

16. Villains in the Bible 181

17. The Coming of the Messiah 193

18. The Joyful Mysteries of Christ's Life 209

19. The Luminous Mysteries of Christ's Life 219

20. The Sorrowful Mysteries of Christ's Life 231

21. The Glorious Mysteries of Christ's Life 243

22. The Early Church (St. Peter) 253

23. The Early Church (St. Paul) 265

Catholic Prayers 275

Glossary 277

Bibliography 283

Index 285

Preface

The Catholic Church is *the* Bible Church. It was the Catholic Church that preserved the manuscripts of the Bible and has been their custodian for 2,000 years. It was the Catholic Church that decided which books of those in circulation were truly inspired by God and belonged in the Bible. It was the Catholic Church that gathered these sacred writings together by the second and third centuries, translated them into many languages, and protected them from being lost or destroyed. If it were not for the Catholic Church, there would be no Bible.

The word "bible" (from the Greek word *biblion*) means book, but it is actually a library of sacred writings which contains the truth of God's revelation and which was composed by human authors under the inspiration of the Holy Spirit. These writings of the Old and New Testaments are also called Sacred Scripture or the Word of God, although the latter term encompasses the entire content of divine revelation that is found in the Holy Bible and proclaimed in the Church.

While the *Catechism* says that "all Sacred Scripture is but one book, and this one book is Christ" (n. 134), it also says (n. 108) that "the Christian faith is not a 'religion of the book.' Christianity is the religion of the 'Word' of God, a word which is 'not a written and mute word, but the Word which is incarnate and living' [St. Bernard, *S. missus est hom.* 4, 11: PL 183, 86]. If the Scriptures are not to remain a dead letter, Christ, the eternal Word of the living God, must, through the Holy Spirit, 'open [our] minds to understand the Scriptures'" [cf. *Lk* 24:45].

The Church venerates these inspired writings, said the Second Vatican Council in its document on Divine Revelation, because "they impart the word of God himself without change, and make the voice of the Holy Spirit resound in the words of the prophets and apostles .... For in the sacred books, the Father who is in heaven meets his children with great love and speaks with them; and the force and power in the word of God is so great that it remains the support and energy of the Church, the strength of faith for her sons, the food of the soul, the pure and perennial source of spiritual life" (*Dei Verbum*, n. 21).

Sacred Scripture is the family album of humanity, the story of our ancestors in the Faith, but mostly it is the wonderful saga of God's never-ending love and mercy for his people. The Bible teaches us how God has worked in the lives of those whose story is chronicled from Genesis to Revelation, and how he will work in our lives. As the *Catechism* tells us, "Man is made to live in communion with God in whom he finds happiness" (n. 45).

The Bible is one volume, with one story line that leads inexorably to the fullness of revelation in Jesus Christ, who came to earth so that we could go to heaven. As *Dei Verbum* said:

> Jesus perfected revelation by fulfilling it through his whole work of making himself present and manifesting himself: through his words and deeds, his signs and wonders, but especially through his death and glorious resurrection from the dead and final sending of the Spirit of truth. Moreover, he confirmed with divine testimony what revelation proclaimed: that God is with us to free us from the darkness of sin and death, and to raise us up to life eternal (n. 4).

The Bible is not so much about when certain people lived or when and how certain events occurred, but rather it is about God's role in salvation history, the ways in which he time and again remained faithful to his people and brought good out of evil, and how he will ultimately bring salvation to those who love and trust and obey him.

The purpose of reading the Bible is to make us holy, and this goal can be accomplished only through prayer, study, meditation, and application of the lessons learned. One must read and reread Scripture to develop a love for God's word and to understand what God is trying to tell us. Passages must be read not only by themselves, but in the context of the entire Bible.

As indicated by the story of Philip explaining a passage from Isaiah to the Ethiopian court official on the road to Gaza (cf. Acts 8:26-39), one cannot interpret Scripture by oneself, but must seek sound instruction from the teaching office of the Church (the magisterium) to make sure that a passage is understood correctly. Quoting from *Dei Verbum* (n. 12), the *Catechism* says that "Sacred Scripture must be read and interpreted in the light of the same Spirit by whom it was written" (n. 111).

Keep in mind the warning of St. Peter, who said that even in Paul's letters "there are some things hard to understand that the ignorant and unstable distort to their own destruction, just as they do the other scriptures" (2 Peter 3:16).

The teaching office of the Church, said the document on Divine Revelation, "is not above the word of God, but serves it, teaching only what has been handed on, listening to it devoutly, guarding it scrupulously, and explaining it faithfully by divine commission and with the help of the Holy Spirit" (n. 10).

Why didn't God make everything in the Bible clear? Perhaps because, in the words of Pope Pius XII, "God wished difficulties to be scattered throughout the Sacred Books by him in order that we might be urged to read and scrutinize them more intently and, experiencing in a salutary manner our own limitations, we might be exercised in due submission of mind" (*Divino Afflante Spiritu*, n. 45).

Fortunately, we live in a time when there is an enormous variety of materials available to help us understand the Bible. There are commentaries, dictionaries, concordances, maps, and numerous books and articles written in a popular vein so as to reveal to the ordinary Catholic the riches contained in the Bible. Many of these resources are listed in the bibliography.

Catholics will also benefit from reading *Dei Verbum*, the aforementioned Vatican II Constitution on Divine Revelation, as well as the pertinent sections on the Bible that can be found in the *Catechism of the Catholic Church*.

Those using this text should also be familiar with four companion volumes in this series: *Catholicism and Reason* (Creed and Apologetics), *Catholicism and Life* (Commandments and Sacraments), *Catholicism and Society* (Marriage, Family Life, and Social Justice), and *Catholicism and Ethics* (Medical/Moral Issues). Each text, including this one, is supported by a leader's/ catechist's manual.

Bearing in mind the statement of St. Jerome that "ignorance of the Scriptures is ignorance of Christ," we offer this survey of salvation history with the hope and prayer that it will put the reader firmly on the road to heaven. We also offer a familiar prayer that would be beneficial before reading this text or the Bible itself:

Come, Holy Spirit, fill the hearts of your faithful and enkindle in them the fire of your love. Send forth your Spirit and they shall be created, and you shall renew the face of the earth.

The Blessed Trinity

The Trinity is the central mystery of our Catholic Faith and the source of all the other mysteries. It was Jesus himself who revealed to us that there is one God in three divine Persons: God the Father, God the Son (Jesus), and God the Holy Spirit. It is beyond human understanding how there can be three Persons, but only one God, but we accept this teaching because it was revealed to us by Jesus, who is Truth itself and who can neither deceive nor be deceived.

When we make the Sign of the Cross, we make it in the *name*, not the names, of the Father and of the Son and of the Holy Spirit, for there is only one God in the Most Holy Trinity. All three Persons are equally God — the Father is completely God, the Son is completely God, and the Holy Spirit is completely God. While they are distinct from each other, they are united in one nature or one substance. Thus, it would be wrong to say or to imply that only the Father is God, for the Son and the Spirit are one and equal with the Father.

As the *Catechism of the Catholic Church* (n. 253) says, "The divine persons do not share the one divinity among themselves but each of them is God whole and entire: 'The Father is that which the Son is, the Son that which the Father is, the Father and the Son that which the Holy Spirit is, i.e., by nature one God'" [Council of Toledo XI (675): DS 530:26].

Because of the unity that exists among the three divine Persons, says the *Catechism* (n. 255), " 'the Father is wholly in the Son and wholly in the Holy Spirit; the Son is wholly in the Father and wholly in the Holy Spirit; the Holy Spirit is wholly in the Father and wholly in the Son'" [Council of Florence (1442): DS 1331].

Chapter 1

Bible Questions and Answers

Before undertaking this survey of salvation history, it might be well to answer some commonly asked questions about the Bible. This will help the reader to understand the origins and nature of the sacred writings that have been passed down to us.

Q. Who wrote the Bible?

A. While God is the true author of the Bible, he entrusted the writing and compilation of the Scriptures to human authors who, over a period of more than a thousand years and under the inspiration of the Holy Spirit, set forth those religious truths that God wanted to communicate to us. "Therefore, since everything asserted by the inspired authors or sacred writers must be held to be asserted by the Holy Spirit," said *Dei Verbum*, "it follows that the books of Scripture must be acknowledged as teaching firmly, faithfully, and without error that truth which God wanted put into the sacred writings for the sake of our salvation" (n. 11).

Q. How do we know the Bible is the Word of God?

A. We know this because the Catholic Church, which Jesus established and guaranteed would always teach the truth, tells us that the Bible is the inspired Word of God. Here are the steps leading to that conclusion:

(1) If we look at the Bible as a collection of books about religious history, we find in existence today several thousand partial and complete manuscripts, in many languages, going back over two thousand years. A comparison of those manuscripts with each other, with the writings of Jewish and secular historians, and with archaeological findings in the Middle East shows that the Bible gives us an accurate account of many persons, places and events.

(2) If we look at the four Gospels as reliable history books (*Dei Verbum*, n. 19, says, "Holy Mother Church has firmly and with absolute constancy held, and continues to hold, that the four Gospels just named, whose historical character the Church unhesitatingly asserts, faithfully hand on what Jesus Christ, while living among men, really did and taught for their eternal salvation until the day he was taken up into heaven"), they tell us about a man named Jesus who claimed to be God and proved his claim with many spectacular miracles, including his own Resurrection from the dead. The Gospels tell us that Jesus established a Church (cf. Matthew 16:18), promised that it would last until the end of the world (cf. Matthew 28:20), and said that it would always teach the truth (cf. John 14:16-17).

(3) For about three centuries after Christ, many manuscripts were circulated as the inspired Word of God. The Catholic Church ended this confusion at the Councils of Hippo in 393 and Carthage in 397 by declaring which books were truly inspired by God. The Church at that time gave us the very same Bible that Catholics use today — with 46 books in the Old Testament and 27 in the New Testament — and that canon or list of books has been reaffirmed by several councils of the Church since then.

Q. Why are there only 66 books in Protestant Bibles instead of the 73 books in Catholic Bibles?

A. The discrepancy is in the Old Testament, where Protestant Bibles are missing the seven books of Judith, Tobit, Wisdom, Ecclesiasticus (Sirach), Baruch, and 1 and 2 Maccabees, along with parts of Esther and Daniel. Here is the background:

When the Old Testament was translated into Greek about two centuries before Christ by seventy-two Hebrew scholars (hence the description of this translation as the "Septuagint," a word meaning "seventy"), it contained all the books Catholics recognize today. But around the end of the first century A.D., a group of rabbis in Palestine compiled an Old Testament canon that excluded the seven books mentioned above.

Jews and Protestants today use this Palestinian canon for their Old Testament, although some Protestant Bibles contain the seven books under the heading of "Apocrypha," which to them means not inspired by God. There is no truth to the charge that the Catholic Church "added" these books to the Old Testament section of the Bible. They were there at the time of Jesus, who

THE BOOKS OF THE BIBLE

Old Testament

The Law (Torah)	Wisdom Books	Prophets
Genesis	Job	Isaiah
Exodus	Psalms	Jeremiah
Leviticus	Proverbs	Lamentations
Numbers	Ecclesiastes	Baruch
Deuteronomy	Song of Songs	Ezekiel
	Wisdom	Daniel
Historical Books	Sirach	Hosea
		Joel
Joshua		Amos
Judges		Obadiah
Ruth		Jonah
1 and 2 Samuel		Micah
1 and 2 Kings		Nahum
1 and 2 Chronicles		Habbakuk
Ezra		Zephaniah
Nehemiah		Haggai
Tobit		Zechariah
Judith		Malachi
Esther		
1 and 2 Maccabees		

New Testament

Matthew	1 and 2 Timothy
Mark	Titus
Luke	Philemon
John	Hebrews
Acts of the Apostles	James
Romans	1 and 2 Peter
1 and 2 Corinthians	1, 2, 3 John
Galatians	Jude
Ephesians	Revelation
Philippians	
Colossians	
1 and 2 Thessalonians	

frequently quoted from the Septuagint version. In fact, of the 350 quotations from the Old Testament that appear in the New Testament, 300 are from the Septuagint.

Q. Who divided the Bible into chapters and verses?

A. For many centuries, it was very difficult to read the Bible because there were no divisions into chapters and verses and no punctuation. But in the thirteenth century, Stephen Langton, the Archbishop of Canterbury, was credited with dividing the books of the Bible into chapters. Another three centuries went by before one Robert Etienne (also known as Robert Stephens) completed the division of the chapters into verses around 1551.

Q. What do we mean by the divine inspiration of the Holy Scriptures?

A. Divine inspiration refers to that special influence that God exerted on the human writers of the Bible that enabled them to express the ideas he wanted expressed while using their own human faculties. In the words of *Providentissimus Deus*, Pope Leo XIII's encyclical on the study of Sacred Scripture:

> God so moved the inspired writers by his supernatural operation that he incited them to write, and assisted them in their writing, so that they correctly conceived, accurately wrote down, and truthfully expressed all that he intended and only what he intended; and only thus can God be the author of the Bible.

Q. What do we mean by the inerrancy of the Bible?

A. Inerrancy means that the books of the Bible, whose authors wrote under the inspiration of the Holy Spirit, teach the truth. In the words of the *Catechism* (n. 107):

> "Since therefore all that the inspired authors or sacred writers affirm should be regarded as affirmed by the Holy Spirit, we must acknowledge that the books of Scripture firmly, faithfully, and without error teach that truth which God, for the sake of our salvation, wished to see confided to the Sacred Scriptures" [*DV* 11].

To those who would restrict this inerrancy just to those parts of the Bible that deal with faith and morals, Pope Pius

XII, in his encyclical *Divino Afflante Spiritu,* said that such an attitude is wrong. He referred back to *Providentissimus Deus* and quoted Leo XIII as having said that divine inspiration is not only "essentially incompatible with error but excludes and rejects it as absolutely and necessarily as it is impossible that God himself, the Supreme Truth, can utter that which is not true. This is the ancient and constant faith of the Church" (n. 3).

Q. What is meant by the literary forms of the Bible?

A. This means that the authors of the books of the Bible chose those forms or literary styles that were current when they wrote and that were best suited to their goal of expressing the truths that God wanted expressed. So the Bible is made up of history, biography, poetry, songs, parables, proverbs, prophecies, allegories, letters, etc. It is important when trying to discern the meaning of a Scripture passage to know what the author's intention was, what his culture was like, and the ways in which writers of that time expressed themselves.

Q. What are the senses of Scripture?

A. This refers to the four-fold sense that will help us to understand what we read in the Bible. The two general categories are the literal sense and the spiritual sense, and the spiritual sense is divided into the allegorical sense, the moral sense, and the anagogical sense. Here is an explanation of each sense:

(1) Literal sense — This is the meaning conveyed by the words themselves when we use sound methods of interpretation. All the other senses are based on the literal sense.

(2) Allegorical sense — This is when we can recognize, through stories and actual events, certain things in the Old Testament as pointing toward something in the New Testament. Thus, the Israelites' escape through the waters of the Red Sea from slavery in Egypt points toward the waters of Christian Baptism, which free us from slavery to sin.

(3) Moral sense — This refers to those events in Scripture that ought to instruct and convince us to lead a holy life. Thus, the calamities that struck the Israelites in the desert are a warning against idolatry and immorality.

(4) Anagogical sense — This enables us to view passages in the Bible as pointing toward heavenly things. Thus, the Church on earth is seen as a sign of the new and eternal Jerusalem that will reach fulfillment in heaven.

Q. What is meant by typology or the use of types in Scripture?

A. Typology is the typical sense of Scripture, whereby certain persons and things prefigure or foreshadow other persons and things. For example, Adam, Melchizedek, Moses, and David are types of Christ, as are the paschal lamb and the bronze serpent that Moses raised on a pole to cure the Israelites who were bitten by poisonous snakes. The manna in the desert is a type of the Eucharist, and Jonah's time in the belly of the great fish foreshadows the three days Jesus spent in the tomb.

The Church from its earliest years, says the *Catechism*, "has illuminated the unity of the divine plan in the two Testaments through typology, which discerns in God's works of the Old Covenant prefigurations of what he accomplished in the fullness of time in the person of his incarnate Son" (n. 128).

"Christians therefore read the Old Testament in the light of Christ crucified and risen," says the *Catechism* (n. 129). "Such typological reading discloses the inexhaustible content of the Old Testament; but it must not make us forget that the Old Testament retains its own intrinsic value as Revelation reaffirmed by our Lord himself" [cf. *Mk* 12:29-31].

The study of types makes clear what St. Augustine meant when he said that the New Testament lies hidden in the Old, and the Old Testament is unveiled in the New.

Q. Should individuals try to interpret the meaning of Scripture on their own?

A. Not unless they want to add to the confusion that already exists among thousands of Christian communities that differ on the meaning of various passages in the Bible. Catholics are blessed to have a teaching office (the magisterium) that is guided by the Holy Spirit in the task of interpreting the Word of God, whether written in the Bible or handed on through Tradition.

Sacred Tradition with a capital "T" is what St. Paul was talking about when he told the Thessalonians to "hold fast to the traditions that you were taught, either by an oral statement or by a letter of ours" (2 Thessalonians 2:15). See also his comments in 2 Timothy 2:2.

Think of Scripture, Tradition, and the magisterium as three legs on a stool. Remove one leg and the stool tips over, so all three elements are vital to a correct interpretation of the Bible. In the words of *Dei Verbum:*

It is clear, therefore, that sacred Tradition, sacred Scripture, and the teaching authority of the Church, in accord with God's most wise design, are so linked and joined together that one cannot stand without the others, and that all together and each in its own way under the action of the one Holy Spirit contribute effectively to the salvation of souls (n. 10).

It is good to keep in mind the warning of St. Augustine, that "heresies would not have arisen unless men had read good Scripture badly, and rashly asserted their own mistakes to be the truth."

Q. Has the Church ever forbidden Catholics to read the Bible?

A. The Church has always encouraged Bible reading, but in the past has, on rare occasions, restricted the use of erroneous translations of the Bible, such as those which the Albigensians published in France in the thirteenth century to promote their immoral views about marriage, fornication, and ritual suicide.

Some critics of the Catholic Church have said that her practice centuries ago of chaining Bibles in churches was an indication of her desire to keep the Bible away from the people. On the contrary, the reason for keeping Bibles chained in churches was to protect from theft the very few and very valuable copies in existence before the invention of printing.

What do those who make this accusation think when they see telephone directories chained near public telephones — that the phone company is trying to keep people from reading the directories?

Q. What are the Dead Sea Scrolls?

A. They are a collection of manuscripts, written mostly in Hebrew, that were discovered between 1947 and 1956 in eleven caves near the northwest corner of the Dead Sea at a place called Qumran. Dating from the first century before and the first century after Christ, about one-fourth of the manuscripts are from the Old Testament.

There are ten complete scrolls, including the entire text of Isaiah, and thousands of fragments from every Old Testament book, except Esther, but no scrolls from the New Testament. Scholars will continue their study of these manuscripts and fragments for years to come.

Q. What are the Gnostic gospels?

A. The Gnostic gospels are documents discovered in the Egyptian village of Nag Hammadi in 1945-1946 that were apparently written some 100 to 300 years after Jesus. These documents (e.g., the *Gospel of Thomas*, the *Gospel of Philip*, the *Gospel of Mary*, the *Gospel of Judas,* and others) present Jesus not as the God-man of Christianity, but rather as a guru and spiritual master. They don't provide any of the historical details about Christ that we find in Matthew, Mark, Luke, and John, but instead portray him as a phantom-like creature who speaks in words that only the Gnostic elite can understand.

The *Gospel of Thomas*, which has no narrative and consists of 114 sayings allegedly spoken by Jesus, begins: "These are the secret words which the living Jesus spoke." Some of the sayings are identical or similar to what we find in the true Gospels, but others bear no resemblance to the thoughts of the Jesus we know and were surely invented in Gnostic circles.

Gnosticism comes from the Greek word *gnosis*, which means knowledge, and the Gnostics believed that there were two worlds — the good world of the spirit and the evil world of matter. Thus, they were hostile to the physical realm and to the human body, and they rejected the Incarnation of Jesus, as well as his Passion, Death, and Resurrection.

They viewed salvation not as overcoming sin through God's assistance, but as overcoming ignorance through a hidden self-knowledge that only Gnostics possessed. They considered themselves superior to the ignorant masses of people

Some modern-day commentators have used these bogus gospels to argue that Jesus was romantically involved with Mary Magdalene (some even go so far as to say that Jesus and Magdalene were married), that she and not Peter was the chief Apostle, and that the Church of the first century was led equally by male and female bishops and priests.

There is no historical evidence to support these theories. For more on them, see Philip Jenkins' book *Hidden Gospels*.

Q. Do the various numbers in the Bible have special significance?

A. Yes, numbers are used in the Bible to convey certain ideas. The number three appears many times and represents unity, as in the human race stemming from Noah's three sons and the Trinity being three divine Persons in one God. The number seven signifies completeness or perfection, as in seven days of the week or when the Israelites marched around the city of Jericho seven times on the seventh day, with their priests blowing horns, before the walls collapsed (Joshua 6:1-20).

Conversely, attributing the number 666 to the Beast (Revelation 13:18) comes from the idea that, since the number six is one less than the perfect number seven, the number 666 implies imperfection in the extreme, that is, total evil.

The number twelve has to do with fullness of divine rule, as in the twelve tribes of Israel and the twelve Apostles. And forty is a number indicating trial or testing, as in forty days of rain at the time of Noah, Israel's forty years in the desert, and Jesus' forty days of prayer and fasting before beginning his public life, which is why we pray and fast for forty days every Lent.

Q. How do you answer those who claim that there are contradictions in the Bible that make it an unreliable source of information? For example, these critics point to the Resurrection accounts that have one group of women saying there were two angels at the tomb, and another group saying there was only one angel. Or in one place it says that Judas hanged himself, but in another it says that Judas fell headlong to the ground and his insides spilled out.

A. These are not really contradictions, but rather different reports from different people. Just as eyewitnesses to a bank robbery may differ on how many men were in the getaway car, so, too, one group of women at the tomb of Christ may have seen two angels, while the other group saw only one. What is important is that both groups saw at least one visitor from heaven, and were agreed that the tomb in which the Lord had been buried was empty.

Similarly, the two accounts of the death of Judas don't necessarily contradict each other. Perhaps the branch from which Judas was hanging broke off the tree, dropping him headlong to the ground and causing his insides to spill out. These inconsistencies in minor details in no way undermine the truthfulness of Sacred Scripture.

Q. What is a good translation of the Bible to use?
A. Whichever Catholic translation you find easiest to read and understand. The citations in this book are taken from the

New American Bible, which is the version used for the readings at Mass, but there are other good Catholic translations as well.

Q. How should I get into the Bible? Should I start on page one and continue to the end?

A. If you start on page one, you will run out of gas long before you complete the first five books (the Pentateuch). Just trying to get through the rituals and laws of legal purity in Leviticus, not to mention the census figures and offerings in Numbers, will discourage you. However, there are some good plans for reading the Bible that will have you alternating between the New Tesatment and the Old Testament, between the Gospels and Exodus, between the letters of Paul and John and the Psalms and Proverbs.

One good plan is that of Jeff Cavins, who has prepared a 24-week video series to illustrate what he calls a "Bible Timeline." He recommends reading fourteen chronological books of Bible history that will give a reader the big picture. The books are Genesis, Exodus, Numbers, Joshua, Judges, 1 and 2 Samuel, 1 and 2 Kings, Ezra, Nehemiah, 1 Maccabees, Luke, and the Acts of the Apostles.

Mr. Cavins says that a person can complete the fourteen historical books in about one hundred days by reading only four chapters a day. His plan, which is called *The Great Adventure*, is available from St. Joseph Communications, P.O. Box 720, West Covina, CA 91793. Their toll-free number is (800) 526-2151.

Another good plan is offered by Catholic Scripture Study International. Contact them at www.catholicscripturestudy.com.

<u>WORDS TO REMEMBER</u>

* Bible	* canon	* Septuagint
* Apocrypha	* Torah	* inspiration
* inerrancy	* literary forms	* typology
	* senses of Scripture	* magisterium
* Tradition	* Dead Sea Scrolls	* Gnostic Gospels

Chapter 2

The Big Picture: From Adam to Christ

> The LORD is our God,/ who rules the whole earth.
> He remembers forever his covenant,/
> the pact imposed for a thousand/ generations.
> — Psalm 105:7-8

Have you ever worked a jigsaw puzzle? Not a small child's version with a dozen large pieces, but rather one with hundreds of tiny pieces? Even when you have a picture of what the puzzle should look like, it is still a huge challenge, requiring much patience and perseverance, to fit all the pieces together correctly.

Salvation history is like a giant jigsaw puzzle, with hundreds of persons, places, and events spread over thousands of years, and it can seem confusing and almost incomprehensible at times. Only God knows what the entire puzzle will look like at the final judgment, but we can get a pretty good idea of how the pieces fit together so far by studying the Bible prayerfully and relying on the magisterium of the Church for authoritative guidance.

It is the purpose of this chapter to paint a simplified version of the big picture before getting into more detail in subsequent chapters. But what this brief survey of salvation history attempts to show is how God out of love has revealed and given himself to us and "has thus provided the definitive, superabundant answer to the questions that man asks himself about the meaning and purpose of his life. God has revealed himself to man by gradually communicating his own mystery in deeds and in words" (*Catechism*, nn. 68-69).

A long time ago, when the world began
Adam and Eve disobeyed God's plan.

The story of creation tells us that everything God created was good — the sun and the moon, the earth and the sea, plant life and animals — but the creation of the first man and woman was

A SALVATION TIMELINE
(All dates are approximate)

B.C. (Before Christ)

1850 — God calls Abraham

1700 — Joseph in Egypt

1700-1270 — Israel in Egypt

1270 — Passover and Exodus

1270-1230 — In the Wilderness

1230 — Joshua enters Promised Land

1225-1025 — Time of the Judges

1030 — Saul chosen as first King

1010 — Reign of David begins

970 — Reign of Solomon begins

931 — The Kingdom is divided

721 — Fall of Northern Kingdom (Israel)

587 — Fall of Southern Kingdom (Judah)

587-538 — Exile in Babylon

538 — Return from Exile

538-332 — Persian Empire

332-63 — Greek Empire

63 — Roman Empire

4 — Birth of Jesus*

A.D. (Anno Domini — In the Year of Our Lord)

30 — Death and Resurrection of Jesus

30 — Coming of the Holy Spirit on Pentecost

64-67 — Martyrdom of Sts. Peter and Paul

A calendar error in the sixth century misdated the year in which Jesus was born "very good" (Genesis 1:31). The man was called Adam because that is the Hebrew word for man; the woman was called Eve because she was to be the mother of all the living. They were created in a state of holiness, justice, and immortality.

But into the peace and harmony of the Garden of Eden came a fallen angel in the guise of a serpent. He tempted our first parents into disobeying God's command not to eat the fruit of the tree of knowledge of good and evil lest they die. Adam and Eve believed the lie of the devil that eating the fruit would make them "like gods," and they succumbed to a temptation that was rooted in pride and disobedience.

When the couple realized what they had done, they hid from God, just as we try to hide from God when we sin. God banished them from paradise and told them to expect a life of hard work and pain and suffering before they died. But he also promised to put enmity between Satan and the woman and between the devil's offspring and hers.

The Church has always seen this passage from Genesis 3:15 as a promise of a Redeemer, Jesus, who would be the offspring of the woman named Mary and who would "destroy the works of the devil" (1 John 3:8).

Things got worse after Abel and Cain so God sent forty days of rain.

The effects of that Original Sin and fall from grace became obvious in the next generation as Cain murdered his brother Abel out of jealousy because the Lord looked more favorably on Abel's offering. God had tried to warn Cain not to let the "demon lurking at the door" (Genesis 4:7) stir up resentment in him, but Cain gave in to temptation and killed his brother. How many times since then have men and women allowed jealousy to fester into hatred, and hatred into murder?

Although God sent Cain to wander restlessly over the earth, he did not abandon him, but rather put a mark (perhaps a tattoo) on him and warned that anyone who killed Cain would be avenged sevenfold.

Meanwhile, the wickedness and rebellion against God spawned by Satan became so great and so widespread that God decided to send a flood that would wipe out everything he had created, sparing only a good and blameless man named Noah, along with his wife, his three sons, and their wives.

While following the Lord's directions to build an ark to ride out the flood, Noah was surely laughed at by his neighbors, just as those today who try to follow the Lord's directions (Commandments) are ridiculed. Those who seek to put God first in their lives, to worship him every Sunday, to show respect and reverence for all human life and for the Creator's plan for sexuality can expect the disdain of the culture in which we live. But as St. Peter said when the disciples were told to stop teaching in the name of Jesus, "We must obey God rather than men" (Acts 5:29).

Throughout the Flood there was still a spark, our race was saved on Noah's Ark.

Whether the Flood covered all the earth, or only that part of the world where Noah lived, is open to speculation. What is not open to speculation, however, is that God once again sought to save humanity from its sinfulness, with the water prefiguring Baptism and the ark the Church. He promised Noah, who had offered sacrifices to the Lord immediately upon reaching dry land, that never again would he destroy the earth by the waters of a flood. He didn't say, however, that he would never destroy the world again, and St. Peter suggests that the destruction of the earth the next time will be by fire (2 Peter 3:7).

As a sign of his intentions, God set a rainbow in the sky so as to "recall the everlasting covenant that I have established between God and all living beings — all mortal creatures that are on earth" (Genesis 9:16). By this covenant and the one with Abraham, "God formed his people and revealed his law to them through Moses" (*Catechism*, n. 72). This foreshadowed a future covenant with David and the "new and everlasting covenant" that would be established in Jesus (cf. *Catechism*, n. 73).

To Noah and his sons, God gave the same command he had given Adam and Eve: "Be fertile, then, and multiply; abound on earth and subdue it" (Genesis 9:7). But the consequences of Original Sin continued to plague the human race and, before long, prideful men began constructing a tower in Babel that would reach to the heavens and enable them to play God. The temptation to play God is still a problem for humanity today.

So the Almighty confused their language, making it impossible for them to communicate with each other, and their tower project collapsed. He then scattered people throughout the world, and their disunity has continued until the present day, causing

Jesus, while he was on earth, to pray for that day when there would be one flock and one shepherd (cf. John 10:16).

Though God still cared, we were in a jam;
he made a pact with Abraham.

God intervened again in human history around 1,850 years before Christ when he called a man named Abram and his wife Sarai to leave their homeland and travel to a faraway country. "I will make of you a great nation,/" God told Abram, "and I will bless you;/ I will make your name great,/ so that you will be a blessing" (Genesis 12:2). He promised to make his descendants as numerous as the stars in the sky and changed his name to Abraham, which means "father of a host of nations."

As a sign of the covenant with Abraham, God decreed the rite of circumcision for every male child eight days after birth. That covenant remained in effect until the new covenant established by Jesus. After that time, Gentile converts to the Catholic Church were not obligated to be circumcised (cf. Acts 15:28).

The one thing missing from the lives of Abraham and Sarai (later Sarah) was children, so God provided the elderly couple with a son named Isaac. But when Isaac was twelve, God tested Abraham's faith by asking him to sacrifice the child of his old age. However, just as Abraham was about to slay his son, a messenger from heaven told Abraham not to kill the boy, and the patriarch offered in Isaac's stead a ram that had been caught in a nearby thicket.

The heavenly messenger conveyed God's approval of Abraham's willingness to sacrifice even his beloved son (just as the Father would later request the sacrifice of his own beloved Son, Jesus), and reiterated the promise that Abraham's descendants would be "as countless as the stars of the sky and the sands of the seashore" (Genesis 22:17).

Along came Isaac and Jacob his son,
these patriarchs thought the battle won.

Abraham deeded everything to Isaac, who married Rebekah and became the father of twin sons, Esau and Jacob. Although Esau emerged first from his mother's womb, which entitled him to a position of honor in the family and double the share of his father's possessions, he later sold his birthright to Jacob for a bowl of stew. Jacob then pretended to be Esau and deceived his aged and nearly blind father into giving him the special blessing that should have gone to the first-born son.

Esau was furious with Jacob and intended to kill him, but Rebekah warned Jacob to flee the country to escape the wrath of Esau. It would be many years before the brothers would be reconciled. Meanwhile, Jacob journeyed to Haran and sought to marry a woman named Rachel, the daughter of his uncle Laban. Laban promised Rachel to Jacob if he would serve him for seven years, but after seven years, Laban deceived Jacob and married him to Rachel's older sister, Leah. A week later, Jacob also maried Rachel and worked another seven years for his uncle.

Jacob eventually had twelve sons and, after a struggle one night with an angel, his name was changed to Israel. He passed on to his sons the blessing he had received from Isaac, and they became the leaders of the twelve tribes of Israel. Of all Jacob's sons, Joseph was his favorite, much to the dismay of his brothers, who were jealous of him and who, when the opportunity arose, sold Joseph into slavery in Egypt for twenty pieces of silver (Jesus would be sold for thirty pieces of silver) and told Jacob that he had been killed by a wild animal.

The story of Joseph is one of the most fascinating stories in the Bible and a good example of how God can bring good out of evil. Joseph's skill as an administrator and his ability to interpret dreams so impressed Pharaoh, the king of Egypt, that he put Joseph in charge of all the land and crops in Egypt. By storing up grain during the abundant years, Joseph was able to provide food for the people during the years of famine.

So it was that some of Joseph's brothers came down to Egypt to obtain food for their starving people back home. They did not recognize Joseph, but he recognized them and, after putting them through some anxious moments, finally revealed his identity to them. Joseph then arranged for Jacob, his brothers, and their extended family to move to Egypt, where they lived in peace and prosperity for many years.

But then came slavery under Pharaoh's hand
'til Moses led them to the Promised Land.

It wasn't long after Joseph's death that a new Pharaoh, who had never heard of Joseph, began to persecute and enslave the Israelites. After many years of hardship and oppression, God heard the cries of his people and raised up a man named Moses to lead them back to the Promised Land. Like Jesus, Moses as a baby had escaped death at the hands of an evil ruler and eventually saved God's people from slavery in Egypt, just as Jesus would come out of Egypt with Mary and Joseph and eventually lead all people away from their slavery to sin.

Moses was an unlikely and unwilling instrument of the Lord at first, but with the constant and unwavering assistance of God, he was able to lead the people of Israel through forty years of trials and temptations in the desert to the borders of Canaan, the Promised Land. An outstanding event on their journey, and one of the most important events in the Book of Exodus, as well as the entire Old Testament, was the Passover, where God struck down the oldest child in each family in Egypt as a final warning to Pharaoh to let his people go.

The oldest child in the Israelite households was spared after the blood of the lamb was smeared over the doors of the houses, and the Lord passed over those homes. This was a great foreshadowing of Jesus, the Lamb of God, whose blood shed on the cross would make it possible for all humanity to escape the everlasting death of sin.

Once the people passed miraculously through the waters of the Red Sea and escaped their Egyptian pursuers, they should have reached the Promised Land in a matter of months. But their continual apostasy, their continual rebellion against God, and their continual refusal to put aside false gods and to love the true God with all their hearts, minds, and souls kept them wandering in the desert for forty years.

God established still another covenant at Mount Sinai by giving Moses the Ten Commandments, but the people turned back to the gods of Egypt and worshiped a golden calf. When Moses came down from Sinai with the tablets on which the Commandments had been inscribed, his face was radiant, just as the body of Jesus became radiant during his Transfiguration on the mountain as he conversed with Moses and Elijah about his coming Death in Jerusalem (cf. Luke 9:28-36).

Despite their apostasy and ingratitude, however, God still watched out for the people of Israel. He guided them with a cloud by day and fire by night. When they complained about hunger and thirst, God gave them water from a rock and a special food called manna from heaven, which was a foreshadowing of the Holy Eucharist, the true bread from heaven that is Jesus.

Though Moses had for years tried to act as God's spokesman to his "stiff-necked people," he would not be privileged to set foot in the Promised Land because he had on one occasion showed a lack of trust in God. The Lord had told him to order a rock to give forth water, but Moses, in a moment of doubt, instead struck the rock twice with Aaron's staff.

So God sent Joshua and the Judges too to guide his people as Israel grew.

The task of leading the people of Israel into the Promised Land of Canaan fell to Moses' successor Joshua, whose name meant "Yahweh saves" and who was a type of Jesus. He conquered the land of Canaan, beginning with the famous overthrow of the city of Jericho, whose walls came tumbling down. The extermination of the Canaanites to make room for Israel may seem unfair and even wrong, but it was tolerated to fulfill the promise made to Abraham and because the holiness of Israel would have been threatened by the sinfulness of the Canaanites.

The Israelites should not have been able to conquer the militarily powerful Canaanites, but God was on their side. When Israel obeyed God, it triumphed; when it disobeyed God, it suffered military disaster.

Following the death of Joshua, God raised up twelve Judges to settle the land and guide his people. They were not judicial authorities as such, but rather military commanders sent to protect the nation from its enemies, and the best known of them were Barak, Gideon, and Samson. Samson, who had taken a Nazarite vow not to cut his hair, drink wine, or touch a corpse, was a type of John the Baptist.

Throughout the books of Joshua and Judges, we find what some have called the cycle of sin, whereby the sinfulness of the people was followed by slavery, suffering, and salvation before the cycle started all over again. Others describe the cycle as one of sin, punishment, repentance, and liberation. But whatever words are used, the pattern is one that continues to plague the human race down to the present time.

Yet still they sinned and they complained when Kings David and Solomon reigned.

The people of Israel were not happy with God as their sovereign, so they asked for a king to rule over them. God told the prophet

Samuel to grant their request, but also to warn them that a king would force their sons into military service, make them do his plowing and harvesting, take the best of their crops for his own officials, and ultimately make both males and females his slaves.

The people refused to listen to Samuel's warning and demanded that they be like other nations in having a king to rule them and lead them into battle. So Samuel anointed Saul the first king of Israel around the year 1030 B.C. But Saul was not the king he could have been; he often failed to trust God completely and frequently turned away from him.

God informed Samuel of his displeasure with Saul and told him to go to Bethlehem and anoint one of the sons of Jesse as the successor of Saul. That son, who was just a shepherd boy at the time, was David. He slew the Philistine giant Goliath and joined the staff of Saul, but Saul was extremely jealous of David and even sought to kill him.

However, David repeatedly escaped Saul's wrath, even passing up an opportunity to kill the king, and finally succeeded him after Saul and his sons were killed in battle with the Philistines. Warfare continued between the families of Saul and David, but David finally prevailed and began his 40-year reign (1010-970) over the nation of Israel by bringing the Ark of the Covenant to Jerusalem, making the city both the religious and political capital of Israel.

Though David sinned terribly by committing adultery with Bathsheba and having her husband killed, he later repented of his sins and became the greatest of Israel's kings and a spiritual prototype of Jesus, who also came from Bethlehem and would establish an everlasting kingdom. That is why Jesus would be called Son of David, although he was far superior to David.

David was succeeded as king by his son Solomon, who also ruled for almost forty years (970-931) and erected the magnificent temple in Jerusalem. The reign of Solomon got off to a good start as he used well the wisdom and understanding that God had granted him. But then he turned away from God, multiplying wives and concubines and gold and silver and bringing in foreign religions that led the people away from the true God.

It was Solomon's misrule that set the stage for a series of mostly bad kings, for the division of Israel into two kingdoms, and for the eventual fall of Jerusalem and the exile of the Israelite nation.

On many kings God did not smile,
first came division and then exile.

Solomon's oppressive rule was continued by his son Rehoboam, and this led to a revolt by Jereboam and division of the nation into the Northern Kingdom of Israel (with ten tribes) and Southern Kingdom of Judah (with two tribes). There was no link to David in the North since Jereboam was not of the royal family, so the lineage of David would be continued in the South.

Things got very confusing over the next two centuries, with nineteen kings and nine successive family dynasties in the North and twenty kings and one family dynasty in the South. Not surprisingly, the enemies of Israel took advantage of this division. First, the Assyrians conquered the North in 721 B.C. and deported its leading officials. They invaded Judah, but did not capture Jerusalem at that time.

When Assyrian power declined, the Babylonians took their place and, under Nebuchadnezzar, captured Jerusalem in 597 and deported King Jehoichin and his leading citizens to Babylon. Nebuchadnezzar destroyed Jerusalem in 587 and deported the rest of the populace to Babylon. Israel had gone from the height of power and splendor under David and Solomon to the depths of ruin and destruction and exile.

So God sent prophets to prepare the way
for the Messiah who would come some day.

As we have seen, God continually showed his love and concern for his people by raising up spiritual and political leaders to guide them. He also raised up great prophets, men from all walks of life who not only predicted the future, but more importantly called people back to God and to a holy life. We will have more to say about individual prophets in later chapters, but for now let's just mention some of those who preached before and during the exile.

Amos and Hosea (formerly known as Osee) were the prophets of the Northern Kingdom, with Amos prophesying that the destruction of Israel would not be total, that a remnant would survive. His predictions would be cited by St. Stephen just before his martyrdom (cf. Acts 7:42-50). Hosea was the last prophet before the fall of the North, and he compared Israel's infidelity to the Lord to his own failed marriage. He said that God would use the exile as a period of purification and then take Israel back as his spouse, just as Hosea had taken his wife Gomer back.

Isaiah and Micah were contemporaries in Jerusalem in the eighth century, and Isaiah prophesied in 701 that Yahweh would protect Jerusalem from the Assyrian armies. His prophecy came true as the Assyrians marched up to the walls of Jerusalem and then turned around and left.

Micah predicted that the unfaithful would suffer desolation, but also that God would bring forth a new king, one who would come from Bethlehem (cf. Micah 5:1) and would gather his people together again. It was this prophecy that led the Magi to Bethlehem at the time Jesus was born.

Jeremiah was in Jerusalem when it fell to the Babylonians in 597. He was allowed to remain there after many citizens were deported, and he finally fled to Egypt with other refugees in 582. He is a type *par excellence* of Jesus in that he remained celibate at God's command and was put to death by those to whom he preached. What happened to Jeremiah, Jerusalem, the Temple, and the Babylonians parallels what happened to Jesus, Jerusalem, the Temple, and the Romans.

Ezekiel preached to the people in exile. His famous "dry bones" vision (cf. 37:1-14) told them that God would breathe new life into Israel and return the exiles to Jerusalem. The vision also foreshadowed the resurrection of the body. The prophet is further noted for his parables of the good shepherd (34:1:31), the replacement of our "stony hearts" with natural hearts (36:26), and the waters of new life flowing from the Temple (47:1-12).

As the prophets had foretold, the people of Israel were allowed to return from exile in 538 by the Persian King Cyrus, and they were able to rebuild the Temple under the guidance of Ezra and Nehemiah and with the benevolence of Cyrus and his successor Darius I. God has a way of using worldly rulers to help carry out his plans.

The centuries leading up to the coming of the Messiah had been foreseen by the prophet Daniel, who in a dream saw four kingdoms arising on earth, those of Babylon, Persia, Greece, and Rome. He saw the last of these kingdoms being overcome by "One like a son of man coming,/ on the clouds of heaven" whose "dominion is an everlasting dominion/ that shall not be taken away,/ his kingship shall not be destroyed" (Daniel 7:13-14).

Jesus would associate this prophecy with himself during his trial before the Sanhedrin (Mark 14:62).

And then one night, after years of them,
Christ was born in Bethlehem.

After thousands of years of waiting, and hundreds of prophecies in the pages of the Old Testament, the "fullness of time" had arrived for the Messiah to appear on the scene. However, this long-awaited and anxiously anticipated event did not occur in a palace in one of the major cities in the world, but rather in a cave in the obscure town of Bethehem in the hills of Judea.

The birth of this new and everlasting King was not witnessed by earthly kings and their courts, but by a teenage mother and her husband, a few animals, and some shepherds. There were no news reporters or television cameras to herald the coming of the Messiah, only some angels giving glory to God.

Yet no greater or more earth-shaking event had ever happened, or would ever happen, in the entire history of the human race than the Incarnation of Jesus, when God the Son took on human flesh and, for some thirty-three years, taught us how to live if we wished to enjoy eternal life in heaven.

His mother Mary was the new Eve because she had said yes to God the Father, unlike Adam's wife. Jesus was the new Adam because what Adam had lost at the tree in the Garden of Eden, Jesus would win back on the tree of the cross. The shadow of the cross was there in Bethlehem as one of the Magi gave the newborn Child a gift of myrrh, a burial ointment indicating that suffering would be a part of this Child's life.

His life was threatened immediately by a king named Herod, who had heard about the birth of this new King and who sought to eliminate all rivals. But an angel warned Joseph to take Mary and Jesus into Egypt to escape the slaughter of all male children under the age of two in the region of Bethlehem. God then brought his Son out of Egypt after Herod had died, just as he had brought the Israelite people out of Egypt thirteen hundred years earlier.

Mary and Joseph settled in the Galilean town of Nazareth upon their return from Egypt, and Jesus grew up there, working as a carpenter with his foster father and advancing in "wisdom and age and favor before God and man" (Luke 2:52). The only event in his young life that has been recorded for us is the time when he was twelve years old and remained behind in the Temple in Jerusalem, listening to the religious leaders, asking them questions, and astounding them with his understanding and answers. He would astound them again twenty years later.

He was God's Son, he was God's Word,
he spread God's love to all who heard.

Around the age of thirty, Jesus began his public life by spending forty days praying and fasting in the desert, where he would repel three temptations by Satan to turn away from his mission of saving the world from its sins. His cousin John the Baptist paved the way for Jesus by recalling the prophecy of Isaiah to "prepare the way of the LORD!" (Isaiah 40:3), by calling him "the Lamb of God, who takes away the sin of the world" (John 1:29), and by telling his own disciples: "He must increase; I must decrease" (John 3:30).

There were those at the time of our Lord, just as there are many today, who thought of Jesus as just a good man, and they refused to recognize him as God. The problem with that attitude is that Jesus said he was God on many occasions, and proved it by fulfilling scores of prophecies about the Messiah from the Old Testament and performing dozens of recorded miracles.

If Jesus were not the God he claimed to be, then he was either a liar or a lunatic, which means he could not have been a good man. But everything we know about him shows him to have been an extraordinarily good man. He was a skilled debater who defeated every attempt to trip him up or to make him look foolish and a spellbinding storyteller who got his message across with parables about good shepherds and good Samaritans and runaway sons, about fishermen, farmers, laborers, tax collectors, and hypocritical religious leaders.

The Son of God preached a strong moral code, one that called for keeping the Ten Commandments, demonstrating love first of all for God and then for others and even for enemies, treating others the way we would want to be treated ourselves, and reaching out to the least of our brothers and sisters, those who are hungry or naked or thirsty, sick or in prison or homeless.

Jesus' perfect humanity was illustrated by his desire to do the will of his Father. "In Christ, and through his human will," says the *Catechism* (n. 2824), "the will of the Father has been perfectly fulfilled once for all. Jesus said on entering into this world: 'Lo, I have come to do your will, O God' " [Heb 10:7; Ps 40:7]. So, too, in his Agony in the Garden, Jesus prayed, "not my will but yours be done" (Luke 22:42).

Doing the will of his Father encompassed Jesus' compassion and tenderness for the sick and suffering, his mercy and forgiveness toward sinners, but also his courage and fearlessness when facing down those who would turn the Temple into a den of thieves or who would impose heavy burdens on the people while they themselves lived an easy life. No man with all of these virtues and admirable qualities could possibly be a liar or a lunatic. Jesus' flawless personality, which stems from his relationship with the Father and the Holy Spirit, is one of the strongest arguments for his claim to be a divine messenger and the Messiah.

But Jesus was more than just an extraordinary man; he was also God. Unlike any other man in history, he demonstrated this by fulfilling prophecies that pertained to the Messiah. He was born in Bethlehem (Micah 5:1) of a virgin mother (Isaiah 7:14). Kings came to adore him (Psalm 72:10), he was betrayed for thirty pieces of silver (Zechariah 11:12-13), his hands and feet were pierced with nails (Isaiah 53:5), and he was led like a sheep to the slaughter (Isaiah 53:7).

But Jesus showed his divinity even more with spectacular miracles that could only be performed by a messenger from God or by God himself. How else could Jesus have changed water into wine, walked on water, calmed the wind and the sea, fed thousands with a handful of loaves and fishes, cured people of all kinds of ailments, and even raised three persons from the dead if he were just another preacher or prophet? He was indeed the Christ, the anointed one sent by God to save the world.

He died for women, he died for men.
On Easter morn, he rose again.

The Passion and Death of Jesus on Good Friday is one of the best-known events in human history, and the cruelty of his Crucifixion was dramatically portrayed in the Mel Gibson movie, *The Passion of the Christ*. Viewers of that movie realized perhaps for the first time the depths of Jesus' love for humanity and the unbelievable horror of sin.

Fortunately for the world, the story of Jesus did not end on Good Friday. If it had, he would have been just another victim of the Roman Empire and would not have earned even a footnote in history. The reason why we know of Jesus today, and the pillar on which our whole religion rests, is the Resurrection of Jesus on Easter Sunday morning. By walking out of his grave and overcoming the power of death, the Lord foreshadowed the resurrection of our bodies at the end of the world.

There are many who believe that Jesus died on the cross, but do not think he rose from the dead. However, there are good reasons to believe, such as the fact that the tomb was empty on Sunday morning and no corpse was ever found, that Jesus was seen over the next forty days by more than 500 people, and that the Apostles who had abandoned Jesus on Good Friday now were willing to go out and die in order to spread his teachings and to persuade the world that he had risen from the dead.

People are not willing to sacrifice their lives for a lie, but they might be willing to die for the truth, for their belief in the words of Jesus that those who die in his friendship will enjoy eternal communion with God in heaven.

He started a Church with Peter and Paul and promised his Church would never fall.

When Jesus changed Simon's name to Peter and gave him the keys to the kingdom of heaven, he said that the gates of hell would never prevail against his Church, and he promised to back up in heaven whatever decisions Peter and his successors made on earth (cf. Matthew 16:13-19). On another occasion, Jesus asked Peter to "feed my sheep" (John 21:17), recalling again the image of the good shepherd who feeds his flock the solid food of truth and not the poison of error.

But it wasn't until Christ sent the Holy Spirit down on the Apostles on Pentecost that Peter and the others were given the Spirit's gifts of wisdom, understanding, knowledge, and fortitude to help them spread the Kingdom of God throughout the hostile Mediterranean world. This Holy Spirit, "whom Christ the head pours out on his members," says the *Catechism,* "builds, animates, and sanctifies the Church. She is the sacrament of the Holy Trinity's communion with men" (n. 747).

The Church of Christ has survived for 2,000 years and has prevailed over all kinds of hostility from without and sinfulness from within. She will continue to do so, not because she is lucky or wealthy or powerful, but because she was founded by the Son of God himself and promised his protection until the end of the world (cf. Matthew 28:20), and because she is guided by the Holy Spirit. "From the beginning to the end of time, whenever God sends his Son," says the *Catechism*, "he always sends his Spirit: their mission is conjoined and inseparable" (n. 743).

SALVATION HISTORY

A long time ago, when the world began
Adam and Eve disobeyed God's plan.

Things got worse after Abel and Cain,
so God sent forty days of rain.

Throughout the Flood there was still a spark,
our race was saved on Noah's Ark.

Though God still cared, we were in a jam.
He made a pact with Abraham.

Along came Isaac and Jacob his son,
these patriarchs thought the battle won.

But then came slavery under Pharaoh's hand
'til Moses led them to the Promised Land.

So God sent Joshua and the Judges too
to guide his people as Israel grew.

Yet still they sinned, and they complained
when Kings David and Solomon reigned.

On many kings God did not smile,
first came division and then exile.

So God sent prophets to prepare the way
for the Messiah who would come some day.

And then one night, after years of them,
Christ was born in Bethlehem.

He was God's Son, he was God's Word,
He spread God's love to all who heard.

He died for women, he died for men,
on Easter morn, he rose again.

He started a Church with Peter and Paul
and promised his Church would never fall.

If Jesus were here, this is what he'd say,
love God and others every single day.

Confess your sins and grace will flood,
be sure you eat my Body and Blood.

And go to church, make sure you pray,
you'll get to heaven with little delay.

Now some folks sing, and some folks can't,
and this sure isn't Gregorian chant.

But my good friends, please take it from me,
it is salvation history!

The temptation in the Garden of Eden.

Chapter 3

Creation, Fall and Flood: From Adam to Noah

> When I see your heavens, the work of your fingers,
> the moon and stars that you set in place —
> What are humans that you are mindful of them,
> mere mortals that you care for them?
> — Psalm 8:4-5

When the first missions to outer space took place in the 1960s, they captured the imagination of millions of people around the globe. The very idea of landing on the moon, the competence and bravery of those first astronauts, were taken out of the realm of science fiction and put in the real world. As the first crew approached the surface of the moon, the world waited to hear their first words. From space came the message — old, old words now thrillingly new: "In the beginning God created heaven and earth." Imagine, men of science quoting the first line of the Bible!

Of course, there can be no conflict between scientific truth and religious truth since God is the author of both. But what happened in the beginning? To find that out, we must look at the first eleven chapters of the Book of Genesis. Some have sought to characterize these chapters as mythical or fictional stories, but the Catholic Church teaches otherwise.

Addressing this issue in his 1950 encyclical *Humani Generis,* Pope Pius XII conceded that the eleven chapters do not conform to modern historical methods, but he said that they "do nevertheless pertain to history in a true sense" in that they use "simple and metaphorical language adapted to the mentality of a people little cultured" in order both to state "the principal truths which are fundamental for our salvation, and also to give a popular description of the origin of the human race and the Chosen People" (n. 38).

The Holy Father said that "whatever of the popular narrations have been inserted into the Sacred Scriptures must in no way be considered on a par with myths or other such things, which are more the product of an extravagant imagination than of that striving for truth and simplicity which in the Sacred Books, also of the Old Testament, is so apparent" (n. 39).

Echoing Pius XII forty-two years later, the *Catechism of the Catholic Church* (n. 390) said that "the account of the fall in Genesis 3 uses figurative language, but affirms a primeval event, a deed that took place *at the beginning of the history of man* [cf. *GS*13.1]. Revelation gives us the certainty of faith that the whole of human history is marked by the original fault freely committed by our first parents" [cf. Council of Trent: DS 1513; Pius XII: DS 3897; Paul VI: AAS 58 (1966), 654].

Whatever figurative language or popular narrations were used by the author of Genesis, Catholics are required to believe the following truths:

(1) God created everything out of nothing, and everything he created was good. God is in no way responsible for evil, but he permits evil to exist because he respects the free will of his creatures and because, in some mysterious way that we will not understand until the next life, he is able to bring good out of evil, for example, our redemption through Jesus' Death on the cross.

(2) He created the first man and woman in a special way, and Adam and Eve enjoyed not only friendship with God, but also a state of holiness, justice, and immortality.

(3) Our first parents disobeyed God's command at the instigation of Satan and lost their original holiness and their harmony with each other and with creation, and brought death into human history.

(4) Because we are descendants of Adam, Original Sin is transmitted to us. It is not a personal fault of ours, but rather a deprivation of original holiness and justice. Human nature is not totally corrupted or depraved, as some have suggested, but it is weakened and prone to sin. Baptism takes away Original Sin, but we must wage a constant spiritual battle to overcome the effects of this sin.

(5) God promised a Redeemer (Genesis 3:15), a promise that was fullfilled in Jesus. In the words of the evangelist: "For God so loved the world that he gave his only Son, so that everyone who believes in him might not perish but might have eternal life" (John 3:16).

The Days of Creation

Although the work of creation is usually attributed solely to God the Father, the Church teaches that it was the combined action of the Father, Son, and Holy Spirit (cf. *Catechism*, nn. 291, 316). Everything was made out of nothing by God (cf. John 1:1-3), but through the Son (cf. Colossians 1:16-17) and with the Spirit, whom the Nicene Creed says is "the giver of life."

Genesis describes the creation of the world as having taken place over six days, but Genesis is not about the when and the how of creation, but rather the who (God and us) and the why (to share his love and his glory with us). "In the creation of the world and of man," says the *Catechism*, "God gave the first and universal witness to his almighty love and his wisdom, the first proclamation of the 'plan of his loving goodness,' which finds its goal in the new creation in Christ" (n. 315).

So while the language may be symbolic and figurative, the order of creation shows a hierarchy from the less perfect to the more perfect. Thus, plants and vegetative life, and animals and birds and sea creatures, are subordinate to man, who is the summit of God's creation, the only creature willed by God for its own sake. And while we are given dominion over creation, we are to be good stewards of what God has made available to us.

The earth was a dark and formless and lifeless wasteland until God replaced chaos with order and harmony. He brought light where there was darkness, separated the oceans from the land, and filled the earth with all kinds of plants and trees, animals, birds, and creeping things — and he saw how good all of this was.

But it wasn't until

> God created man in his image;
> in the divine image he created him;
> male and female he created them.
> — Genesis 1:27

that he found all of his creation "very good" (Genesis 1:31). What higher compliment could be paid to human beings than to be made in the image of the Creator himself? Of course, this does not mean that we image God physically, since he is a spirit, but rather that we image him in our spiritual nature.

We image our God in our ability to think, to choose, and to love. We have been given the power to seek the truth with our reason and intellect, to make good moral choices using the grace and guidance God provides us, and to love God and others in the same selfless manner that Jesus did. Who better to imitate than Jesus, whom St. Paul calls "the image of the/ invisible God" (1 Colossians 1:15)?

Just as in the sacrament of Baptism the visible sign of water, for example, illustrates the invisible reality of Original Sin being washed away, so, too, the visible Jesus shows us the reality of the invisible Father. What was Jesus' response when the Apostle Philip asked him to show them the Father? The Lord replied: "Have I been with you for so long a time and you still do not know me, Philip? Whoever has seen me has seen the Father" (John 14:9).

Scripture tells us that on the seventh day God rested. This does not mean that God was tired and needed rest, but rather that we need to rest from our labors and to devote one day of the week to the worship of the One who brought us into existence and who in his providence watches over us 365 days a year.

For the people of Israel, the seventh day of the week was Saturday, so that became their day of rest and worship. But because Jesus rose from the dead on Sunday, the early Church began celebrating the Lord's Day on the first day of the week (cf. Acts 20:7) and has continued that practice for 2,000 years.

The First Man and Woman

The second chapter of Genesis gives us more information about the creation of Adam and Eve and provides us with the origins of marriage. After Adam had been formed out of the clay of the ground and life had been breathed into him (the only other time the Bible mentions God breathing on humans is on Easter Sunday night, when Jesus breathed on the Apostles before giving them the power to forgive sins — cf. John 20:22), God commissioned him to care for the Garden of Eden.

God told Adam that he was free to eat from all the trees in the garden, "except the tree of knowledge of good and bad. From that tree you shall not eat; the moment you eat from it you are surely doomed to die" (Genesis 2:17). The Creator had invited Adam to name all the animals and to seek companionship with them, but none of them were suitable companions for him.

"It is not good for the man to be alone," said God. "I will make a suitable partner for him" (Genesis 2:18). He cast Adam into a deep sleep, took out one of his ribs, and built that rib into a woman. When he brought the woman to him, Adam exclaimed with delight:

> "This one, at last, is bone of my bones
> and flesh of my flesh;
> This one shall be called 'woman,'
> for out of 'her man' this one has been taken."
> — Genesis 2:23

The symbolism of this account is very important for it shows the equal dignity of man and woman. Eve was taken from a rib of Adam to show her closeness to his heart and her place at her husband's side as his loving companion. There was no tension between them as indicated by Adam's joy at the sight of his partner, and God established the marriage covenant with the familiar words one still hears today at weddings:

> That is why a man leaves his father and mother
> and clings to his wife, and the two of them
> become one body.
> — Genesis 2:24

In the next verse, the author of Genesis makes the important observation that "the man and his wife were both naked, yet they felt no shame." Some commentators have interpreted the nakedness of Adam and Eve as evidence that their sin involved sex, but that is not true. They were not ashamed of their nakedness at first because they saw each other as persons to be loved and their sexual desire as a free, sincere, and total gift to each other.

But once they rebelled against God, their sexual desire became self-seeking and they viewed each other as objects to be used for sexual pleasure, thus corrupting the Creator's original plan. Love was replaced by lust and woman, then and now, covers her body not because it is bad, but to protect it from the lustful looks of those who fail to respect her God-given dignity as a person.

This was explained in greater detail by Pope John Paul II in a series of 129 weekly talks that have become known as the "Theology of the Body."

Sex and Marriage

One of the authors of this text has a friend who speaks to teenagers about chastity and following the Creator's plan for sex. Linda Thayer tells young people that sex is <u>S.L.I.C.</u> — **S**acred, **L**ife-giving, **I**ntimate, and **C**ommitted to marriage — and backs up her presentation with quotations from the first two chapters of Genesis.

Thus, sex is <u>sacred</u> because we are created in God's image ("God created man in his image;/ in the divine image he created him;/ male and female he created them" — Genesis 1:27).

Sex is <u>life-giving</u> because we are called to populate the earth ("God blessed them, saying to them: 'Be fertile and multiply; fill the earth and subdue it. Have dominion over the fish of the sea, the birds of the air, and all the living things that move on the earth' " — Genesis 1:28).

Sex is <u>intimate and fulfilling</u> because men and women were made for each other to be a communion of persons cooperating as spouses and parents in the work of the Creator ("The LORD God said: 'It is not good for the man to be alone. I will make a suitable partner for him' " — Genesis 2:18).

Sex is <u>committed to marriage</u> because marriage is part of God's plan and provides the stable, loving, nurturing environment in which children can be properly raised ("That is why a man leaves his father and mother and clings to his wife, and the two of them become one body" — Genesis 2:24).

Thousands of years later, Jesus reaffirmed what was said in the Book of Genesis, elevated marriage to a sacrament, and asserted that the marriage union was to last forever ("Have you not read that from the beginning the Creator 'made them male and female' and said, 'For this reason a man shall leave his father and mother and be joined to his wife, and the two shall become one flesh'? So they are no longer two, but one flesh. Therefore, what God has joined together, no human being must separate" — Matthew 19:4-6).

This is the Creator's plan for marriage, the union of one man and one woman for life. Modern-day attempts to redefine marriage as the union of two men or two women fly in the face of what God established from the beginning and must be rejected by those who recognize the divinely ordained nature of marriage as a vital pillar of modern society.

Temptation and Fall

So what happened to disrupt this idyllic scene in the Garden of Eden, this original state of holiness, justice, immortality, and participation in the divine life? A fallen angel, whom the Bible calls the devil and Satan (cf. Revelation 12:9), appeared in the garden disguised as a serpent and tempted our first parents to rebel against God, just as he and the other fallen angels had themselves rebelled against the Creator and been driven out of heaven.

For good reason would Jesus call Satan the "father of lies" (John 8:44) for the devil set out to deceive Adam and Eve. Don't worry about God's prohibition against eating the fruit of the tree in the middle of the garden, Satan told Eve. "You certainly will not die! No, God knows well that the moment you eat of it your eyes will be opened and you will be like gods who know what is good and what is bad" (Genesis 3:4-5).

Therein lies the root of all sin, the desire to be "like gods." Pride heads the list of the seven deadly or capital sins for a good reason: it leads the creature to think that he knows better than the Creator what is good and bad. "Yes, God," we are prone to say, "I know you have said that (anger, lust, covetousness, gluttony, envy, and sloth, etc.) are wrong, but these things are not wrong for me at this particular time in my life. I know better than you what is best for me right now."

So Eve listened to the Tempter, ate some of the fruit (the type of fruit is not mentioned), and gave some to Adam, who also ate it. "Then the eyes of both of them were opened, and they realized that they were naked; so they sewed fig leaves together and made loincloths for themselves" (Genesis 3:7). Sin, which always looks so appealing before we commit it, takes on an entirely different appearance afterwards.

Pay careful attention to the following exchange between God and our first parents because their unwillingness to take responsibility for their actions has been typical of human beings ever since. Think, for example, of a time when you did something wrong and tried to blame it on someone else.

When Adam and Eve heard God coming, they hid. We often try to hide from God, sometimes in drugs, alcohol, sex, or other addictions. "Where are you?" (3:9), God asked, just as he constantly asks us the same question, wanting to know where we are in our relationship with him. Adam and Eve answered that they had hidden themselves because they were naked. God said that they could only have known of their nakedness if they had eaten the forbidden fruit, and he inquired of Adam why he had done so.

"The woman whom you put here with me — she gave me fruit from the tree, so I ate it" (3:12), said Adam. Not my fault, he said, putting the blame on Eve. She had gone from the woman of his dreams ("This one, at last, is bone of my bones/ and flesh of my flesh") to the temptress who led him into sin.

So God put the same question to Eve. Did she confess her guilt and express sorrow for her sin? No, she blamed the serpent for tricking her into eating the fruit.

God then meted out punishment first to the serpent and then to the offending couple. He told the serpent that he would crawl on his belly and eat dirt for the rest of his life. He told Eve that she would suffer pain in childbearing, and Adam that he would have to endure hard work "until you return to the ground,/ from which you were taken;/ For you are dirt,/ and to dirt you shall return" (Genesis 3:19).

Talk about going from riches to rags! Adam and Eve had apparently lost everything — the grace of original holiness, their happy and harmonious existence, their freedom from pain and suffering and toil, and their immortality. Their disobedience brought not only sin into the world, but also death (cf. Romans 5:12). Was there any light to be glimpsed at the end of this dark tunnel?

The Good News

Just when all seemed lost, a merciful God promised to send a Redeemer who would atone for the sin of Adam and Eve and raise mankind up from its fallen state. The key passage, which is called the *Protoevangelium* (or "first gospel"), can be found in God's words to Satan as recorded in Genesis 3:15:

> I will put enmity between you and the woman,
>   and between your offspring and hers;
>   He will strike at your head,
>   while you strike at his heel.

Christian tradition has seen in this passage the first announcement of the Messiah and Redeemer, the seed of the woman who will bring about the final victory over Satan, sin, and death.

Jesus will become the "new Adam," who by "becoming obedient to death,/ even death on a cross" (Philippians 2:8) will offer complete satisfaction for the disobedience of the old Adam.

"In conclusion," said St. Paul, "just as through one transgression condemnation came upon all, so through one righteous act acquittal and life came to all. For just as through the disobedience of one person the many were made sinners, so through the obedience of one the many will be made righteous" (Romans 5:18-19).

The same Christian tradition sees the woman of Genesis 3:15 as Mary, the mother of Jesus and the "new Eve." Writing in the second century, St. Irenaeus said that "the knot of Eve's disobedience was untied by Mary's obedience." Her connection with the woman of Genesis will also be made clear when Jesus calls his mother "woman" at the wedding feast in Cana (John 2:4) and at the foot of the cross (John 19:26).

Because of Mary's role as the "new Eve" and Mother of the Redeemer, it has also been the Church's constant belief that, from the moment of her conception, she was free from Original Sin. This dogma is known as her Immaculate Conception. To the objection that Mary could not have escaped Original Sin since she refers in the Magnificat to "God my savior" (Luke 1:47), implying her need to be saved from sin, the Church responds that she was redeemed by her Son's Death on the cross in a special way — by anticipation. Thus, God prevented her from contracting Original Sin at all, and she "remained free of every personal sin her whole life long" (*Catechism*, n. 493).

The Bad News

While the blood of Jesus and the water of Baptism free us from Original Sin, the consequences of that sin continue to plague the world. The sin may be taken away, but its deleterious effects remain. In addition to suffering and death, those effects include an inclination toward sin, what theologians call "concupiscence." This means that our intellects are darkened, so that we don't always see clearly what God wants us to do, and our wills are weakened, so that we often struggle to do what is right.

St. Paul acknowledged this problem when he talked about how easy he found it to do the wrong thing, and how difficult to do the right thing (cf. Romans 7:15). Only through prayer and the sacraments, especially Penance and the Holy Eucharist, can we overcome sinful inclinations.

It didn't take long for the effects of Original Sin to impact the children of Adam and Eve. When it came time for their sons Abel, a shepherd, and Cain, a farmer, to make an offering to God, the Lord looked more favorably on Abel's offering, much to the consternation of Cain. So great was Cain's resentment that he invited his brother out into the field and killed him.

"Where is your brother Abel?" God asked Cain in an effort to get him to own up to what he had done. "I do not know," Cain responded and then asked a question that has been repeated many times down through the years, "Am I my brother's keeper?" (Genesis 4:9). The unspoken answer, of course, is that he was — just as we are — responsible for the care of our brothers and sisters. For whatever we do for the least of them, as Jesus said, we do for him (cf. Matthew 25:40).

God first demanded to know what Cain had done, again giving him the opportunity to confess his sin, and then said: "Listen: Your brother's blood cries out to me from the soil!" (Genesis 4:10). He then sentenced Cain to become "a restless wanderer on the earth" (4:12), and when Cain expressed fear that this punishment would be too much to bear and that he might be killed on sight, God put a mark on Cain (perhaps a tattoo) and banished him from the garden with the warning that anyone who killed him would be avenged sevenfold.

The murder of Abel is the first of four sins in the Bible which cry out to heaven for vengeance. The other three are sodomy or homosexual behavior (cf. Genesis 18:20), oppression of the Israelites in Egypt (cf. Exodus 2:23), and defrauding laborers of their wages (James 5:4). These are not necessarily the worst sins that can be committed — in the early Church, the worst sins included murder, adultery, blasphemy, and apostasy — but they have been singled out because the cries of their victims were heard by God.

Noah and the Flood

The lawlessness of mankind continued to worsen over the succeeding generations and God decided to wipe out all of his creatures to put an end to this wickedness that had virtually inundated the earth. Only Noah, whom the Bible describes as "a good man and blameless in that age" (Genesis 6:9), and his family were to be spared. They were instructed to build an ark, whose dimensions were approximately 440 by 73 by 44 feet, to ride out the flood, and were also told to bring with them two of all living creatures, one male and one female.

One can imagine the ridicule that was directed at Noah as he constructed this huge ship on dry ground, but he trusted in God and persevered, finishing the ark just before the rains began and the flood waters covered the earth. Whether it actually rained for forty days and forty nights, or whether the flood covered the entire earth or only that region where Noah lived, the story illustrates the enormity of sin and the dire consequences of rebellion against God.

But it also illustrates the faithfulness and providence of God toward those who are loyal to him. After the waters receded and Noah had offered on an altar of sacrifice one of every clean animal and clean bird, the Lord blessed Noah and his three sons, Shem (from whose line would come Abraham), Ham, and Japheth, and told them to "be fertile and multiply and fill the earth" (Genesis 9:1). He also established an "everlasting covenant" with them and with all their descendants and said that he would put a rainbow in the clouds as a sign of his covenant and of his intention never again to destroy all living creatures with a flood.

God refuses to turn his back on us, no matter what we do, and he continues to show his solicitude for the human race. In the words of the fourth Eucharistic Prayer used at Mass:

> Even when he disobeyed you and lost
> your friendship
> you did not abandon him to the power
> of death,
> but helped all men to seek and find you.
> Again and again you offered a covenant to man.

In the story of Noah we also find types of Baptism, which washes away sin, and of the Church, the ark of salvation, which Jesus promised would survive all manner of calamities, external and internal, and lead its faithful members to heavenly glory.

The Tower of Babel

In the time following Noah, all peoples spoke the same language, but it was not long before some of them, tempted again by pride to be "like gods," decided to build a city and a tower that would reach to the sky. They hoped to outshine God by creating a culture apart from him and to make a name for themselves.

But the Lord, realizing that if these men succeeded in building their tower, "nothing will later stop them from doing whatever they presume to do" (Genesis 11:6), confused their language so that they could not communicate with one another and then scattered them all over the earth.

This division into many nations, says the *Catechism* (n. 57), "is intended to limit the pride of fallen humanity [cf. Acts 17:16-27], united only in its perverse ambition to forge its own unity as at Babel" [cf. *Wis* 10:5; *Gen* 11:4-6].

<u>WORDS TO REMEMBER</u>

* Original Sin   * Sabbath   * Theology of the Body
* concupiscence   * capital sins   * Protoevangelium

Jacob's stairway to heaven.

Chapter 4

The Patriarchs: Abraham and Isaac

> Recall the wondrous deeds he has done,
> his signs and his words of judgment,
> You descendants of Abraham his servant.
>
> — Psalm 105:5-6

There is a story of a mountain climber who lost his grip as he neared the top and began falling. In desperation, he grabbed onto a branch sticking out of the mountain and hung there hundreds of feet above the ground. He started shouting, "Is there anyone up there who can help me?"

"Yes," came a loud voice. "This is God. I can help you."

"Oh, am I glad you heard me, God. Tell me what to do."

"Let go of the branch with your right hand."

While somewhat skeptical, the climber did what God wanted and then asked, "Okay, God, now what should I do?"

"Let go with your left hand."

To which the climber replied, "Is there anyone else up there?"

The mountain climber's lack of faith in God is in sharp contrast to that of the first of the great patriarchs chosen by God to inaugurate the history of salvation. Abram was a shepherd living in Haran (modern-day Syria) when God called him to leave his homeland and travel to the land of Canaan (modern-day Israel). If he would obey the call, God promised (Genesis 12:2-3):

> I will make of you a great nation,
> and I will bless you;
> I will make your name great,
> so that you will be a blessing.
> I will bless those who bless you
> and curse those who curse you.
> All the communities of the earth
> shall find blessing in you.

Because Abram did what the Lord directed him to do, he is considered the model of faith and obedience, the one who is called "our father in faith" in the first Eucharistic Prayer at Mass. He more than fulfills the definition of faith that we find in the Letter to the Hebrews: "Faith is the realization of what is hoped for and evidence of things not seen" (Hebrews 11:1).

His obedience of faith would be perfectly embodied many generations later by the Virgin Mary, who would courageously say yes to becoming the mother of Jesus, believing the words of the angel Gabriel that "nothing will be impossible for God" (Luke 1:37). We call Mary "blessed" in imitation of her kinswoman Elizabeth, who said at the time of the Visitation: "Most blessed are you among women, and blessed is the fruit of your womb" (1:42). And Mary responded prophetically by saying that "from now on will all ages call me blessed" (Luke 1:48).

The Priest Melchizedek

Traveling with Abram and his family was his nephew Lot, who had settled on the Jordan Plain near the city of Sodom, whose inhabitants were notorious for being "very wicked in the sins they committed against the LORD" (Genesis 13:13). When Abram learned that a group of kings had seized all the food supplies and possessions of Sodom and Gomorrah and had taken Lot prisoner, he mustered more than 300 men, pursued his nephew's captors, defeated them in battle, and rescued Lot.

When Abram returned from his victory, he was greeted by the king of Salem (later Jerusalem), Melchizedek, who brought out bread and wine, and being a priest of God Most High, he blessed Abram with these words:

> Blessed be Abram by God Most High,
> the creator of heaven and earth;
> And blessed be God Most High,
> who delivered your foes into your hand
> (Genesis 14:18-20).

Here we see the reason why Melchizedek is mentioned in the first Eucharistic Prayer. His offering of a sacrifice of bread and wine to God prefigures the offering of bread and wine by Jesus, who is also a King and Priest, at the Last Supper and the offering of bread and wine by the priest at every Mass.

Covenant with Abraham

When Abram was ninety-nine years old, the Bible tells us, the Lord appeared to him for the purpose of establishing a covenant with him, a solemn agreement by which Abram would become the father of many nations. God said that from now on, Abram would be called Abraham "for I am making you the father of a host of nations. I will render you exceedingly fertile; I will make nations of you; kings shall stem from you" (Genesis 17:5-6).

God said that this covenant with Abraham and his descendants was a pact that would endure throughout the ages, and that the sign of this covenant would be the circumcision of every male when he was eight days old. The rite of circumcision remained a required religious ritual until Jesus came to establish a new and everlasting covenant. After that, Gentile converts to Christianity were not required to undergo circumcision.

This had been a major controversy in the early Church and it was fiercely debated at the Council of Jerusalem around the year 49. After hearing arguments from Paul and Barnabas and Peter, a letter was drafted to those of Gentile origin, saying that "it is the decision of the holy Spirit and of us not to place on you any burden beyond these necessities, namely, to abstain from meat sacrificed to idols, from blood, from meats of strangled animals, and from unlawful marriage" (Acts 15:28-29).

In addition to establishing a covenant with Abraham, God also promised that he and his elderly, childless wife Sarah (formerly Sarai) would be blessed with a son the following year. Neither of them thought this likely because of their age, but a short time later, a mysterious heavenly visitor confirmed what God had promised and asked a skeptical Sarah, "Is anything too marvelous for the LORD to do" (Genesis 18:14). Another heavenly visitor would speak similar words many years later to a young woman in the town of Nazareth (cf. Luke 1:37).

Destruction of Sodom and Gomorrah

Meanwhile, as Abraham walked with the Lord, they looked down on the city of Sodom and the Lord said that "the outcry against Sodom and Gomorrah is so great, and their sin so grave, that I must go down and see whether or not their actions fully correspond to the cry against them that comes to me" (Genesis 18:20-21). Abraham tried to intercede for Sodom, asking the Lord if he would spare the city if there were 50 innocent people there.

The Lord said that he would, so Abraham persisted, eventually getting the Lord to say that he would not destroy the city if only ten innocent people could be found there. Apparently, there were not ten innocent people in Sodom, for two angels told Lot that God had sent them to destroy the city.

The angels, who appeared in the form of young men, accepted Lot's invitation to stay overnight at his house. During the night, however, the men of the city stormed the house, demanding to "have intimacies" with the two men. They were prevented from breaking into the house by a blinding flash of light that dazed them. As dawn was breaking, the angels warned Lot to flee from the area with his wife and two daughters and not to look back.

The next morning, Lot arrived at the city of Zoar just as the Lord rained down sulphurous fire on Sodom and Gomorrah, destroying those cities of the Plain and all their inhabitants. But Lot's wife looked back, and she was turned into a pillar of salt (cf. Genesis 19:26).

Homosexual Acts

There are those today who contend that the sin of Sodom (from which comes the word "sodomy") and Gomorrah was not homosexuality, but rather inhospitality to the angelic visitors. This contention is not supported by the account in Genesis 19 and is contrary to the teaching of the Catholic Church. For example, in describing homosexual acts as "acts of grave depravity," the *Catechism* (n. 2357) cites in a footnote the following biblical passages: Genesis 19:1-29, Romans 1:24-27, 1 Corinthians 6:10, and 1 Timothy 1:10. See also Jude 7.

Anyone who is familiar with St. Paul's graphic description of homosexual acts in the first chapter of Romans would be hard-pressed to believe that such acts are morally acceptable expressions of love on a par with the use of sex as God intended.

It should be noted, however, that while condemning homosexual actions as gravely depraved, the *Catechism* says that those who commit these actions, and all those with a homosexual inclination, "must be accepted with respect, compassion, and sensitivity" (n. 2358). It also says that homosexuals are called to chastity and to "unite to the sacrifice of the Lord's Cross the difficulties they may encounter from their condition" (n. 2358).

God's Strange Request

As God had promised, Abraham and Sarah had a son whom they named Isaac. When the boy was about twelve years old, God made a strange request of Abraham. He told him to take Isaac to the land of Moriah and offer him up as a holocaust on a hill that God would point out to him. So Abraham cut some wood for the fiery sacrifice and set out with Isaac and two servants. As they neared the place, Abraham told the servants to remain with the donkey while he and his son went on ahead. He placed the wood on Isaac's shoulders, and he himself carried a knife and the implements to start the fire.

As they walked along, Isaac asked a very appropriate question of his father: "Here are the fire and the wood, but where is the sheep for the holocaust?" Abraham answered that "God himself will provide the sheep for the holocaust" (Genesis 22:7-8)

When they reached the hill in Moriah, Abraham built an altar of stones, placed the wood on it, and much to Isaac's surprise, tied him up and put him on top of the wood. But just as Abraham was about to slaughter his son with the knife, a messenger from the Lord said, "Abraham, Abraham .... Do not lay your hand on the boy. Do not do the least thing to him. I know now how devoted you are to God, since you did not withhold from me your own beloved son" (Genesis 22:11-12).

Abraham then spotted a ram caught by its thorns in a thicket, so he took the ram and offered it to God as a sacrifice in place of Isaac. The Lord's messenger praised Abraham for his faith and trust in God and told him, "I will bless you abundantly and make your descendants as countless as the stars of the sky and the sands of the seashore; your descendants shall take possession of the gates of their enemies, and in your descendants all the nations of the earth shall find blessing — all this because you obeyed my command" (Genesis 22:17-18).

God's request was a test of Abraham's faith, as the author of Hebrews (11:17-19) points out, but it was also a warning to the people of Israel not to imitate the Caananite practice of sacrificing a first-born child to the pagan gods. The story is a preview of God providing his own Son, Jesus, as a sacrificial offering, the Lamb of God instead of a ram. And like Isaac, Jesus will also be rescued from death, in his glorious Resurrection on Easter Sunday. It may take God a long time to carry out his plan, but he will carry it out.

Following Abraham's Example

Are there lessons for us in the story of Abraham? Is our faith strong enough to do what God wants, especially when it goes contrary to our desires, or to the opinions of our families and friends, or to the culture in which we live? For example, there is much talk today about a crisis in religious vocations. Is this due to the failure of God to call young men and women to the priest-hood and the consecrated life? Or is it a failure on the part of young people to pay attention to God's call? And even when men and woman show an interest in devoting their lives to God, do they receive encouragement from family and friends, or disdain and even ridicule?

Is our faith strong enough to resist what Pope John Paul II called the "culture of death"? We may be horrified at the Ca-naanite practice of killing their children, but are we horrified at the tens of millions of unborn children who have been aborted and sacrificed on the altar of convenience? What are we doing to halt this silent holocaust, or to assist women who are faced with unwanted or problem pregnancies? Many women have said that they would never have had their abortion if someone had tried to talk them out of it.

Do we act promptly in following God's commands, as Abraham did, or in responding to reasonable requests by parents, teach-ers, and those in positions of legitimate authority? Which one of the two sons in Jesus' parable (cf. Matthew 21:28-32) do we resemble? Recall that a father told his sons to go out and work in the vineyard. The first one said that he would not, but later changed his mind and went. The second said that he would, but did not go. To his credit, the first son eventually did what his father wanted, but only after causing his father some trouble.

Abraham's faith made him a blessing for all the nations; Mary's faith made her "blessed among women." Their faith is an example of what the *Catechism* describes as "an assent of the intellect and will to the self-revelation God has made through his deeds and words" (n. 176).

The Story of Isaac

As Abraham was nearing the end of his life, he wanted to make sure that Isaac would not marry a Canaanite woman, so he sent a servant with ten camels and many other gifts to visit relatives near the city of Nahor to obtain a wife for Isaac. As the servant stood near a watering place, praying that God would help his mission turn out favorably, a beautiful young woman named Rebekah came to the spring to fill her jug. The servant went with her to her father's house and explained why he was there. The father agreed to the proposal and sent Rebekah, along with her maids, with the servant back to the Negeb region of southern Palestine where Isaac was living, and Rebekah became his wife.

Because Rebekah was found to be sterile, Isaac prayed to the Lord on behalf of his wife, and she subsequently delivered twin boys, Esau and Jacob. Even in the womb, the two jostled each other so much that Rebekah asked the Lord about it. He responded with a prediction of things to come:

> Two nations are in your womb,
> two peoples are quarreling while still within you;
> But one shall surpass the other,
> and the older shall serve the younger
> (Genesis 25:23).

At the time of the delivery, Esau was the first to emerge, and then came Jacob, gripping Esau's heel. Esau, who was his father's favorite, grew up to be a hunter, while Jacob, who was his mother's favorite, kept to his tents. Once when Jacob was cooking a stew, Esau came in from the field very hungry and asked for some of the stew. "First, give me your birthright in exchange for it" (Genesis 25:31), said Jacob, and he made Esau swear that he would do so. So Esau, who cared little for his birthright, sold it to Jacob for a bowl of stew, thus giving to his younger brother the inheritance rights that belonged to the first-born son (cf. 25:29-34).

Before he died, Isaac made plans to convey the blessing he had received from Abraham to his son Esau. He sent him out to hunt some game so that a special meal could be prepared for the ceremony of conferring the blessing. But Rebekah had overheard Isaac's words and, after Esau had left, she conspired with Jacob to deceive her husband, who was nearly blind.

She prepared an appetizing dish for Isaac and seasoned it so he would think the game had just been caught. Then she got some of Esau's clothes for Jacob to wear and had her smooth-skinned younger son cover his arms and neck with animal skins in imitation of Esau's hairy body. Jacob doubted that the deception would work, and feared that it would bring a curse on him rather than a blessing, but Rebekah said, "Let any curse against you, son, fall on me!" (Genesis 27:13).

Jacob's Deception

When Jacob brought the meal to his father, Isaac asked, "Which of my sons are you?" and Jacob answered, "I am Esau, your first-born. I did as you told me. Please sit up and eat some of my game, so that you may give me your special blessing" (Genesis 27:18-19). Isaac was surprised that the game had been caught and prepared so quickly, and he thought the voice sounded like Jacob's, but the hairy hands felt like Esau's. He asked again if it were really Esau, and Jacob said yes.

After he had eaten the meal, Isaac asked Jacob to come closer and kiss him and, when he smelled the fragrance of the clothes, he gave him this blessing:

> May God give to you
> of the dew of the heavens
> And of the fertility of the earth
> abundance of grain and wine.

> Let peoples serve you,
> and nations pay you homage;
> Be master of your brothers,
> and may your mother's sons bow down to you.

> Cursed be those who curse you,
> and blessed be those who bless you
> (Genesis 27:28-29).

Shortly after Jacob had left his father's presence, Esau returned from hunting, prepared a meal, brought it to Isaac, and asked for the special blessing. When his father realized what had happened, he gave the bad news to Esau, who was furious at the deception, saying that Jacob had now supplanted him twice, once by taking away his birthright and now by taking away his blessing. He asked for another blessing, but Isaac told him that he had already made Jacob his master and had given him everything.

Isaac did, however, tell Esau that while he would live by the sword and serve his younger brother, the day would come when "you shall throw off his yoke from your neck" (Genesis 27:40). Not surprisingly, Esau bore a grudge against Jacob and threatened to kill him. When Rebekah learned of the threat, she warned Jacob and told him to flee at once to the home of her brother Laban and to stay there until Esau's fury subsided.

No one should think that Jacob's deceiving of his father and cheating Esau out of his blessing were praiseworthy things to do. In fact, his actions would later be condemned by the prophets Hosea (12:4) and Jeremiah (9:3). Consider these strong words of Jeremiah:

> Be on guard, everyone against his neighbor;
> put no trust in any brother.
> Every brother apes Jacob, the supplanter,
> every friend is guilty of slander.

Furthermore, as punishment for the deception, Jacob and his mother would remain separated for the rest of their lives. The story offers us another illustration of how God, while never sanctioning sinful actions such as Jacob's lies to his father, uses weak and sinful people to accomplish his ultimate goal of salvation for all who are faithful to him and to his purposes. He was able to bring good out of the situation so that Jacob could continue the line from Abraham to Jesus.

Jacob's Stairway

On his way to his uncle Laban's home, Jacob stopped at a place that would come to be known as Bethel. He had a dream there during the night of a stairway that rested on the ground but reached to the heavens, and he saw angels going up and down the stairway. He heard the Lord say that he would give Jacob and his descendants the land he was standing on and that "in you and your descendants all the nations of the earth shall find blessing. Know that I am with you; I will protect you wherever you go, and bring you back to this land. I will never leave you until I have done what I promised you" (Genesis 28:14-15).

When Jacob awoke from this sleep, he built a memorial on the spot and vowed that if God remained with him and protected him on his journey, gave him enough bread to eat and clothing to wear, and brought him back safely to his father's house, "the LORD shall be my God. This stone that I have set up as a memorial stone shall be God's abode. Of everything you give me, I will faithfully return a tenth part to you" (Genesis 28:21-22).

The symbolism of the stairway, sometimes called Jacob's Ladder, was that his mission was to serve as God's link between heaven and earth. We by virtue of our Baptism and our Confirmation are also supposed to act as God's missionaries on earth, helping others by our words and actions to ascend the stairway to heaven.

<u>WORDS TO REMEMBER</u>

* faith	* Melchizedek	* covenant
* circumcision	* sodomy	* birthright

Joseph reveals himself to his brothers.

Chapter 5

Jacob (Israel)
and Joseph

Oh, that from Zion might come
the deliverance of Israel,
That Jacob may rejoice, and Israel be glad
when the LORD restores his people!
— Psalm 14:7

There is a current saying that "what goes around comes around." It means that while a person may get away with something the first or second time, sooner or later their deception will catch up with them. The story of Jacob is an ancient example of this modern adage. Or as the Bible might put it, a person will reap what he sows.

Jacob had barely arrived at his uncle Laban's property when he met his younger daughter Rachel, who was tending her father's sheep. He told her who he was, and she took him to Laban, who embraced him fervently and listened to the story of what had happened with Isaac and Esau.

After a month there, Laban asked Jacob what his wages should be, and Jacob said that he would serve Laban for seven years if he could then marry Rachel. Laban agreed and, when the seven years had passed, gave a feast. After much eating and drinking, Laban brought his older daughter Leah, who was veiled, to Jacob's darkened tent, where the marriage was consummated.

Jacob was stunned in the morning to find that he had married Leah, and he asked Laban, "How could you do this to me! Was it not for Rachel that I served you? Why did you dupe me?" (Genesis 29:25). Laban answered that it was the custom in his country to marry off the older daughter first, but he told Jacob that if he finished a week of bridal festivities with Leah, he would allow him to marry Rachel. A week later, Jacob also married the younger daughter and worked another seven years for his uncle.

The Bible doesn't tell us whether Jacob saw the irony in his new situation. Imagine him criticizing Laban for deception involving an older and younger sibling, when Jacob had done the same thing to Esau! Jacob had taken advantage of Isaac's darkened eyes, just as Laban took advantage of Jacob's darkened vision. Sometimes it is easy for us to find fault with others, but we have a hard time recognizing our own faults.

Jesus had this in mind when he asked, "Why do you notice the splinter in your brother's eye, but do not perceive the wooden beam in your own eye? How can you say to your brother, 'Let me remove that splinter from your eye,' while the wooden beam is in your eye? You hypocrite, remove the wooden beam from your eye first; then you will see clearly to remove the splinter from your brother's eye" (Matthew 7:3-5).

The Children of Jacob

In another bit of irony, Leah was able to have children, while Rachel was not, and she bore Jacob three sons, hoping that her husband would become attached to her, but Jacob loved Rachel. Because she was envious of Leah, Rachel gave one of her maidservants to Jacob, and she bore him two children. Leah then gave her maidservant to Jacob as a consort, and two more sons were born. This was certainly not acceptable conduct in the eyes of God, but it was permitted in order to increase the Lord's family and eventually to make up the twelve tribes of Israel.

Finally, after much pleading and praying, Rachel conceived a son whom she named Joseph. Not long after that, the Lord told Jacob to return to the land of his fathers, and the future patriarch, who had quietly built up his own flocks and possessions, informed Laban of his intentions.

When Jacob learned that Laban's sons were plotting against him for using their father's property to increase his own wealth, he decided to flee the country with Rachel and Leah and their children. It was three days before Laban learned of the flight, and he mustered a force to pursue Jacob, catching up with him in the highlands of Gilead.

After some explaining and negotiating, the two men agreed to a pact, with the Lord as their witness, that would allow Jacob and his wives and children to return to his homeland. "May the LORD keep watch between you and me when we are out of each other's sight," said Laban. "If you mistreat my daughters, or take other wives besides my daughters, remember that even though no one else is about, God will be witness between you and me" (Genesis 31:49-50). They set up a mound of stones near the memorial stone as a reminder that neither of them would cross into the other's territory with hostile intent.

Struggle with an Angel

Now that he and Laban had worked out their problems, Jacob faced another obstacle — the hostility of his brother Esau, who was encamped not far away with an army of tribesmen. Jacob was frightened of Esau and sent him a peace offering of hundreds of animals. In the course of the night, Jacob got into a wrestling match with an angel that continued until the break of dawn. When the angel found that he could not overpower Jacob, he struck his hip and dislocated it from the socket.

The angel then asked Jacob to let go of him, but Jacob demanded that the angel bless him first. What is your name, the angel asked, and he said Jacob. Then the angel said: "You shall no longer be spoken of as Jacob, but as Israel, because you have contended with divine and human beings and have prevailed." Jacob named the place Peniel "because I have seen God face to face ... yet my life has been spared" (Genesis 32:29, 31).

The change of a name always indicates that something significant has happened. Thus, Abram became Abraham, the father of a host of nations; Simon will become Peter, the rock on which the Church of Christ will be built; and Saul will become Paul, the apostle to the Gentiles. So, too, Jacob will now be known also as Israel, and the people and land will go by that name.

At Baptism and Confirmation, we (or our parents) choose names, preferably the name of a saint in heaven whom we can both imitate and seek their guidance and protection. So careful thought should be given to the names we select, as well as to those whom we offer the privilege of being godparents or sponsors. Those to be asked cannot be one's parents. They must be at least sixteen years of age, have received the sacraments of the Holy Eucharist and Confirmation, and be living the life of a faithful Catholic since they are to serve as role models for the child they are sponsoring.

Reconciliation with Esau

When Jacob saw Esau approaching with four hundred men, he divided his children among his two wives and their maidservants and went on ahead of them, bowing seven times as he neared Esau. His brother then ran to Jacob, embraced him, and kissed him. Esau asked about Jacob's large family and why he had sent so many animals to Esau. Jacob said that it was to gain Esau's favor, but his brother said that was not necessary and that he should take the presents back. Jacob, however, said that God had blessed him with abundance, and he pleaded with Esau to keep the animals, which Esau agreed to do.

Esau then offered to travel along with Jacob's entourage, or at least to leave some of his men as an escort, but Jacob declined his offer because he said that they would be traveling very slowly. So the two formerly estranged brothers parted on good terms, and Jacob eventually settled near Shechem in Canaan. When their father Isaac died, the brothers were there to bury him.

Shortly after Jacob's return to Canaan, God asked him to go back to Bethel to erect an altar "to the God who appeared to you while you were fleeing from your brother Esau" (Genesis 35:1). Jacob told his family to get rid of any foreign gods, to purify themselves, and to accompany him to Bethel. When he arrived there, God said that his name would now be Israel and told him:

I am God Almighty;
be fruitful and multiply.
A nation, indeed an assembly of nations,
shall stem from you,
and kings shall issue from your loins.
The land I once gave
to Abraham and Isaac
I now give to you;
And to your descendants after you
will I give this land (Genesis 35:11-12).

The sons of Jacob, from whom would come the twelve tribes of Israel, were those of Leah (Reuben, Simeon, Levi, Judah, Issachar, and Zebulun), of Leah's maid (Gad and Asher), of Rachel's maid (Dan and Napthali), and of Rachel (Joseph and Benjamin). Rachel died after giving birth to Benjamin and was buried on the road to Bethlehem.

The Story of Joseph

Joseph was Jacob's favorite son because he was the child of his old age, and his brothers were jealous of him and even hated him. On two occasions, Joseph had dreams about sheaves of wheat bowing to his sheaf, and about the sun, moon, and eleven stars bowing down to him. When he told his brothers about the dreams, they were incensed at the thought that they would have to bow before him.

One day, after the brothers had gone to tend the sheep, Jacob sent Joseph to check on them and report back to him. When the brothers saw Joseph at a distance, they plotted to kill the "master dreamer" by throwing him into a cistern and then telling their father that wild animals had gotten him. "We shall then see what comes of his dreams," they said (Genesis 37:20).

However, one of the brothers, Judah, tried to save Joseph's life by persuading the others not to kill him, but to sell him to a group of Ishmaelites who were traveling in a caravan on their way to Egypt. The brothers agreed, and Joseph was sold for twenty pieces of silver, ten less than the price Judas would be paid for betraying Jesus. They then took Joseph's tunic, a gift from his father, smeared it with animal blood, and brought it to Jacob, pretending that they didn't know whose tunic it was.

Jacob was distraught over the apparent death of his son and refused all consolation, saying that "I will go down mourning to my son in the nether world" (Genesis 37:35).

The Onan Incident

The saga of Joseph in the Book of Genesis is interrupted by an incident involving a man named Onan, who was struck dead by God for spilling his seed on the ground during marital relations (hence the term Onanism for the vice of trying to prevent life from being conceived by withdrawal during intercourse). Onanism was the general term for contraception for centuries, and it wasn't until the birth-control debates of the 1960s that the interpretation of the Onan account as anti-contraception was challenged by those who wanted to see the Catholic Church change her teaching to allow contraceptive practices.

The modernist argument is that Onan was not struck dead for contraception, but for violating the Levirate law that required a man to marry his brother's widow if the brother died before they had children. However, the Levirate-only interpretation is not supported either by Scripture or by the Church's tradition and, in fact, two other persons who violated that law — Onan's father Judah and his brother Shelah — were not struck dead.

This had led John Kippley, author of the book *Sex and the Marriage Covenant,* to conclude:

> When three people are guilty of the same crime, but only one of them receives the death penalty from God, common sense requires that we ask if that one did something the others did not do. The answer is obvious: Only Onan went through the motions of the covenantal act of intercourse, but then defrauded its purpose and meaning; only Onan engaged in the contraceptive behavior of withdrawal (p. 311).

Joseph in Egypt

Upon his arrival in Egypt, Joseph was sold as a slave to Potiphar, chief steward to Pharaoh, the king of Egypt. His personable and enterprising attitude impressed Potiphar, and he soon placed Joseph in charge of his household and all his possessions and, with the Lord's blessing on him, everything Joseph did turned out well.

Meanwhile, Potiphar's wife became enamored of the handsome young man and she invited him to lie with her. Joseph refused, saying that it would be a betrayal of the authority and trust her husband had placed in him. "How, then," he asked, "could I commit so great a wrong and thus stand condemned before God?" (Genesis 39:9).

But the wife continued her efforts to seduce Joseph, and he tried to avoid her. One day, however, when he came to the house to do his work, and none of the servants were there, she grabbed him by the cloak and begged him to lie with her. When he ran outside, the wife screamed for the servants.

"Look!" she shouted. "My husband has brought in a Hebrew slave to make sport of us! He came in here to lie with me, but I cried out as loud as I could. When he heard me scream for help, he left his cloak beside me and ran away outside" (Genesis 39:14-15). She later told the same story to her husband, who became enraged, seized Joseph, and threw him into the jail where the royal prisoners were kept.

In refusing to commit adultery, Joseph showed what an honorable and God-fearing man he was. He was faced with a strong temptation and could have tried to justify his actions by saying that he needed to pacify the wife to keep his job. But instead he did the right thing, not the expedient thing. He would be an excellent role model today for those who are tempted to commit adultery.

The Interpreter of Dreams

But again the Lord remained with Joseph, making the chief jailer well-disposed toward him. The head jailer, recognizing Joseph's abilities, put him in charge of all the prisoners and, as in Potiphar's house, everything ran smoothly. In the jail with Joseph were two former employees of the Pharaoh, his chief cupbearer and his chief baker, who had caused the Pharaoh some offense and were dispatched to the royal jail.

One night, both of them had strange dreams and, when Joseph asked them the next day why they seemed so distressed, they recounted their dreams to him. In his dream, said the cupbearer, he saw a grapevine with branches. He said that he squeezed the juice out of the grapes and put it in Pharaoh's cup.

What this means, said Joseph, is that in three days the Pharaoh will restore you to your job and you will hand him his cup as you once did. He also asked the cupbearer to mention his name to Pharaoh so he could get out of jail, for "the truth is that I was kidnapped from the land of the Hebrews, and here I have not done anything for which I should have been put into a dungeon" (Genesis 40:15).

In his dream, said the baker, he had three wicker baskets on his head, with all kinds of bakery products in the top basket, but birds were pecking at the food. Joseph must have hesitated to give his interpretation of this dream, since he had to tell the baker that in three days, Pharaoh would have him impaled on a stake, and the birds would peck the flesh from his body.

Three days later, Joseph's interpretations proved to be true, as the baker was executed and the cupbearer got his old job back. However, he forgot all about Joseph and never mentioned his name to Pharaoh.

Two years went by, and then one night Pharaoh had two dreams. In the first, he saw seven fat cows standing on the banks of the Nile when seven emaciated cows came out of the river and ate up the fat cows. In the second dream, Pharaoh saw seven fat, healthy ears of grain growing on a single stalk when seven thin, unhealthy ears swallowed them up.

The king summoned all the sages and soothsayers in Egypt to his palace, but none could interpret his dreams. Then the cupbearer remembered Joseph and told Pharaoh about him, so Pharaoh had Joseph brought from the jail.

After listening to the dreams and making it clear that "it is not I ... but God who will give Pharaoh the right answer" (Genesis 41:16), Joseph said that both dreams had the same meaning. He said that the seven healthy cows and the seven healthy ears represented seven years of great abundance in Egypt, while the seven scrawny cows and the seven withered ears represented seven years of famine in the land.

He recommended to Pharaoh that grain should be stored up during the good years so that there would be plenty of food for the bad years. Pharaoh was so pleased with Joseph's advice that he put him in charge of agriculture over the whole land and, under Joseph's capable leadership, plenty of food had been accumulated when the years of famine arrived.

The Brothers of Joseph

The famine that affected Egypt had also gripped surrounding countries as well and, when word of Egypt's surplus reached those countries, people traveled there to obtain rations of grain. So it was that Jacob sent all of his sons except Benjamin, the youngest, down to Egypt to purchase grain for the land of Canaan.

As God had planned it, Joseph's brothers had to appeal to him, as governor of the land, for a portion of grain. The brothers did not recognize Joseph, so many years had passed, but he knew who they were, and he recalled the dreams he had as a youth that showed his brothers bowing down to him. But he concealed his identity from them and first accused them of being spies and then questioned them about their father and their family. Upon learning that one brother was not with them, Joseph said that he would not sell them any grain unless they sent for Benjamin.

Joseph then kept one brother, Simeon, in prison as a hostage and gave provisions to the others to take back to their starving families. Reuben saw their situation as punishment for what they had done to Joseph, saying that "now comes the reckoning for his blood" (Genesis 42:22). When they stopped for the night on the way back to Canaan, they were amazed to find the money they had used to pay for the grain hidden in the sacks and asked, "What is this that God has done to us?" (Genesis 42:28).

When the brothers told Jacob all that had happened and that the governor of Egypt wanted them to bring Benjamin back with them as a sign that they were honest men and not spies, Jacob said no. He said that he has already lost Benjamin's full brother Joseph, and would not risk losing Benjamin, too.

However, as the famine grew more severe, and they had used up all the rations from the first journey, Jacob relented after Judah promised to protect Benjamin. So back they went to Egypt with double the money and numerous gifts. When Joseph saw Benjamin with his other brothers, he had Simeon released from jail and had a meal prepared for all of them, with the largest portions being served to Benjamin.

However, he decided to test them once more, instructing his head steward to fill their bags with grain and put each one's money at the mouth of his bag, but to put in Benjamin's bag a silver goblet belonging to Joseph. After the brothers had begun their return journey, Joseph sent men after them to accuse them of stealing money and the silver cup. The soldiers also told the brothers that the one in whose bag the cup was found would become Joseph's slave.

The brothers were distraught at this turn of events and, when they returned to the city, they begged Joseph to change his mind. Judah told him that his aged father would die of grief if Benjamin did not return, and he offered to remain as a slave in Egypt in place of Benjamin. Joseph could no longer control himself and he told them, "I am your brother Joseph, whom you once sold into Egypt" (Genesis 45:4).

His brothers were dumbfounded, but he told them not to be distressed, that "it was really for the sake of saving lives that God sent me here ahead of you ... to ensure for you a remnant on earth and to save your lives in an extraordinary deliverance. So it was not really you but God who had me come here; and he has made of me a father to Pharaoh, lord of all his household, and ruler over the whole land of Egypt" (Genesis 45:5-8).

It is easy to see why the story of Joseph has such appeal, illustrating as it does the marvelous providence of God, who is able to bring good out of evil, to bring salvation for the starving people of Israel, just as he would later bring salvation to a spiritually starving world through the evil perpetrated against his Son. It is not always easy to see the silver lining in the cloud, and the temptation is often to blame and berate God, or at least to ask, "Why me?" or "How could God let this happen to me?"

It may be a cliche to say that patience is a virtue, but if we can be patient and trust in God, as Joseph did, a great reward awaits us, if not in this life, then in the next. Remember the words of St. Paul: "I consider that the sufferings of this present time are as nothing compared with the glory to be revealed for us" (Romans 8:18).

From Canaan to Egypt

When his sons told Jacob that Joseph was alive and ruler of all the land in Egypt, he was stunned. "My son Joseph is still alive!" Jacob exclaimed. "I must go and see him before I die" (Genesis 45:28). So Israel and all his descendants and all his possessions migrated to Egypt, and he was affirmed in his journey by the Lord himself, who said in a vision:

> I am God, the God of your father. Do not be afraid to go down to Egypt, for there I will make you a great nation. Not only will I go down to Egypt with you; I will also bring you back here, after Joseph has closed your eyes" (Genesis 46:3-4).

Joseph told Pharaoh when his family arrived in Egypt, and the king said that the land of Egypt was at their disposal. They settled in the region of Goshen, where they soon acquired property and increased in numbers. Seventeen years after their arrival, as Jacob's life neared its end, he called all his sons together and gave each of them an appropriate message and asked to be buried in the same cave where Abraham and Sarah, Isaac and Rebekah, and Leah were buried.

After the burial of their father in Canaan and their return to Egypt, Joseph's brothers became fearful that he might still be holding a grudge against them, so they approached him and said that Jacob had told them to beg forgiveness for what they had done to their brother. Joseph broke into tears, reassured them of his forgiveness, and reminded them again that what had happened to him was part of God's plan for the survival of his people.

WORDS TO REMEMBER

* Israel	* Tribes of Israel	* Onanism
* Providence	* Levirate law	* godparents

Chapter 6

Angels in the Bible

For God commands the angels
to guard you in all your ways.
— Psalm 91:11

In *Where Angels Walk*, her first book about modern-day angelic appearances, Joan Wester Anderson tells of an experience her son Tim had on a bitterly cold and snowy Christmas Eve in 1983 when he and two college roommates were driving from Connecticut to Illinois. After dropping off one friend, Don, in Fort Wayne, Indiana, Tim and Jim started off on the final leg of their journey.

They were traveling along a rural access road to the Indiana tollway when their car died at the top of a small hill in the middle of nowhere. There was no traffic coming along in either direction, and no houses or other buildings anywhere in sight. The cold was seeping into the stalled car and, even if there had been a farmhouse in view, the young men might not have survived the wind-chill of 80 degrees below zero trying to reach it.

"Well, God," Tim thought to himself, "you're the only one who can help us now." Four hours away, in her suburban Chicago home, Tim's mother, not knowing the danger her son was in but thinking that he might be in trouble since she had not heard from him, was also praying, "God, send someone to help them."

As Tim and Jim were growing numb and beginning to get drowsy, they saw headlights right behind their car. They hadn't noticed any vehicle approaching and wondered if they were dreaming, but then there was a knock on the driver's window and a man, with everything but his eyes covered with a furry parka and a scarf, asked if they needed a tow.

"Yes! Oh, yes. Thanks!" they said, and then watched the stranger drive around the front of the car and hook up the chains. They asked him if he could tow them back to Don's house, and he agreed, stopping only at a pay phone so Tim could tell Don what had happened and to expect them shortly.

When they reached Don's street, the driver maneuvered around the cul de sac in front of Don's house and stopped. Tim and Jim raced into the house and asked if Don could lend them some money to pay the driver of the tow truck. "What tow truck?" said Don, looking out the window. "I don't see any tow truck."

Tim and Jim looked back toward the street, but the only vehicle in front of the house was their car. They hadn't heard any chains being removed or the sound of an engine moving away, and there were no receding taillights in the distance. They ran outside and looked at the drifting snow on the road, but only saw one set of tire tracks, and they belonged to Tim's car.

Was it really an angel who had saved their lives, or is there another explanation to account for their rescue by the mysterious stranger? Mrs. Anderson says that the family may never know for sure, but the incident led her to solicit other people's accounts of similar happenings, and she has since published five books containing dozens of true stories of heavenly guardians.

Widespread Interest in Angels

Although we live in an oftentimes cynical and irreligious culture, there is a considerable interest in angels. Many books have been written about them, along with numerous newspaper and magazine articles, and there have been movies and television programs that were enormously popular. Think, for example, of the movie *It's a Wonderful Life*, where a bumbling angel named Clarence saves the life of a Jimmy Stewart character bent on suicide. Or the long-running TV shows *Highway to Heaven* and *Touched By An Angel*.

Angels are mentioned some 300 times in the Bible, but before getting to that, what do we know about angels in general? We know that the word angel means "messenger" and that they are pure, created, and highly intelligent spirits who do not have bodies, although they can and do take on human form. They are often portrayed as chubby little babies with wings, but in reality are of such great majesty and power that their first words to humans are usually "do not be afraid," implying that their appearance on earth can be rather frightening or intimidating.

They are, according to the *Catechism* (n. 329) primarily servants and messengers of God who " 'always behold the face of my Father who is in heaven' " and who "are the 'mighty ones who do his word' " [*Mt* 18:10; *Ps* 103:20].

God created a multitude of angels, and they have been present since creation and have played a vital role in the history of salvation. The Church has traditionally divided angels into nine categories or choirs, ranking them from the highest to the lowest as follows:

Seraphim
Cherubim
Thrones
Dominations
Virtues
Powers
Principalities
Archangels
Angels

Only three angels are mentioned by name in Holy Scripture, and they are the archangels Michael, Gabriel, and Raphael, whose feast day the Church celebrates on September 29th. The Bible also tells us (Matthew 18:10) that each one of us receives a special guardian angel when we are born, and the feast day of the Guardian Angels is October 2nd. Many Catholics learned the following prayer as children and continue to recite it today:

Angel of God, my guardian dear,
to whom God's love commits me here.
Ever this day be at my side
to light and guard, to rule and guide. Amen.

Since angels are powerful beings sent by God to watch over and guide us, it would be very prudent for each of us to pray to our guardian angel every day and not to hesitate to invoke his protection in time of trouble. We can also pray to the guardian angels of other persons and ask heavenly intercession for them. It is said that Blessed Pope John XXIII always prayed to the guardian angel of any important person with whom he was meeting. It would be foolish to neglect this source of love and guidance that God has provided for us.

Another Catholic tradition that is based on Scripture and has been popular for centuries is that of praying the Angelus three times a day: at 6 a.m., 12 noon, and 6 p.m. Here is how the prayer should be said:

The Angelus

V. The angel of the Lord declared to Mary.
R. And she conceived of the Holy Spirit. **Hail Mary**
V. Behold the handmaid of the Lord.
R. Be it done to me according to your word. **Hail Mary**
V. And the Word was made flesh.
R. And dwelt among us. **Hail Mary**
V. Pray for us, O holy Mother of God.
R. That we may be made worthy of the promises of Christ.

Let us pray. Pour forth, we beseech you, O Lord, your grace into our hearts, that we to whom the Incarnation of Christ, your Son, was made known by the message of an angel, may by his Passion and cross be brought to the glory of his Resurrection, through the same Christ our Lord. Amen.

The Archangel Raphael

The first archangel mentioned by name in the Bible is Raphael, who played a key role in the lives of Tobit, a wealthy Israelite living among the captives deported to Nineveh from the northern kingdom of Israel in 721 B.C., and his son Tobiah. A generous and virtuous man who had performed many charitable deeds for his people but who had suffered setbacks and had gone blind, Tobit pleaded with God to end his life. But then he remembered that he had left a large sum of money with a man in far-off Media, and he asked his son to travel there to bring back the money.

Meanwhile, in Media, a young woman named Sarah was also praying for death because each of her seven husbands had died on their wedding night at the hands of a demon named Asmodeus. The prayers of Tobit and Sarah were heard "in the glorious presence of Almighty God" (Tobit 3:16), and the archangel Raphael was sent from heaven to help both of them.

Before departing for Media, Tobiah was given some fatherly advice: "Through all your days, my son, keep the Lord in mind, and suppress every desire to sin or to break the commandments. Perform good works all the days of your life, and do not tread the paths of wrongdoing. For if you are steadfast in your service, your good works will bring success, not only to you, but also to all those who live uprightly" (Tobit 4:5-6).

Looking around for someone who knew the roads to Media, Tobiah came upon Raphael, who was disguised as an ordinary man named Azariah and who offered to serve as Tobiah's guide. That night, while camping beside the Tigris River, Tobiah stepped into the river to wash his feet, and a large fish attacked him. Raphael told him to seize the fish and cut it open, taking out its gall, heart, and liver, because they make "useful medicines" (Tobit 6:5). Tobiah did as he was instructed.

As they neared the town of Ecbatana in Media, Raphael told Tobiah that they would be staying with a relative named Raguel, who had a courageous and beautiful daughter named Sarah, and that Tobiah should seek to marry her. But, Tobiah objected, "I have heard that this woman has already been married seven times, and that her husbands died in their bridal chambers .... And I have heard it said that it was a demon who killed them. So now I too am afraid of this demon" (Tobit 6:14-15).

Do not worry, said Raphael, who then instructed the young man to take the fish heart and liver and place them on the fire in the bridal chamber. He said that when the demon smelled the odor they give off, he would flee and never again come near Sarah. So they went to the house of Raguel, who was overjoyed to learn that Tobiah was the son of a noble and good man like Tobit, and who quickly consented to the marriage with Sarah.

After placing the fish heart and liver on the embers in the bridal chamber that night, which drove the demon away, Tobiah invited his wife to pray along with him that God would have mercy on them and grant them deliverance. He recalled that God had created Adam and Eve, saying that it was not good for the man to be alone and that he should have a partner like himself, and then prayed in these words:

> Now, Lord, you know that I take
> this wife of mine not because of lust,
> but for a noble purpose.
> Call down your mercy on me and on her,
> and allow us to live together to a happy old age
> (Tobit 8:7).

The couple enjoyed a peaceful night in the bridal chamber, much to the surprise of Raguel, who had dug a grave during the night in which to bury Tobiah. Raguel praised God the next day for sparing his son-in-law and began a 14-day wedding celebration, during which time Raphael visited the man who had been holding Tobit's money and brought the money to Raguel's house.

After the celebration was over, Tobiah, Sarah, and Raphael began the homeward journey, with Raphael promising Tobiah that the gall from the fish, when rubbed on Tobit's eyes, would shrink the cataracts and restore his sight. The promise was fulfilled when they reached Nineveh, and Tobit rejoiced to see his son and his new wife.

When the wedding celebration there had ended, Tobit said that Tobiah should give Raphael some money for his services and even suggested half of what they had brought back from Media. But when the two men attempted to compensate Raphael, he revealed his true identity to them: "I am Raphael, one of the seven angels who enter and serve before the Glory of the Lord." He told them that his help "was not out of any favor on my part, but because it was God's will. So continue to thank him every day; praise him with song" (Tobit 12:15, 18).

The Archangel Gabriel

When the time had come for the Messiah to enter into human history, the archangel Gabriel appeared twice in Israel, first to the elderly priest Zechariah and then to a young maiden named Mary. Zechariah was serving in the sanctuary of the Temple in Jerusalem when Gabriel appeared to him and announced that his prayers and those of his wife Elizabeth had been answered and that they would have a son whom they would name John.

The angel said that John "will be great in the sight of [the] Lord. He will drink neither wine nor strong drink. He will be filled with the holy Spirit even from his mother's womb, and he will turn many of the children of Israel to the Lord their God. He will go before him in the spirit and power of Elijah to turn the hearts of fathers toward children and the disobedient to the understanding of the righteous, to prepare a people fit for the Lord" (Luke 1:15-17).

Zechariah doubted the words of Gabriel because he and his wife were advanced in age, so the angel rendered him speechless until the time the promise was fulfilled. When John was born, it was expected that he would be named after his father, but Zechariah called for a tablet and wrote, "John is his name" (Luke 1:63). At that moment, his speech was restored and he delivered his famous canticle of praise (cf. Luke 1:68-79).

Three months earlier, Gabriel had startled a young virgin in Nazareth, who was betrothed to a man named Joseph, by appearing to her and asking her to become the mother of Jesus. He told her that this Child "will be great and will be called Son of the Most High, and the Lord God will give him the throne of David his father, and he will rule over the house of Jacob forever, and of his kingdom there will be no end" (Luke 1:32-33).

Mary was profoundly disturbed by the angel's words because she had vowed to remain a virgin all of her life, but Gabriel quieted her fears by saying that this Child would be conceived not in the usual human way but miraculously by the power of the Holy Spirit. Mary, the New Eve, responded to this request from God by saying, "Behold, I am the handmaid of the Lord. May it be done to me according to your word" (Luke 1:38).

The Archangel Michael

In chapter 12 of the Book of Revelation, we read that "war broke out in heaven; Michael and his angels battled against the dragon. The dragon and its angels fought back, but they did not prevail and there was no longer any place for them in heaven. The huge dragon, the ancient serpent, who is called the Devil and Satan, who deceived the whole world, was thrown down to earth, and its angels were thrown down with it" (12:7-9).

The Church has traditionally seen this passage as referring to the rebellion of the bad angels against God and their expulsion from heaven by the archangel Michael. The *Catechism* (n. 391) teaches that Satan and his comrades were " 'created naturally good by God, but they became evil by their own doing' [Lateran Council IV (1215): DS 800]." Why they rebelled is not clear, although it may have been the same motive as that suggested by the tempter in the Garden of Eden — "You will be like gods" (Genesis 3:5).

In any case, their conscious and deliberate rejection of God is irrevocable and unforgivable, and there is no chance for repentance, just as there will be no chance for repentance for humans after death if they have died in a state of hostility toward God (cf. *Catechism*, n. 393).

One morning in 1886, after celebrating Mass, Pope Leo XIII, who reigned from 1878-1903, reportedly had a terrifying vision of the power the devil would wield in the coming century. So he composed the following prayer:

St. Michael, the archangel, defend us in battle.
Be our protection against the wickedness
and snares of the devil. Rebuke him, O God,
we humbly beseech you, and do you, O prince
of the heavenly host, by the power of God,
drive into hell Satan and all the evil spirits
who roam through the world
seeking the ruin of souls. Amen.

Angels in the Old Testament

The participation of angels in Old Testament events is considerable. In Genesis, they visited with Abraham (18:2ff) and Lot (19:1ff) and urged Lot to flee the region before God destroyed the cities of Sodom and Gomorrah (19:15-22). They are mentioned in Jacob's dream as "God's messengers" going up and down the stairway to heaven (28:12), and an angel, after a nocturnal wrestling match, informs Jacob that from now on his name will be Israel (32:29).

In Exodus 14, the angel of the Lord led Moses and his people toward the Red Sea and then moved behind them to shield them from the pursuing Egyptians. In the Sinai wilderness, God promised to send "an angel before you, to guard you on the way and bring you to the place I have prepared. Be attentive to him and heed his voice. Do not rebel against him, for he will not forgive your sin. My authority resides in him. If you heed his voice and carry out all I tell you, I will be an enemy to your enemies and a foe to your foes" (Exodus 23:20-22).

In the Book of Judges, an angel scolded the Israelites for making pacts with the inhabitants of Canaan and for not pulling down their altars to pagan gods, and said that "I will not clear them out of your way; they shall oppose you and their gods shall become a snare for you" (2:3). An angel appeared to Gideon and commissioned him to save Israel from the power of Midian, promising that "I shall be with you ... and you will cut down Midian to the last man" (6:16).

Another angel appeared to a woman in Zorah who had never been able to have children and told her that she would bear a son who would begin the deliverance of Israel from the power of the Philistines. That son would be called Samson (Judges 13:24).

In the First Book of Kings, an angel of the Lord ordered the prophet Elijah, who was hiding from those seeking to take his life, to eat and drink and begin his 40-day journey to the mountain of God in Horeb (19:7) In the Second Book of Kings, an angel instructed Elijah to tell the king of Samaria that he would die from an injury sustained in a fall because he had sent messengers to the pagan god Baalzebub to ask whether he would recover from his fall (1:16).

In First Chronicles, the Lord sent an angel to destroy the city of Jerusalem because King David had conducted a census of the people against the Lord's wishes, but relented at the last minute from imposing this punishment (21:15). In Second Chronicles, an angel of the Lord struck down 185,000 men in the Assyrian camp (32:21 and Isaiah 37:36).

In the Book of Daniel, an angel delivered Shadrach, Meshach, and Abednego from a fiery death (3:95), and saved Daniel from being mauled to death in a lion's den (6:22). And the prophet Zechariah was repeatedly informed by angels about the future of Jerusalem and the people of Israel.

Angels in the New Testament

If angels were important in the millennia leading up to the coming of the Messiah, it is not surprising that they accompanied Jesus from his Annunciation to his Resurrection and Ascension. We have already noted Gabriel's appearances to Zechariah and Mary, and angels were in Bethlehem on the night Jesus was born, informing shepherds of the Birth of the Savior and Messiah and singing, "Glory to God in the highest/ and on earth peace to those on whom his favor rests" (Luke 2:8:14).

Following the Annunciation, an angel had informed Joseph in a dream that it was all right to take Mary into his house since the Child she was carrying had been conceived by the power of the Holy Spirit (Matthew 1:20). After the birth in Bethlehem, another angel warned Joseph to take Mary and Jesus into Egypt because the evil King Herod was seeking to kill the Child (Matthew 2:13). He complied immediately with the angelic warning, and the Holy Family remained in Egypt until an angel informed Joseph that Herod had died and that it was safe to returrn home (Matthew 2:19).

At the start of his public life, Jesus was tempted by Satan in the desert after forty days of prayer and fasting. Angels came and ministered to Christ following the ordeal (Matthew 4:11). The presence of Satan in the Garden of Gethsemane is not specifically mentioned in the Gospels but, as Mel Gibson dramatized in his movie *The Passion of the Christ*, it seems likely that the tempter was there trying to persuade Jesus to abandon his mission to save the world from sin. In any case, we know that during his ordeal in the Garden, an angel from heaven came to strengthen him (Luke 22:43).

We also know that Jesus wished to suffer his agony to the fullest since he rejected the idea of calling on his Father to send thousands of angels to rescue him from the soldiers who had arrested him (Matthew 26:53).

It was not unusual for the Lord to talk about angels during his public ministry. He warned against leading little children into sin, "for I say to you that their angels in heaven always look upon the face of my heavenly Father" (Matthew 18:10). He said that a day would come when "you will see the sky opened and the angels of God ascending and descending on the Son of Man" (John 1:51). And after telling one of his parables, Jesus said that "there will be rejoicing among the angels of God over one sinner who repents" (Luke 15:10).

Angels will also be very much involved at the end of world, said Christ. They will gather up all the evildoers and cast them into "the fiery furnace, where there will be wailing and grinding of teeth" (Matthew 13:42). On that day, he said, "the Son of Man will come with his angels in his Father's glory, and then he will repay everyone according to his conduct" (Matthew 16:27).

This second coming won't be as quiet and obscure as the first one either, said Jesus, saying that "he will send out his angels with a trumpet blast, and they will gather his elect from the four winds, from one end of the heavens to the other" (Matthew 24:31). So much for the modern theory of the "Rapture," which contends that God will quietly and secretly snatch people up to heaven while they are going about their everyday activities.

Angels were also present to celebrate Jesus' rising from the dead on Easter morning, appearing first to the guards at the tomb and then to the women who came to prepare the body for burial (Matthew 28:2-7, Mark 16:5-7, Luke 24:4-7), and also to Mary Magdalen (John 20:12-13). Their message was the same to all the followers of Christ: He has risen from the dead as he promised, and they would see him soon in Galilee.

Forty days after the Resurrection, Jesus met with the disciples on a mountain in Bethany and commissioned them to spread his teachings throughout the world. As they watched him ascend into heaven, two angels appeared and said: "Men of Galilee, why are you standing there looking at the sky? This Jesus who has been taken up from you into heaven will return in the same way as you have seen him going into heaven" (Acts 1:11).

Angels in the Early Church

According to the Acts of the Apostles, St. Luke's account of the first decades of the Catholic Church's existence, angels continued to guide and protect the followers of Christ. They twice freed Peter from jail (5:19 and 12:7); told Philip to speak to an Ethiopian on the road to Gaza so the deacon could explain to him the passage from Isaiah 53:7-8 about a sheep being led to the slaughter, a reference to Jesus, and then baptize him (8:26-39); and told the Gentile Cornelius to summon Peter to his house in Caesarea, where Peter would baptize Cornelius and his relatives and friends (10:3-6).

An angel also struck Herod Antipas dead because he had accepted the praise of a crowd which said that he was "the voice of a god, not of a man" (12:22), and told St. Paul that neither he nor any of the passengers on a ship caught in a terrible storm would lose their lives because "you are destined to stand before Caesar [in Rome]; and behold, for your sake, God has granted safety to all who are sailing with you" (27:24).

In his Second Letter to the Corinthians, Paul cautioned against believing demons posing as angels. He warned about "false apostles, deceitful workers, who masquerade as apostles of Christ. And no wonder, for even Satan masquerades as an angel of light. So it is not strange that his ministers also masquerade as ministers of righteousness. Their end will correspond to their deeds" (11:13-15).

In the letter to the Hebrews, the author counseled mutual love among the faithful, saying, "Do not neglect hospitality, for through it some have unknowingly entertained angels" (13:2).

In the Second Letter of Peter, the prince of the Apostles reminded his readers that "God did not spare the [bad] angels when they sinned, but condemned them to the chains of Tartarus and handed them over to be kept for judgment" (2:4). Tartarus is a term borrowed from Greek mythology that refers to the regions of hell.

In verse 6 of his letter, Jude echoed Peter by saying that "the [bad] angels too, who did not keep to their own domain but deserted their proper dwelling, he has kept in eternal chains, in gloom, for the judgment of the great day."

In the last book of the Bible, the Book of Revelation, there are dozens of mentions of angels, beginning with the one who made God's revelation known to John (1:1), to the ones watching over the seven churches of Asia, to the four angels standing at the four corners of the earth and holding back the four winds (7:2), to the seven angels blowing trumpets in heaven (8:2), to the three angels bringing the "everlasting good news ... to every nation, tribe, tongue, and people" (14:6).

In the final chapter of Revelation, the author says, "It is I, John, who heard and saw these things, and when I heard and saw them I fell down to worship at the feet of the angel who showed them to me. But he said to me, 'Don't! I am a fellow servant of yours and of your brothers the prophets and of those who keep the message of this book. Worship God'" (22:8-9).

WORDS TO REMEMBER

* angel   * choirs of angels   * archangel
* Angelus   * guardian angels   * Raphael
* Gabriel   * Michael

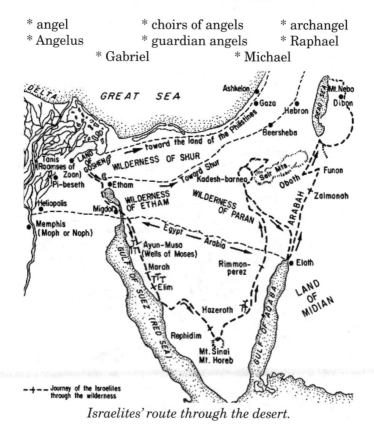

Israelites' route through the desert.

Chapter 7

Out of Egypt:
Moses and the Exodus

> He split the sea and led them across,
> piling up the waters rigid as walls.
> God led them with a cloud by day,
> all night with the light of fire.
> — Psalm 78:13-14

The use of types in Scripture, as noted in Chapter 1, means that certain persons and events in the Old Testament prefigure or foreshadow persons and events in the New Testament. This typology is particularly evident in the parallels between Moses and Jesus. Consider just the following examples:

- As infants, both escaped death at the hands of an evil king
- Little is known about the childhood of either one
- Moses was a shepherd; Jesus was the Good Shepherd
- Both were often rejected by their own people
- Moses led people from slavery in Egypt; Jesus led people from their slavery to sin
- Moses received the law on a mountain; Jesus fulfilled the the law in his Sermon on the Mount
- Moses led his people to the Promised Land of Canaan; Jesus leads his people to the promised land of heaven
- Moses used the blood of a lamb to save his people from death; Jesus is the Lamb of God whose blood saves us from eternal death

Oppression in Egypt

As long as the memory of Joseph remained in Egypt, the people of Israel prospered. But then a new king came to power who knew nothing of Joseph and who was alarmed at how numerous and strong the Israelites had become. He instituted two policies: (1) force the Israelites into slave labor building the cities of Pithom and Rameses, and (2) have the Hebrew midwives who assisted in the birth of children throw the boy babies into the river, but let the girls live. The midwives, however, feared God more than Pharaoh and let the boys live.

And so it was that a Hebrew woman had a son and hid him for three months. When she could conceal him no longer, she put him in a papyrus basket sealed with pitch and set him afloat in the reeds along the river, while her daughter Miriam watched to see what would happen. The basket floated down to where Pharaoh's daughter was bathing, and she sent her handmaid to fetch it.

As soon as Pharaoh's daughter saw the baby boy and expressed concern about him, Miriam approached and asked her if she should find the child's mother to nurse him. Yes, said Pharaoh's daughter, and Miriam went and got her mother. She nursed her son for a time and then brought him back to Pharaoh's daughter, who adopted the boy and named him Moses, "for ... 'I drew him out of the water' " (Exodus 2:10).

Moses grew up in Pharaoh's household, but remained a Hebrew at heart and was disturbed at the oppression of his people. One day he saw an Egyptian strike a Hebrew and, looking about and seeing no one, Moses killed the Egyptian and buried him in the sand. The following day he saw two Hebrews fighting and, when he intervened, one of the combatants asked, "Who has appointed you ruler and judge over us? Are you thinking of killing me as you killed the Egyptian?" (Exodus 2:14).

Moses became frightened and, when he learned that Pharaoh had heard of the affair and sought to kill him, he fled to the land of Midian, became a shepherd, and married a woman named Zipporah. Meanwhile, the oppression of the Hebrews increased in Egypt, and they groaned and cried out for relief.

A Reluctant Emissary

After many years as a shepherd for his father-in-law Jethro, Moses one day was leading the sheep near Horeb, the mountain of God, when he saw a strange sight — a bush that was on fire but that was not being consumed. As he approached the bush, God called out to him, saying, "Come no nearer! Remove the sandals from your feet, for the place where you stand is holy ground. I am the God of your father, the God of Abraham, the God of Isaac, the God of Jacob" (Exodus 3:5-6).

Moses was afraid to look at God, but the Lord told him that he had heard the cry of his people against their slavemasters, and he was going to send Moses to lead them out of Egypt. But Moses wanted to know how someone like him could go to Pharaoh and lead the Israelites to freedom, and God said, "I will be with you" (Exodus 3:12).

But when he went to the Israelites to tell them that the God of their fathers had sent him, Moses persisted, what name should he give to God. God replied, "I am who am.... This is what you shall tell the Israelites: I AM sent me to you." He added, "This is my name forever;/ this is my title for all generations" (Exodus 3:14-15).

God was telling Moses that he was a personal God, one who was personally and intimately interested in the well-being of his people, not some aloof and uncaring god. The kind of God of whom Jesus spoke when he said that not even a sparrow falls to the ground "without your Father's knowledge. Even all the hairs of your head are counted. So do not be afraid; you are worth more than many sparrows" (Matthew 10:29-31).

During his public ministry, Jesus on occasion associated himself with this title for God, as when he said that he knew Abraham and that Abraham was glad when he saw Jesus' day. How could he have seen Abraham when Jesus was not yet fifty years old, his enemies asked, and Christ replied: "Amen, amen, I say to you, before Abraham came to be, I AM" (John 8:58).

This reply so infuriated his foes that they picked up stones to throw at him, so Jesus left the Temple area and hid.

Moses was still skeptical that the Israelites would even listen to him or believe that God had spoken to him. So the Lord performed two miracles to convince Moses: he changed his staff into a serpent and then back to a staff again, and he afflicted Moses' hand with leprosy and then restored it to health again. God also overcame his chosen envoy's last objection, that he was too slow of speech and tongue to impress anyone, by appointing his brother Aaron, an eloquent speaker, to be Moses' spokesman.

Return to Egypt

After performing various signs for the people to persuade them that God had commissioned him, Moses went back to Egypt, and he and Aaron asked Pharaoh to let their people go out into the desert to offer sacrifice to the Lord. Pharaoh refused the request that would take the people away from his building projects, and he ordered his slavemasters to increase the workload of the people. No longer would he provide straw for the making of bricks; the people would have to gather the straw themselves and meet the same daily quota of bricks as when the straw had been supplied to them.

So Moses and Aaron renewed their demand to Pharaoh and demonstrated the power their God had given to them by having Aaron's staff turn into a snake. It seemed like a standoff when Pharaoh's magicians were able to work the same wonder, but then Aaron's staff swallowed up those of the magicians. Pharaoh remained obstinate, however, as God had foretold, so Moses initiated a string of ten plagues to show Pharaoh that God was serious in seeking freedom for his people.

The plagues began with water turned into blood, and that was followed by swarms of frogs, gnats, and flies; by pestilence that killed all the livestock in Egypt; by festering boils; by giant hailstones that ruined all the crops; by a swarm of locusts that ate up any vegetation left from the hailstorm; and by a dense darkness throughout the land that lasted for three days.

After some of the plagues, Pharaoh appeared willing to relent and let the people go, but once the plague stopped he reverted to his previous stand. So God imposed the final and deadliest plague by decreeing that at midnight he would go forth throughout Egypt and strike down every first-born in the land, bringing about such "loud wailing throughout the land of Egypt, such as has never been, nor will ever be again" (Exodus 11:6).

The First Passover

To protect the families of the Israelites, God told Moses to instruct the people to slaughter a one-year-old male lamb without blemish and to smear the blood of the lamb on the doorposts and lintel of every house. Each family was then to eat the lamb's roasted flesh with unleavened bread and bitter herbs, and to eat "like those who are in flight. It is the Passover of the LORD. For on this same night I will go through Egypt, striking down every first-born of the land, both man and beast, and executing judgment on all the gods of Egypt — I, the LORD! But the blood will mark the houses where you are. Seeing the blood, I will pass over you; thus, when I strike the land of Egypt, no destructive blow will come upon you" (Exodus 12:11:13).

God also decreed that this day would become a memorial feast for the people of Israel, which all generations would celebrate as a perpetual institution to remind them of God's saving actions. It was just such a Passover meal that Jesus celebrated with his Apostles the night before he died. Only at that meal the Lamb of God instituted a new and everlasting covenant, gave himself to them under the appearances of bread and wine in the Holy Eucharist, and commanded that his followers throughout the centuries "do this in memory of me" (Luke 22:19).

That is why all Catholics should take part every week in the Holy Sacrifice of the Mass — not just to fulfill an obligation, not just because weekly Mass attendance is a precept of the Church, not just because parents or teachers encourage us to participate — but simply and solely because the Son of God, on the night before he willingly laid down his life for our sins, commanded us to celebrate this banquet in remembrance of him.

Joyful participation in holy Mass is our best way of praising God, thanking him for all his blessings, asking his help for our needs and those of others, and making reparation for our sins and the sins of the world.

When Pharaoh saw the havoc that had been wreaked on his country, including the death of his own son, he summoned Moses and Aaron and told them to leave Egypt quickly and take all their people, flocks, and herds with them. The Lord had made the Egyptian people well-disposed toward the Israelites, and they showered them with articles of silver and gold and other things. Jacob had come down to Egypt with about seventy people (cf. Exodus 1:5) some 430 years earlier; now Moses would be leading about 600,000 Israelites, not counting children, out of Egypt.

Miracle at the Red Sea

Setting out for the Red Sea by way of the desert road and carrying the bones of Joseph, who had asked his people to swear that they would return his remains to the land of Canaan, the Israelites were guided by the Lord. He preceded them during the day by means of a column of cloud, and illuminated their way at night with a column of fire. Thus, they were able to travel day and night.

Meanwhile, Pharaoh had changed his mind about letting them go and sent his entire army after them, hundreds and hundreds of chariots and warriors. When the Israelites saw the

Egyptians coming, they berated Moses for getting them into this predicament and said that they would be better off serving the Egyptians than to die in the desert. But Moses assured them that "the LORD himself will fight for you; you have only to keep still" (Exodus 14:14).

Then the angel of the Lord, who had been leading them, went around behind the Israelites, as did the column of cloud that had been in front of them. The cloud became dark and obscured the Egyptians' view, and the night passed without the two rival camps coming any closer to each other.

Moses then stretched out his hand over the sea while the Lord swept the sea with a strong east wind so that it turned into dry land. The Israelites marched through the sea on the dry path, with walls of water on both sides of them, and the Egyptians followed in pursuit. The Lord then cast a glance at the Egyp-tians through the fiery cloud that so rattled them that their chariot wheels became clogged, and they sounded retreat.

The Lord told Moses to stretch his hand out again over the sea and the waters flowed back to their normal depth, covering the chariots and charioteers of Pharaoh's whole army. Not a single member of the army survived. When the Israelites saw all the bodies of the dead Egyptians lying on the seashore, "they feared the LORD and believed in him and in his servant Moses" (Exodus 14:31).

They then sang a lengthy song to the Lord (cf. Exodus 15:1-18), which began with these verses:

> I will sing to the LORD, for he is gloriously triumphant;
> horse and chariot he has cast into the sea.
> My strength and my courage is the LORD,
> and he has been my savior.
> He is my God, I praise him;
> the God of my father, I extol him.

This joy and excitement would not last long, however, and the people would soon start complaining again.

Manna from Heaven

After miraculously crossing through the Red Sea, the Israelites came to the appropriately named Wilderness of Sin. They had gone for several days without water and, once again, complained to Moses: "Would that we had died at the LORD's hand in the land of Egypt, as we sat by our fleshpots and ate our fill of bread! But you had to lead us into this desert to make the whole community die of famine!" (Exodus 16:3).

So Moses turned to the Lord for help, and God promised to "rain down bread from heaven" for the people. "I have heard the grumbling of the Israelites," he told Moses. "Tell them: In the evening twilight you shall eat flesh, and in the morning you shall have your fill of bread, so that you may know that I, the LORD, am your God" (Exodus 16:12).

Every evening after that, quail covered the camp and, in the morning, there were on the ground bread-like wafers. When asked what the wafers were, Moses told them that this was the bread which God had given them to eat. This, of course, was a foreshadowing of another bread that would come down from heaven, the bread of life that is Jesus and that comes to us in the Holy Eucharist. Unlike those who ate the manna in the desert and still died, however, the bread from heaven that Jesus gives will enable those who receive it to live forever (cf. John 6:58).

Along with providing the bread, God gave instructions on how it was to be obtained. Each day a person was to collect enough bread for those in his tent, and no one was to keep any bread overnight, or it would become wormy and rotten. On the sixth day, they were to gather enough food for two days since no manna would be provided on the Sabbath.

Water from the Rock

The next complaint was about lack of water, so Moses asked God in frustration, "What shall I do with this people? A little more and they will stone me!" (Exodus 17:4). God told him to order a nearby rock to yield its water for the people to drink, but instead of speaking to the rock, Moses exhibited a weakening of his faith in God and struck the rock twice with his staff.

The water gushed out in abundance, but the Lord said to Moses and Aaron: "Because you were not faithful to me in showing forth my sanctity before the Israelites, you shall not lead this community into the land that I will give them" (Numbers 20:12). That place became known as Massah and Meribah because the Israelites "quarreled there and tested the Lord, saying, " 'Is the LORD in our midst or not?' " (Exodus 17:7).

Not long after that, a people known as Amalekites engaged the Israelites in battle. Moses had ordered Joshua to pick out certain men to defend the Israelites and had said that he would be standing on the top of the hill with the staff of God in his hand. As long as Moses kept his hands raised up in prayer, the Israelites were winning, but when his hands grew tired and he lowered them, the Amalekites gained the advantage. So Aaron and Hur supported Moses hands, one on each side of him, until sunset, and Joshua was able to defeat the foe completely.

Has it occurred to you that our spiritual leaders today, especially the Holy Father in Rome and our bishops and priests, also grow tired in the constant struggle against a culture that seeks to remove all mention of God from the public square? They need our help to hold up their hands when they grow weary, and they need our prayers, encouragement, praise, and support.

The Covenant at Mount Sinai

Three months after leaving Egypt, the Israelites came to the desert of Sinai and pitched camp at the base of the mountain. God summoned Moses to the top of the mountain and established a covenant with him, just as he had done with Abraham and would do with David. He told him to tell the people:

"You have seen for yourselves how I treated the Egyptians and how I bore you up on eagle's wings and brought you here to myself. Therefore, if you hearken to my voice and keep my covenant, you shall be my special possession, dearer to me than all other people, though all the earth is mine. You shall be to me a kingdom of priests, a holy nation" (Exodus 19:4-6).

So Moses conveyed the Lord's words to the elders of the people, and they promised to do everything that the Lord asked. God then told Moses to have the people sanctify themselves for two days and then he would come down the mountain on the third day. Warn them, God said, not to go up the mountain or to touch its base, or they would be put to death.

On the morning of the third day, the people saw a heavy cloud over the mountain and heard loud claps of thunder and a trumpet blast, so that all trembled in fright. The Lord came down upon the mountain in fire, and those assembled at the base of the mountain could hear Moses talking and God answering him with peals of thunder.

The Ten Commandments

While this great theophany was taking place, Moses went up Mount Sinai and received from God on two tablets of stone the Lord's blueprint for moral living, the Ten Commandments (cf. Exodus 20:2-17 and Deuteronomy 5:6-21). The Church's traditional way of expressing these commandments is as follows (cf. *Catechism*, pp. 496-497):

1. I am the LORD your God: you shall not have strange gods before me.
2. You shall not take the name of the LORD your God in vain.
3. Remember to keep holy the LORD's day.
4. Honor your father and your mother.
5. You shall not kill.
6. You shall not commit adultery.
7. You shall not steal.
8. You shall not bear false witness against your neighbor.
9. You shall not covet your neighbor's wife.
10. You shall not covet your neighbor's goods.

These Ten Commandments are not ten suggestions that we may keep or disregard at will. Nor are they all that is expected of us. The Christian moral life is more about following the person of Jesus (which includes keeping the Commandments) than following a moral code or a set of rules. Christ made that clear when he told the rich young man: "If you wish to be perfect, go, sell what you have and give to [the] poor, and you will have treasure in heaven. Then come, follow me" (Matthew 19:21).

In his Sermon on the Mount (cf. Matthew 5, 6, 7), the Lord said that he had not come "to abolish but to fulfill" the law of God (Matthew 5:17). Thus, he explained, it is not only wrong to kill another person, but if we are unjustly angry, we will be liable to judgment. It is not only wrong to commit the act of adultery, he said, but it is also adultery of the heart if one looks lustfully at another person.

Jesus went well beyond the Ten Commandments in the Sermon on the Mount, as he spelled out for us in great detail his blueprint for virtuous living, beginning with the Beatitudes. In those eight blessings, our Lord esteemed the poor in spirit, those who mourn, the meek, those who are hungry for righteousness, the merciful, the clean of heart, the peacemakers, and those who suffer persecution for conforming their lives to the will of God. He said that those who live the Beatitudes will enjoy their reward in the kingdom of heaven (cf. Matthew 5:10).

According to the *Catechism*, holiness of life is made possible "by union with Christ. When we believe in Jesus Christ, partake of his mysteries, and keep his commandments, the Savior himself comes to love, in us, his Father and his brethren, our Father and our brethren. His person becomes, through the Spirit, the living and interior rule of our activity" (n. 2074).

The Precepts of the Church

To make sure that we would always have the truth available to us, Jesus founded a Church to carry on his work in the world and gave the leaders of this Church the power to make laws in his name, saying to Peter: "Whatever you bind on earth shall be bound in heaven" (Matthew 16:19). For 2,000 years that Church, which St. Paul called "the pillar and foundation of truth" (1 Timothy 3:15), has faithfully promulgated the message and moral code of her Founder.

One expression of that moral code is the Precepts of the Church, which bind Catholics just as much as the Ten Commandments. Those precepts are listed as follows in the *Catechism* (cf. nn. 2042-2043):

1. You shall attend Mass on Sundays and on holy days of obligation and rest from servile labor.
2. You shall confess your sins at least once a year.
3. You shall receive the sacrament of the Eucharist at least during the Easter season.
4. You shall observe the days of fasting and abstinence established by the Church.
5. You shall help provide for the needs of the Church.

While it is valuable to have spelled out for us just what God expects, our interior dispositions are even more important. External observance of the law does not guarantee internal adherence to it. Jesus warned that those would not be saved whose religious practice consisted merely in calling him "Lord, Lord," while failing to do the will of his Father in heaven (cf. Matthew 7:21). It is deeds that count and not words.

The Two Great Commandments

In the Book of Deuteronomy, we find a more complete explanation of the law proclaimed on Mount Sinai. The book has been called Moses' last will and testament because he delivered a number of eloquent sermons to remind the people of what God had done for them and what love and loyalty they owed to him. He reiterated all the laws and statutes that Israel was called to observe and then summed them up with one great commandment:

Hear, O Israel! The LORD is our God, the LORD alone! Therefore, you shall love the LORD, your God, with all your heart, and with all your soul, and with all your strength. Take to heart these words which I enjoin on you today. Drill them into your children. Speak of them at home and abroad, whether you are busy or at rest (Deuteronomy 6:4-7).

Years later, a scribe would ask Jesus which of all the commandments should come first. Virtually repeating the words of Deuteronomy, but adding something else, Jesus replied:

The first is this: "Hear, O Israel! The Lord our God is Lord alone! You shall love the Lord your God with all your heart, with all your soul, with all your mind, and with all your strength." The second is this: "You shall love your neighbor as yourself." There is no other commandment greater than these (Mark 12:29-31).

So God had established his covenant with the people of Israel at Mount Sinai, and he had proclaimed his Commandments to them, but they were still a long way from the Promised Land, both geographically and spiritually.

WORDS TO REMEMBER

* I AM   * plagues   * Passover
      * manna   * Commandments
* Beatitudes   * Precepts of the Church

Worshiping the golden calf.

Chapter 8

In the Wilderness: Ark and Golden Calf

They exchanged their glorious God
for the image of a grass-eating bull.
They forgot the God who saved them,
who did great deeds in Egypt.
— Psalm 106:20-21

There's a well-known short story written many years ago called *The Man Without a Country*. It's about a fictional naval officer named Philip Nolan who got involved with Aaron Burr in some treasonous activities in the early 1800s. Nolan was eventually found guilty and, when the military court asked him if he were sorry for plotting against his country, he said he hoped that he would never see or hear of the United States again.

Shocked at Nolan's outburst, the judge declared a recess in order to think of an appropriate sentence for the defendant. He returned to the courtroom and told Nolan that he was granting him his wish that he would never see or hear of the United States again. Nolan was sentenced to spend the rest of his life on ships traveling around the world. His reading materials would be censored of any reference to the United States, no one on the ships would be allowed to mention anything about America to him, and, whenever the ship he was on neared the shores of the United States, Nolan would be transferred to another ship sailing away from America.

The rest of the story is about Philip Nolan's growing realization of the terrible mistake he had made in denouncing his country. He was especially stricken on one occasion when he came across Sir Walter Scott's poem "Lay of the Last Minstrel," which contains the lines:

Breathes there a man, with soul so dead,
Who never to himself hath said,
This is my own, my native land! ...

Sacrifices to the Lord

Like Philip Nolan, the Israelites were a people without a country, but their God was with them constantly despite their lapses into disloyalty and idolatry. Moses reported to the people what God had said on the mountain, and he erected at the foot of Sinai an altar and twelve pillars representing the twelve tribes of Israel.

After having sent men to sacrifice young bulls on the altar as peace offerings to the Lord, Moses took half of the blood from the animals and splashed it on the altar. He then sprinkled blood on the people, saying, "This is the blood of the covenant which the Lord has made with you in accordance with all of these words of his" (Exodus 24:8).

Blood was essential in Old Testament sacrifices because it was believed that life was located in the blood. And because blood was considered especially sacred, its pouring on the altar and sprinkling on the people symbolized cleansing from sin and reconciliation with God. So the high priest, under the old covenant, would enter into the sanctuary of the Temple (the Holy of Holies) once a year to offer a sacrifice with blood for his own sins and the sins of the people.

But while the blood of animals could bring about legal purification, it would require the blood of the pure and sinless Christ to offer full expiation for our sins and to bring about everlasting redemption. As the author of Hebrews explains:

> But when Christ came as high priest of the good things that have come to be, passing through the greater and more perfect tabernacle not made by hands, that is, not belonging to this creation, he entered once for all into the sanctuary [of heaven], not with the blood of goats and calves, but with his own blood, thus obtaining eternal redemption. For if the blood of goats and bulls and the sprinkling of a heifer's ashes can sanctify those who are defiled so that their flesh is cleansed, how much more will the blood of Christ, who through the eternal spirit offered himself unblemished to God, cleanse our consciences from dead works to worship the living God (9:11-14).

Thus, Christ's covenant surpasses that of Moses because it is ratified by his own blood, not the blood of animals. At the Last Supper on Holy Thursday, he promised that his blood would be "shed on behalf of many for the forgiveness of sins" (Matthew 26:28), and he sealed that promise on Good Friday by pouring out his blood on the cross.

All the elements of a true sacrifice were there on Calvary: an altar, a priest, and a victim being handed over to God. Christ was both the priest and the unblemished victim, and the cross was the altar, representing God, on which was poured the life-giving blood of the victim. That sacrifice is re-presented in an unbloody way (Christ could only die once) at every Mass in every part of the world today. And that Eucharistic sacrifice still involves "thanksgiving and praise to the *Father*; the sacrificial memorial of *Christ* and his Body; [and] the presence of Christ by the power of his word and of his *Spirit*" (*Catechism*, n. 1358).

It should be mentioned that God didn't need sacrifices in Old Testament times; the Israelites needed them to get away from idolatry and for the sake of atonement, thanksgiving, petition, etc. Noting that Jesus in Matthew 9:13 recalled the words of the prophet Hosea ("I desire mercy, not sacrifice"), the *Catechism* says that "the only perfect sacrifice is the one that Christ offered on the cross as a total offering to the Father's love and for our salvation [cf. *Heb* 9:13-14]. By uniting ourselves with his sacrifice we can make our lives a sacrifice to God" (n. 2100).

Ark of the Covenant

While in the presence of the Lord on Mount Sinai, Moses was instructed by God to build a meeting tent or sanctuary that would serve as a portable dwelling place for him among the Israelites until a permanent temple could be built in Jerusalem. That sanctuary tent (cf. Exodus 25-31 for the details on what materials and furnishings were to be used) was to contain the Ark of the Covenant, a small chest about four feet long and two-and-a-half feet wide and deep.

Coverered with gold inside and out, the Ark was to hold the two stone tablets with the Commandments written on them, the staff of Aaron, a jar of manna, and a copy of the book of the covenant. The Israelites frequently carried the Ark into battle as a sign that God was with them (cf. Joshua 6:1-21), and King David brought it to Jerusalem (2 Samuel 6), where it remained until the year 587 B.C., when it disappeared during the Babylonian destruction of the Temple. The search for it was fictionalized in a popular movie called *Raiders of the Lost Ark*.

The Golden Calf

When the people became aware that Moses had been on the mountain for many days, they asked Aaron to make them a god who would be their leader since they didn't know what had happened to Moses. Aaron instructed them to donate all items of jewelry containing gold in them, and then he melted the gold and fashioned the molten metal into a golden calf. The people cried out, "This is your God, O Israel, who brought you out of the land of Egypt" (Exodus 32:4). When he heard this, Aaron also built an altar before the calf.

Meanwhile, on the mountain, God informed Moses that he should go down at once to his people, "for they have become depraved" (Exodus 32:7), and God threatened to destroy them and build a new nation on Moses. But Moses prevailed upon the Lord to withhold his wrath lest the Egyptians say that God had brought them out of the land of Egypt only to exterminate them in the mountains. So God relented in the punishment he had intended to inflict on the Israelites for their idolatry.

Moses then came down from the Sinai height and, hearing the revelry of the people and seeing the golden calf, he smashed the tablets with the Commandments on them, fused the calf in fire and ground it into powder, which he spread on water and made the people drink. He asked Aaron how he could have let such a thing happen, and Aaron's only response was, "You know well enough how prone the people are to evil" (Exodus 32:22).

Moses then addressed the people and said, "Whoever is for the Lord, let him come to me!" (Exodus 32:26). Only the Levites rallied to him, and he told them to slay their rebellious relatives, friends, and neighbors. About three thousand people fell to the sword that day.

The following day, Moses told the people that they had committed a grave sin in worshiping a god of gold and that he would ask the Lord if there were some way they could atone for the sin. But when he asked God to forgive their sin, and even asked to have his own name stricken from the list of God's friends if the Almighty would not forgive the Israelites, the Lord responded:

> Him only who has sinned against me will I strike out of my book. Now, go and lead the people whither I have told you. My angel will go before you. When it is time for me to punish, I will punish them for their sin" (Exodus 32:33-34).

The golden calf was Israel's forbidden fruit. Just as Adam and Eve had turned away from the one, true God to become like gods themselves, so the Israelites had rebelled against the God who had led them out of slavery in Egypt and had turned their worship "to the image of a grass-eating bull" (Psalm 106:20). Note, too, how Aaron said that they were prone to evil, which is one of the effects of Original Sin.

In what way are people today prone to evil? What forbidden fruit do they seek? What golden calf do they worship? Think of some examples in your own life or in the society in which we live. The examples are plentiful.

Moses' Intimacy with God

Despite his anger with those whom God called "a stiff-necked people" (Exodus 33:5), Moses continued to lead them and to encourage them to change their sinful ways. He also remained in intimate contact with the Lord, often consulting with him at the meeting tent. After Moses had entered the tent, a column of cloud would stand at the entrance while God spoke to him, and all the people would rise and worship at the entrance of their own tents.

Once when Moses asked to see the glory of the Lord, he was told that he could not see the face of God and live, but that the Lord would pass before him without showing his face. As the Lord did so, God exclaimed: "The LORD, the LORD, a merciful and gracious God, slow to anger and rich in kindness and fidelity, continuing his kindness for a thousand generations, and forgiving wickedness and crime and sin" (Exodus 34:6-7).

Moses went up Mount Sinai again and stayed for forty days. When he came down bearing two new tablets of Commandments to replace the ones he had broken, the skin on his face had become radiant, and Aaron and the others were afraid to come near him. So he put a veil over his face whenever he entered into the presence of the Lord.

The radiant face of Moses is a foreshadowing of the radiant appearance of Jesus on the Mount of Transfiguration, where his faced changed in appearance and his clothing became dazzlingly white. The eyewitnesses to that event, Peter, James, and John, reported that they saw Jesus conversing with Moses and Elijah, two key figures of the Old Testament, about his coming Passion and Death in Jerusalem (cf. Luke 9:31).

The radiance of Moses' face and Jesus' body is also a foreshadowing of the glorified state our bodies will enjoy in the kingdom of heaven.

Departure from Sinai

Less than two years had passed since the Israelites had escaped from Egypt and made their way to Mount Sinai, and the remainder of their journey should have been accomplished in less time than that. But in fact the journey would take some 38 years because of the people's continued rebellion against God and their refusal to follow the lead of Moses. There was even jealousy on the part of Moses' siblings, Aaron and Miriam.

When the Lord heard that Aaron and Miriam were complaining about Moses being the only spokesman for God and saying that the Lord also spoke through them, God called the three of them together at the meeting tent and explained the primary role of Moses (Numbers 12:6-8):

> Should there be a prophet among you,
> in visions will I reveal myself to him,
> in dreams I will speak to him;
> Not so with my servant Moses!
> Throughout my house he bears my trust:
> face to face I speak to him,
> plainly and not in riddles.
> The presence of the LORD/ he beholds.

So angry was the Lord with them, that after he had departed Miriam was turned into a snow-white leper. Aaron pleaded with God not to charge them with the sin they had foolishly committed, and Moses begged the Lord to heal Miriam. God responded by telling them to confine Miriam outside the camp for seven days and then she would be healed and could return.

Scouting the Land of Canaan

Not long after that, God told Moses to send out twelve men, one from each of the tribes of Israel, to reconnoiter the land of Canaan, to see what kind of land it was, whether the soil was fertile or barren, and whether the people living there were few or many, strong or weak.

The scouting party returned after forty days and reported that the land did indeed flow with milk and honey, but that the inhabitants were fierce and their towns were well-fortified. While two of the scouts, Caleb and Joshua, said that with the Lord's help they would be able to overpower the Canaanites and capture the land, the other ten spread negative reports and stirred up the people to grumble against Moses, to threaten to stone him to death, and to wish that they were back in Egypt.

The Lord was furious at this lack of trust in him and he threatened to wipe out the people of Israel out with a pestilence. Once again, Moses pleaded with God to pardon the rebellious Israelites, and God said that he would, but he added that all of those over the age of twenty, who had seen the signs and wonders he had worked in Egypt and in the desert, would never see the Promised Land, but would die in the desert.

"Forty days you spent in scouting the land; forty years shall you suffer for your crimes: one year for each day," said God. "Thus you will realize what it means to oppose me. I, the LORD, have sworn to do this to all this wicked community that conspired against me: here in the desert they shall die to the last man" (Numbers 14:34-35).

And so it came to pass that all those who opposed God were struck down in the desert. Only Caleb and Joshua survived.

The Bronze Serpent

As the long journey dragged on, the people continued to complain against Moses and objected to "this wretched food" the Lord had provided them. So in punishment, God sent saraph serpents, which bit the people and caused many of them to die. They acknowledged their sinfulness and begged Moses to intercede with God to take the serpents away. The Lord's solution was to have Moses make a saraph serpent and mount it on a pole, and anyone who looked at the bronze serpent would recover from the poisonous snake bites.

Here we have another type of Jesus, who would also be mounted on a cross and, whenever people looked at him, they would be healed of the poison of sin. Here is how Jesus made the connection in his conversation with Nicodemus:

And just as Moses lifted up the serpent in the desert, so must the Son of Man be lifted up, so that everyone who believes in him may have eternal life (John 3:14-15).

On Easter Sunday night, Jesus would make sure that we would have the opportunity to have the poison of sin removed from our lives when he instituted the Sacrament of Penance or Reconciliation. He breathed on the Apostles in the upper room that night and said to them: "Receive the holy Spirit. Whose sins you forgive are forgiven them, and whose sins you retain are retained" (John 20:22-23).

Notice that Jesus did not say, whose sins "I" forgive, although he is ultimately the one doing the forgiving, but rather whose sins "you" forgive. He was extending the power to forgive sins to his priests through the Sacrament of Holy Orders. Notice, also, that in order for a priest to forgive sins, or not to forgive them if he thinks the penitent is not truly sorry or has no intention of avoiding the sin in the future, he must first be told the sins by the penitent.

So if someone asks why Catholics confess their sins to a priest, tell them it's because Jesus said so. Yes, one can seek forgiveness by telling sins directly to God, and we should express sorrow for our sins every night by reciting an Act of Contrition, but the ordinary way for a Catholic to have serious sins forgiven is by telling them to a priest in sacramental Confession.

Recall that the four elements of the Sacrament of Penance are contrition (being sorry for sin), confession (telling the sins), absolution (receiving forgiveness from the priest), and satisfaction (performing some penance, some prayer or good work, to atone for the sin). While telling one's serious sins to a priest is not easy, and requires true humility, it is an unparalleled opportunity to get sound advice on how to live a moral life and to come away with the certainty that our sins have been forgiven.

Our God is a God of unending mercy and forgiveness who is always willing to pardon a sincere penitent, just as he pardoned the people of Israel over and over and over again.

The Call of Joshua

As the people were nearing the land of Canaan, and it seemed as if their sinfulness was growing worse as the Promised Land came within sight (cf. the immorality and idolatry at the Baal of Peor in Numbers 25), the Lord invited Moses to the top of the mountain to see the land that he was giving to the Israelites. He reminded Moses that he would not be allowed to cross into the new land because of his lack of faith at the waters of Meribah.

When Moses asked God to set over the community a man who would be a good shepherd, the Lord told him to lay his hand upon Joshua and commission him before the whole community, investing him "with some of your own dignity, that the whole Israelite community may obey him" (Numbers 27:20). Moses did as the Lord commanded and commissioned Joshua to lead the Israelites into the land God had prepared for them.

While predicting that the Israelites would continue "rendering wanton worship to the strange gods among whom they will live in the land they are about to enter," that the people "will forsake me and break the covenant which I have made with them," and that "many evils and troubles will befall them," God nevertheless told Joshua to "be brave and steadfast, for it is you who must bring the Israelites into the land which I promised them on oath. I myself will be with you" (Deuteronomy 31:16-17, 23).

Moses' Final Instructions

Like all good leaders, including the Son of God himself, who would use his final years on earth to inform, challenge, and inspire his followers, so Moses delivered a series of sermons on the plains of Moab to remind his people of all that had happened to them and to encourage them to do what God expected of them. "I set before you here, this day," said Moses, "a blessing and a curse: a blessing for obeying the commandments of the LORD, your God, which I enjoin on you today; a curse if you do not obey the commandments of the LORD, your God, but turn aside from the way I ordain for you today, to follow other gods, whom you have not known" (Deuteronomy 11:26-28).

The command of the Lord is clear, said Moses. It is not too mysterious and remote, or up in the sky or across the sea, but is rather already in the hearts of the people, waiting to be carried out. "I call heaven and earth today to witness against you," he said. "I have set before you life and death, the blessing and the curse. Choose life, then, that you and your descendants may live, by loving the LORD, your God, heeding his voice, and holding fast to him. For that will mean life for you, a long life for you to live on the land which the LORD swore he would give to your fathers, Abraham, Isaac and Jacob" (Deuteronomy 30:19-20).

That admonition to "choose life" has been adopted as a slogan today by those seeking to protect the dignity of all human life from the moment of natural conception until natural death against the ravages of abortion, euthanasia, cloning, babies created in laboratories, and embryonic stem cell research. That this "culture of death" has been able to spread so rapidly and so far and wide is due in part to the failure of many Catholics to "choose life." They have chased after the false gods of the modern world. Instead of worshiping at the altar of the Lord, they find themselves bowing before the gods of "choice" and "comfort" and "convenience."

As the end neared, Moses went up to the top of Mount Nebo and looked over the Promised Land that he had struggled so mightily to reach, but which he was unable to enter. He died on the mountain and, for thirty days, all Israel mourned him. Writing some years later, the author of the Book of Deuteronomy summed up Moses' impact in these words:

> Since then no prophet has arisen in Israel like Moses, whom the LORD knew face to face. He had no equal in all the signs and wonders the LORD sent him to perform in the land of Egypt against Pharaoh and all his servants and against all his land, and for the might and terrifying power that Moses exhibited in the sight of all Israel (34:10-12).

WORDS TO REMEMBER

* Ark of the Covenant
* bronze serpent
* contrition
* absolution

* golden calf
* Penance/Reconciliation
* confession
* satisfaction

Chapter 9

The Promised Land: Joshua and the Judges

"To you I give the land of Canaan,
your own allotted heritage."
— Psalm 105:11

There is an old Jewish folk tale about two men on horseback on their way to a distant town. One was a believer in God and insisted that the Lord would take care of them. The other was a skeptic and continually demanded proof that God would provide. When they reached their destination, all the inns were filled and they could find no place to stay.

"See," said the skeptic, "I told you that your God wouldn't help us."

"Let's wait and see," the believer replied.

The men had to spend the night outside of town not far from the main road. They tied up their horses to a tree, started a fire, and laid down for the night. When they awoke the next morning, they discovered that rain had put out the fire and a wild animal had driven their horses off.

"Now will you agree with me that your God doesn't care about us?" the skeptic asked. "Else he wouldn't have allowed our horses to be run off."

"I'm sure God had something good in mind for us," the believer countered.

The men then walked into town and learned that, during the night, a group of bandits had raided the community, stolen everyone's belongings, and escaped down the main road.

"There!" the skeptic said. "See if you can find the hand of your God in that."

"Well," the believer said, "if you and I had found a room in town last night, we would have lost everything, too. And if the rain had not put out our fire, and the horses had still been there to make noise, the bandits would have seen or heard us and would have robbed us as well. So I guess God was looking out for us."

Help from Rahab

Like the believer in the story, and like his late mentor Moses, Joshua had great trust and confidence in the God who had promised that he would be with him every step of the way. "I will not leave you nor forsake you," God told Joshua, urging him to "observe the entire law which my servant Moses enjoined on you. Do not swerve from it either to the right or to the left, that you may succeed wherever you go. Keep this book of the law on your lips. Recite it by day and by night, that you may observe carefully all that is written in it; then you will successfully attain your goal" (Joshua 1:5, 7-8).

After hearing these words of support and encouragement, Joshua told the leaders of the twelve tribes to prepare in three days' time to cross the Jordan River into Canaan. He then chose two men to reconnoiter the land, especially around the major city of Jericho. The two spies found lodging in Jericho at the house of a harlot named Rahab and, when the king of Jericho heard that they were there, he ordered Rahab to put them out of her house.

However, the Lord inspired Rahab to hide the two spies and, when the king's men came looking for them, the woman said that they had already left. Once their pursuers were gone, Rahab told the men that she and her countrymen knew of their exploits at the Red Sea and were fearful of them. Nevertheless, she gave them some rope and helped to lower them down from a window in her house, which was built into one of the city walls. She had first extracted from them a promise that, when the Israelites attacked the city, they would spare her and her family. The men replied that if she kept their mission secret, they would show kindess to her after the city had fallen.

Crossing the Jordan

After the spies had reported back to him that the inhabitants of the land were fearful of the Israelites and that the Lord would guarantee them victory, Joshua assembled the people on the banks of the Jordan and, with the Ark of the Covenant at the head of the marchers, led them into the river. As soon as the soles of the feet of the priests carrying the Ark entered the water, the river halted its flow in a solid wall of water, as had also happened at the Red Sea, and all crossed over on dry ground.

After the entire nation had traversed the river, but the priests carrying the Ark were still standing in the river bed, Joshua asked twelve men to gather from the river one large stone each so that he could erect a perpetual memorial on that spot. Once the stones were collected, and the priests had carried the Ark onto the shore, the waters of the Jordan resumed their flow.

The Siege of Jericho

As the Israelites neared the city of Jericho, the Lord ordered Joshua to have them march silently around the walls of the city for six days and then, on the seventh day, to march around the city seven times and have the Levite priests blow their ram's horns while the soldiers shouted as loudly as they could. The directions were followed and the walls of the city collapsed. The Israelite army entered Jericho and killed every one of its inhabitants, except Rahab and her family. Then they burned the city after collecting all the gold and silver, bronze and iron articles and giving them to be put in the treasury of the Lord.

This slaughter of all those in a city, men, women, and children, sounds horribly wrong to us, and it is horribly wrong. On the one hand, however, consider the death toll in just the past century alone. Soviet and Chinese Communism was responsible for killing more than 100 million people in the 20th century. Hitler's victims numbered in the millions and whole cities (Dresden, Hiroshima, Nagasaki) were wiped out during World War II.

Add to that toll those who died in the "killing fields" of Cambodia after the Vietnam War, in the "ethnic cleansing" in Bosnia, in the tribal warfare in Africa, and in the abortion chambers of the world, and you can see that man's inhumanity to man was not restricted to the period before the coming of Christ.

On the other hand, however, it must be noted that the killing by the Israelites was not endorsed by God, but was merely tolerated to give his people the land that had been promised to them and to protect Israel from the idolatry and immorality of the Canaanites. Recall, also, that Moses tolerated the evil of divorce (Deuteronomy 24:1), but this was only because, in the words of Jesus, "of the hardness of your hearts" (Matthew 19:8).

Jesus went on to say that this was not the way it was in the beginning, and that divorce would not be tolerated under the new and everlasting covenant (Mark 10:9-12). He also repudiated the notion of "an eye for an eye and a tooth for a tooth," saying instead to turn the other cheek when someone strikes you (cf. Matthew 5:39) and even to "love your enemies, and pray for those who persecute you" (Matthew 5:44).

The Sin Cycle

The capture of Jericho was not because of military strategy, but because the Lord was with his people. However, some of them disobeyed his command not to steal items of value from the inhabitants and keep them for themselves. God took notice of this and, when the Israelites went into battle at the city of Ai a short time later, they were defeated. When Joshua asked why they had not been successful, God gave him the reason and told him to call everyone together the next day to find out who had stolen the goods and put all Israel into disfavor.

When a man named Achan came forward and admitted to taking and hiding items of gold and silver, he and his entire family were stoned to death for the misery that had been brought on Israel. God told Joshua to attack the city of Ai again, saying that he had delivered the king, the city, and the people, into his power. The Lord's instructions were carried out, and the city was captured and then set on fire after the entire population had been killed.

This same pattern would continue until the Israelites had overcome all their enemies, and well into the future as well. Their military victories would be followed by sinful actions, such as stealing or worshiping idols. The Lord would then withdraw his assistance, allowing the Israelites to undergo suffering and defeat. The people would then express sorrow for their sins and and turn back to the Lord, and the whole cycle would start all over again — from sin to suffering to sorrow to salvation.

We go through the same cycle in our own lives. We are sailing along in God's favor when we see someone or something that we know is "forbidden fruit," but we decide that we have to taste that fruit. It is only after we sin that the fruit doesn't appear so inviting, and our actions have consequences for ourselves and for those around us.

When the suffering and remorse become more than we can handle, we either give in to despair and do something rash, or we humbly admit that we have sinned and seek God's forgiveness and the forgiveness of others whom we have hurt. Once we have confessed our sins, and know with certainty that God has pardoned us, then we are back on the road to salvation. But to stay on that road demands persevering prayer and frequent recourse to the Sacraments that are available to us in the Catholic Church.

Renewal of the Covenant

When Joshua was advanced in years and much of Canaan had been conquered, he divided the land among the tribes of Israel, except for the Levites, the priestly tribe whose inheritance was the Lord. They were given cities in the various regions. Joshua also set up the meeting tent in Shiloh so the people could worship the Lord there. He later gathered all the people at Shechem and reminded them of all the Lord had done for them from the time of Abraham until then.

In a final plea, Joshua said that God would continue to protect them and drive out their enemies before them so long as they remained faithful to him and to the laws of Moses. He warned, however, that if Israel ever abandoned God and allied itself with the people of the conquered lands, intermarrying and intermingling with them, "the anger of the LORD will flare up against you and you will quickly perish from the good land which he has given you" (Joshua 23:16).

The people responded that they would never forsake the Lord to worship other gods, and Joshua said that they were their own witnesses of their vow to remain faithful to God. He then made a covenant with the people and set up a large stone under an oak tree, saying that "this stone shall be our witness, for it has heard all the words which the LORD spoke to us. It shall be a witness against you, should you wish to deny your God" (Joshua 24:27). Joshua then dismissed the people, and shortly after that his life on earth came to an end.

Our Promised Land

Like the people of Israel, we also are on a journey, one that began at our Baptism, that has been strengthened with the sacraments of Confirmation and the Holy Eucharist, and that we hope will end in the promised land of heaven. We have spiritual leaders to guide us and remind us of our destiny — the Holy Father and those bishops and priests who are in communion with him.

Also like the Israelites, we have to fight off temptations from the false gods of this world — wealth, power, fame, pleasure, etc. — and keep our eyes firmly focused on Jesus, who said, "I am the way and the truth and the life. No one comes to the Father except through me" (John 14:6). There will be false messiahs, those who claim to offer a better way to heaven, perhaps one that does not include pain and suffering, but there is only one sure way to the kingdom of God, and that is by way of the cross of Christ. There can be no Easter Sunday without a Good Friday.

The Time of the Judges

With Joshua gone and the land of Canaan mostly settled, and the time of the monarchy still two hundred years away, the people were in need of good leaders to guide them, so God sent a dozen men known as judges. They did not wear black robes and sit in a courtroom; rather, they were military authorities provided by God to protect his people from external dangers that arose because the people once again abandoned the Lord and served false gods known as the Baals. As long as the judge lived, God saved the people from the power of their enemies, but once the judge died, the enemy gained the upper hand until a new judge appeared on the scene.

The judges are usually divided into two groups: the major judges, so called because their lives are treated in some detail and because they are noted for their military prowess, and the minor judges, who are noted more for their administration of justice. Those in the first category are Othniel, Ehud, Barak, Gideon, Jephthah, and Samson. In the second grouping are Shamgar, Tola, Jair, Ibzan, Elon, and Abdon.

Of particular interest are the exploits of Barak, Gideon, and Samson, and we will treat each of them briefly.

Barak and Deborah

Any discussion of Barak necessarily includes Deborah, a prophetess who summoned Barak and ordered him to assemble an army to fight the Canaanite king Jabin and his army general Sisera. Barak said that he would not go unless Deborah accompanied him. "I will certainly go with you," she replied, "but you shall not gain the glory in the expedition on which you are setting out, for the LORD will have Sisera fall into the power of a woman" (Judges 4:9). Apparently, Barak had no problem with that, and Deborah went along on the mission.

Ten thousand soldiers went forth under Barak's command and, with God's help, they routed the enemy and put them all to death. Only Sisera escaped, and he fled to the tent of a woman named Jael, wife of Heber the Kenite, who was friendly with King Jabin. Jael gave Sisera something to drink and covered him with a rug, but when he fell asleep she got a tent peg and a mallet and drove the peg through the general's head. When Barak came in pursuit of Sisera, Jael led him into the tent and showed him the general's dead body.

Deborah then sang a lengthy song that included the words:

> Blessed among women be Jael,
> blessed among tent-dwelling women.
> He asked for water, she gave him milk;
> in a princely bowl she offered curds.
> With her left hand she reached for the peg,
> with her right, for the workman's mallet.
> She hammered Sisera, crushed his head;
> she smashed, stove in his temple.
> At her feet he sank down, fell, lay still;
> down at her feet he sank and fell;
> where he sank down, there he fell, slain.
>
> ... May all your enemies perish thus, O LORD!
> but your friends be as the sun rising in its might!
> (Judges 5:24-27, 31).

The Call of Gideon

The land had been at rest from its enemies for forty years after Barak and Deborah, but the Israelites offended God, and he delivered them into the power of the Midianites. Israel cried out to the Lord for help, and he sent an angel to a man named Gideon and told him that he was to become the champion of his people. "Please, my lord, how can I save Israel?" (Judges 6:15), asked Gideon, saying that he was the most insignificant person in his father's house.

"I shall be with you," the Lord said to him, "and you will cut down Midian to the last man" (5:16). Gideon asked for a sign from God, then went off to prepare a kid goat and some unleavened

112 / CATHOLICISM AND SCRIPTURE

cakes and presented them to the angel, who told Gideon to lay them on a nearby rock. When Gideon did so, a fire came up from the rock and consumed the meat and the cakes. Gideon then asked for two more signs: that a piece of dry fleece become wet from dew when all the ground around it was dry, and later that the fleece alone be dry while all the ground was wet with dew. God granted both signs, and Gideon was ready to do battle.

But now the Lord tested Gideon by telling him to reduce the number of his soldiers from 32,000 to 300, lest Gideon think that it was his own power, and not God's, that brought about the victory. So Gideon divided the 300 into three companies and gave each man a horn and an empty jar with a torch inside it. They surrounded the enemy in the middle of the night and, at Gideon's signal, all began blowing the horns and breaking the jars.

The noise so unnerved the Midianites that they began running around mindlessly, shouting and stabbing each other with their swords, until the whole camp was empty. Gideon and his soldiers then pursued them and subsequently captured and killed them all, as well as other Midianite kings and princes.

St. Paul might have been referring to a man like Gideon when he wrote to the people of Corinth:

> God chose the foolish of the world to shame the wise, and God chose the weak of the world to shame the strong, and God chose the lowly and despised of the world, those who count for nothing, to reduce to nothing those who are something, so that no human being might boast before God (1 Corinthians 1:27-29).

The Shibboleth Incident

During the reign of Jephthah, a judge in Gilead, an incident occurred that added to our language the word "shibboleth," which means a catchword or a slogan. It seems that the men of Gilead had defeated the Ephraimites in battle, but needed some way to make sure that the surviving Ephraimites would not be able to get away. When any man of Gilead asked a man whom he suspected of being an enemy if he were an Ephraimite, and the man said no, the Gileadite would ask him to say "Shibboleth."

If the fleeing person pronounced the word correctly, he would be sent on his way, but if he pronounced it "Sibboleth," he would be seized and killed. The Book of Judges says that 43,000 Ephraimites fell at that time.

Samson and Delilah

The most famous of the judges was Samson, who was born at a time when the Israelites were under the power of the Philistines. Samson's mother had not been able to bear children when an angel of the Lord appeared to her and said that she would conceive a son. The angel said of this son: "No razor shall touch his head, for this boy is to be consecrated to God from the womb. It is he who will begin the deliverance of Israel from the Philistines" (Judges 13:5).

As a young man, Samson was well-known for feats of strength, such as tearing a lion apart with his bare hands (cf. Judges 14:6) and killing 3,000 men with the jawbone of an ass (cf. Judges 15:15). His strength was due to the Nazarite vow he had taken (cf. Numbers 6:1-21), which bound him to avoid wine and strong drink, never to let a razor touch his hair, and never to enter into the presence of a corpse. Other lifelong Nazarites (from a Hebrew word meaning "set apart as sacred") were Samuel (cf. 1 Samuel 1:11) and John the Baptist (cf. Luke 1:15).

The downfall of Samson began when he met a woman named Delilah, who was offered money by the Philistines to find out the secret of Samson's strength. Three times Delilah asked Samson his secret, and he gave her three different reasons, such as binding him with certain kinds of rope or weaving his hair in a certain way. After each reason, she signaled the Philistines to seize him, but each time Samson broke free and avoided capture.

Finally, after hearing so many complaints from Delilah that he was "deathly weary of them," Samson took her into his confidence and said, "No razor has touched my head, for I have been consecrated to God from my mother's womb. If I am shaved, my strength will leave me, and I shall be as weak as any man" (Judges 16:17). As soon as he had fallen asleep, Delilah cut off his hair and, when the Philistines pounced on him, he was unable to resist.

The Philistines gouged out Samson's eyes and took him to a prison in Gaza, but did not pay attention as Samson's hair began to grow back. One day, all the Philistine leaders gathered to offer a great sacrifice to their god Dagon and to celebrate the capture of Samson. They sent for him, had him tied to the columns holding up the roof of the building, and began to mock him. There were about 3,000 men and women looking on as Samson provided amusement.

While they were enjoying the spectacle, Samson prayed to the Lord for strength, that "I may avenge myself once and for all on the Philistines" (Judges 16:28). He pushed hard against two of the middle columns on which the temple rested and brought the whole structure crashing down, killing him and all those in the temple.

His family and kinsmen recovered his body and took him home for burial with his father. Samson had judged Israel for twenty years.

Setting the Stage for Kings

The time of the Judges was coming to an end, and there was a great need in Israel for holy leadership. As the final line of the book puts it: "In those days there was no king in Israel; everyone did what he thought best" (Judges 21:25). The same problem exists today, so we need to follow the spiritual and moral leadership of the Pope so that we will do what is right and not what we think is best.

WORDS TO REMEMBER

* Canaan
* sin cycle
* shibboleth

* Jericho
* Judges
*Nazarite vow

* Levites
* Baals

Chapter 10

Bible Heroes and Heroines

> The LORD is my life's refuge;
> of whom am I afraid?
> — Psalm 27:1

Two brothers were arrested and convicted for stealing sheep. For their punishment, each was branded on the forehead with the letters "ST," which stood for "sheep thief."

One of the brothers was so ashamed at what he had done that he fled to a distant country and tried to stay away from people because they were always asking about the strange brand on his forehead. When he could no longer stand the questions and the stigma, he committed suicide.

The other brother, however, reasoned that he could not escape from the fact that he had been convicted of stealing sheep, so he decided to change his life and work hard to regain his self-respect and the respect of his neighbors. As the years went by, he turned his life around, became a model citizen in his community, and people forgot all about the mark as he earned a reputation for honesty and integrity.

Then one day, a stranger came to town and saw an old man with the letters branded on his forehead. He asked someone what the letters stood for, and the townsman replied: "It all happened before my time, and I don't know the details, but I think the letters are an abbreviation for 'Saint.' "

There are many heroes and heroines in the Bible, some widely acclaimed and others not as celebrated. While much of this book focuses on the major players in salvation history, this chapter will mention some of the lesser lights on the biblical stage. Admittedly, not all of their actions were admirable, and some historical details are questionable, but the lessons to be learned from their stories can be valuable to us today.

The choice of whom to include was purely arbitrary; other men and women could just as easily have been chosen, but here are some of the heroes and heroines that the authors of this text found appealing and inspiring.

Judah

One of Jacob's twelve sons, Judah played a key role in God's plan by talking his brothers out of leaving Joseph to die at the bottom of a cistern. "What is to be gained by killing our brother and concealing his blood?" Judah asked. "Rather, let us sell him to these Ishmaelites, instead of doing away with him ourselves. After all, he is our brother, our own flesh" (Genesis 37:26-27).

Many years went by, during which time Judah married a Canaanite woman and had several children with her, including the ill-fated Onan. There was also his sexual involvement with his daughter-in-law Tamar, who had disguised herself as a temple prostitute. But after this sinful episode, we don't hear from Judah again until he and his brothers were preparing to make a second trip to Egypt to purchase grain for their hungry people. They would have to appeal again to Joseph, their brother, the governor of Egypt, whom they had not recognized on their first trip.

Joseph had told the brothers not to return unless they brought their youngest brother Benjamin with them, but Jacob was adamant in not letting Benjamin go. Judah, however, got his father to change his mind by promising to "stand surety for him. You can hold me responsible for him. If I fail to bring him back, to set him in your presence, you can hold it against me forever" (Genesis 43:9).

During their meeting with Joseph in Egypt, the governor accused Benjamin of stealing a silver goblet that Joseph himself actually had placed in Benjamin's sack as a final test for his brothers. Joseph then said that Benjamin would have to become his slave, but Judah, after saying that the failure to have Benjamin return would "send the white head of our father down to the nether world in grief" (Genesis 44:31), offered to remain in Egypt and become Joseph's slave in place of Benjamin. Joseph then told them who he really was.

In his final testament to his sons, Jacob gave Judah a dominant role in the future of Israel (Genesis 49:8-10), and from the Tribe of Judah came Jesus (cf. Matthew 1:3 and Luke 3:33). Judah was a brave man and also a sinner, but his life is one of many examples of how God can use flawed individuals to facilitate his divine plan.

Tobit

The Book of Tobit concentrates mostly on the exploits of his son Tobiah, but the father should not be overlooked. A pious and wealthy man who had lost his eyesight, Tobit had spent his life performing charitable deeds for others while living among those deported to Nineveh. He gave bread to the hungry and clothing to the naked, and he often provided a decent burial for those of his kinsmen whose bodies had been dumped in the streets.

The theme of the book is that God will deliver those who trust in him, and Tobit is the model of patient acceptance in time of trial. Yes, he prays for death in his grief-stricken state, but he never turns against God. "You are righteous, O Lord,"/ Tobit prays, "and all your deeds are just;/ All your ways are mercy and truth;/ you are the judge of the world" (Tobit 3:2).

As Tobiah was preparing for his journey to Media, he received sound advice from his father, including the importance of alms-giving (4:7-11):

Do not turn your face away from any of the poor, and God's face will not be turned away from you. Son, give alms in proportion to what you own. If you have great wealth, give alms out of your abundance; if you have but little, distribute even some of that. But do not hesitate to give alms; you will be storing up a goodly treasury for yourself against the day of adversity. Almsgiving frees one from death, and keeps one from going into the dark abode. Alms are a worthy offering in the sight of the Most High for all who give them.

Tobit even anticipates, though in negative form, the Golden Rule proclaimed by Jesus: "Do to no one what you yourself dislike" (4:15).

After his eyesight had been restored, Tobit offered this hymn of praise (11:14):

Blessed be God,/ and praised be his great name,
and blessed be all his holy angels.
May his holy name be praised
throughout all the ages....

When his long life of praising God and giving alms was nearing its end, Tobit called together Tobiah and his seven grandsons and admonished them to "serve God faithfully and do what is right before him" (14:9). He then urged them to flee the wicked city of Nineveh as soon as they had buried him and his wife, and warned that Jerusalem would be destroyed and all Israel scattered in foreign lands. But Tobit also prophesied that God would again have mercy on his people and restore them to the land of Israel, where the Temple would be rebuilt for generations to come.

Ruth

In the time of the Judges, a famine struck the land of Israel, and Elimelech of Bethlehem migrated to Moab, a traditional enemy of Israel, with his wife Naomi and two sons. The sons eventually married two Moabite women, Orpah and Ruth, but when Elimelech and the two sons died, Naomi wanted to go back to Bethlehem because she had heard that the Lord had provided food for the people.

Naomi wanted to return by herself and urged Orpah and Ruth to go back to their own homes, but the Gentile Ruth insisted on accompanying Naomi and made this remarkable statement (1:16):

Do not ask me to abandon or forsake you! for wherever you go I will go, wherever you lodge I will lodge, your people shall be my people, and your God my God.

After arriving in Bethlehem at the beginning of the barley harvest, Ruth found work gleaning in the fields of a wealthy landowner named Boaz, a very generous man who had instructed his harvesters to leave some of the standing grain for the poor to gather for themselves. Boaz, who was a kinsman of Elimelech, met Ruth in the fields one day and praised her for her faithfulness to Naomi. He also instructed his harvesters to let Ruth glean among them instead of waiting until they were through.

Boaz was attracted to Ruth and wanted to marry her, but being a righteous man he knew that he had to give a closer relative first claim to her and to the land that had been owned by Elimelech. So he met with the relative at the gate of the city in the presence of ten elders who were to serve as witnesses of the negotiation.

The relative was not interested in purchasing the land, nor in marrying Ruth and raising a family to perpetuate the line of her deceased husband, so Boaz and Ruth were married and had a son named Obed, who became the father of Jesse, the grandfather of David, and an ancestor of Jesus. How accurate were the women of the town when they told Naomi: "Blessed is the LORD who has not failed to provide you today with an heir! May he become famous in Israel!" (Ruth 4:14).

Esther

The story of Esther shows the providence of God in saving his people from destruction as Esther was able to reach a high position in the Persian government that enabled her to help the people of Israel. It also shows her survival skills in the hostile world of the Gentiles, and how one must act in a hostile environment so as not to compromise one's principles. She and her foster father Mordecai demonstrated those traits that Jesus mentioned: "Behold, I am sending you like sheep in the midst of wolves; so be shrewd as serpents and simple as doves" (Matthew 10:16).

Mordecai had ingratiated himself with King Ahasuerus by informing the king of a plot to kill him, but Mordecai's action earned him the hatred of a top adviser to the king named Haman. Meanwhile, during a banquet at the royal palace, Queen Vashti provoked the anger of the king by refusing to appear at the banquet wearing the royal crown, so Ahasuerus put her away and launched a search for a replacement among all the young virgins in the provinces.

When Esther was chosen to be queen, she did not reveal her nationality nor her relationship to Mordecai, who had infuriated Haman by refusing to bow before him. Haman persuaded the king to issue a decree ordering the extermination of all Jews in the land on the 13th day of the 12th month, Adar. Upon learning of the decree, Mordecai asked Esther to plead with the king to rescind the order.

He and Esther both prayed for the Lord's help. Declaring that he would not bow before any man, Mordecai implored God to "spare your people, for our enemies plan our ruin and are bent upon destroying the inheritance that was yours from the beginning. Do not spurn your portion, which you redeemed for yourself out of Egypt" (Esther C:8-9).

Esther, also, after covering herself with dirt and ashes and inflicting punishment on herself, pleaded with God to "give me courage, King of gods and Ruler of every power. Put in my mouth persuasive words in the presence of the lion and turn his heart to hatred for our enemy, so that he and those who are in league with him may perish" (C:23-24).

After three days of prayer, Esther made herself beautiful again and took the risky step of appearing before the king without being summoned. The king, however, treated her gently, saying that he would grant her any request, "even if it is half of my kingdom" (5:3). This promise resembles the promise of another king, Herod, to the daughter of his wife Herodias, that led to the execution of John the Baptist (cf. Mark 6:23).

Queen Esther asked Ahasuerus to come with Haman to a banquet that she would prepare, and then she would make her request known. At the banquet, she asked that her life be spared, along with the lives of her people, who had been scheduled for destruction and extinction. Who is the man who had dared to do this? the king asked, and Esther replied, "The enemy oppressing us is this wicked Haman" (7:6).

Haman stayed behind after the king had left to beg Esther for his life, and he had thrown himself on the couch where the queen was reclining when suddenly the king returned and exclaimed, "Will he also violate the queen while she is with me in my own house?" (7:8). One of the king's court officers told him that Haman had prepared a gallows on which to hang Mordecai, so the king ordered that Haman be hanged from that same gibbet himself.

Ahasuerus then told Mordecai to write another decree in the king's name that would rescind the original order to kill all Jews and, when that decree was promulgated, there was great merriment and celebration by those whose lives had been spared, and "many of the peoples of the land embraced Judaism, for they were seized with a fear of the Jews" (8:17).

The feast celebrating the deliverance of the Jewish people became known as Purim.

Judith

The Book of Judith tells of a beautiful and pious young widow who urged her people not to surrender to the Assyrians, but to trust in God to deliver their city. The army general Holofernes was besieging Bethulia and had cut off the people's water and supplies, and the elders were preparing to hand the city over to the Assyrians.

Inviting three of the elders to visit her at her home, Judith scolded them for promising to surrender the city in five days if the Lord did not intervene and asked who they were to lay down conditions for the Lord. "No, my brothers," she said, "do not anger the LORD our God. For if he does not wish to come to our aid within the five days, he has it equally within his power to protect us at such time as he pleases, or to destroy us in the face of our enemies" (8:14-15).

When one of the elders asked her to pray that the Lord would fill up their cisterns with water so they would not be weakened any further, Judith vowed to "do something that will go down from generation to generation among the descendants of our race" (8:32), and she asked them to let her pass through the gates of the city that night so that she might help save Bethulia.

After donning sackcloth and ashes and praying fervently to the Lord for assistance in her mission, Judith then washed herself clean, dressed herself in beautiful clothes and fine jewelry, and set out with her maid for the enemy camp. She was taken into custody at an outpost of the camp and asked to be conducted into the presence of General Holofernes.

Her demeanor and her beauty so entranced the guards that they took her immediately to the tent of Holofernes and ushered her in. She threw herself at the general's feet, but his servants raised her up. "Take courage, lady; have no fear in your heart!" said Holofernes. "Never have I harmed anyone who chose to serve Nebuchadnezzar, king of all the earth. Nor would I have raised my spear against your people who dwell in the mountain region, had they not despised me and brought this upon themselves" (11:1-2).

Judith responded by saying that, while she was "a God-fearing woman, serving the God of heaven night and day," she would now stay with him, only going out each night to the ravine for a short time to pray to God. She said that "he will tell me when the Israelites have committed their crimes. Then I will come and let you know, so that you may go out with your whole force, and not one of them will be able to withstand you" (11:17-18).

Holofernes was pleased with Judith's words and, on her fourth night in the camp, he invited her to dine with him in the hope of seducing her. But the general drank himself into a stupor and, after all his aides and servants had left him alone with Judith, she took his sword and cut off his head.

Judith gave the head to her maid, who put it inside her food sack, and the two women left the camp ostensibly to pray at the ravine, but instead hurried back to Bethulia, where she showed the head of Holofernes to all the people and praised God for having "shattered our enemies by my hand this very night" (13:14).

All the people were greatly astonished, and Uzziah the elder hailed Judith for what she had done, saying: "Blessed are you, daughter, by the Most High God, above all the women on earth; and blessed be the LORD God, the creator of heaven and earth, who guided your blow at the head of the chief of our enemies. Your deed of hope will never be forgotten by those who tell of the might of God" (13:18-19).

The words of Uzziah would be echoed by Elizabeth centuries later when she would say to the Virgin Mary: "Most blessed are you among women" (Luke 1:42). And Judith's song of thanksgiving and praise to the Lord (cf. 16:1-17) would also resonate in Mary's canticle of praise and thanksgiving known as the Magnificat (cf. Luke 1:46-55).

At dawn the next day, the inhabitants of Bethulia hung the head of Holofernes outside the wall of the city and then launched an attack on the Assyrian camp. When the Assyrians tried to rally their forces and get Holofernes to lead them, they discovered the headless general in his tent. This caused such fear and panic in the camp that the Assyrians broke ranks and fled in all directions. The Israelites pursued them and killed them all and then plundered their camp.

While the details of the story are neither historical nor chronological, they do show that God's strength is not in numbers, that prayer and fasting can overcome an enemy, and that Judith is a model of faith in action.

Eleazar

One of the most inspiring heroes of the Old Testament is a 90-year-old scribe who chose martyrdom rather than violate the Jewish dietary laws. When the soldiers of Antiochus tried to force Eleazar to eat pork, he spat the meat out. Those in charge of the ritual meal, some of whom had known Eleazar for a long time, took him aside and urged him to provide some meat that he could legitimately eat and only pretend to eat the forbidden meat.

He refused this compromise on the grounds that many would think that he had gone over to an alien religion. "Should I thus dissimulate for the sake of a brief moment of life," the old man said, "they would be led astray by me, while I would bring shame and dishonor on my old age. Even if, for the time being, I avoid the punishment of men, I shall never, whether alive or dead, escape the hands of the Almighty. Therefore, by manfully giving up my life now, I will prove myself worthy of my old age, and I will leave to the young a noble example of how to die willingly and generously for the revered and holy laws" (2 Maccabees 6:25-28.

Eleazar was then subjected to brutal torture, with even those who had been kindly disposed to him now hostile because they viewed his principled stand as madness. The author of Second Maccabees said correctly that Eleazar's death was "a model of courage and an unforgettable example of virtue not only for the young but for the whole nation" (6:31).

Following Eleazar's Example

Have you ever wondered if you could give up your life for your Catholic beliefs? Perhaps many of us could when pushed to the wall. But if you could willingly *die* for the Faith, are you also willing to *live* for it? Are you willing to withstand hatred and ridicule and loss of friendships to witness to the teachings of Jesus and his Church?

Are you willing to speak out against abortion and euthanasia, against contraception and cloning, against in vitro fertilization and embryonic stem cell research, against cohabitation before marriage and remarriage after divorce without obtaining a decree of nullity, and against the "gay" lifestyle and same-sex unions? These are all controversial and divisive issues within families and in society, and taking an informed stand against them in our relativistic culture will require the fortitude of an Eleazar and all the other martyrs who over the centuries have put God first in their lives.

Those who are willing to join this long line of faithful witnesses will come to understand what Jesus meant when he said: "Whoever wishes to come after me must deny himself, take up his cross, and follow me. For whoever wishes to save his life will lose it, but whoever loses his life for my sake and that of the gospel will save it" (Mark 8:34-35).

Nicodemus and Joseph of Arimathea

Has anyone ever asked you if you have been "born again"? What those asking want to know is whether you have ever accepted Jesus as your personal Lord and Savior. Your reply should be yes, that you were born again at Baptism and that you accept Jesus as Lord and Savior every time you receive him in Holy Communion. For when the minister of the Eucharist holds up that Host and says, "The Body of Christ," you respond, "Amen." That "Amen" means that you believe what you are about to receive is indeed the Body and Blood, Soul and Divinity of Jesus Christ, the second Person of the Blessed Trinity.

But where does the expression "born again" come from? It comes from a conversation Jesus had late one night with a prominent Pharisee and member of the Jewish Sanhedrin named Nicodemus (cf. John 3:1:21). This man was attracted to the words of Jesus, but wanted to speak to the Lord privately, away from the scrutiny of his colleagues, who were almost unanimously against Jesus.

Nicodemus had witnessed some of Jesus's miracles and had concluded that "no one can do these signs that you are doing unless God is with him." Jesus replied: "Amen, amen, I say to you, no one can see the kingdom of God without being born from above." The Pharisee misinterpreted Jesus and asked, "How can a person once grown old be born again? Surely he cannot reenter his mother's womb and be born again, can he?" (John 3:2-4).

Jesus replied, "Amen, amen, I say to you, no one can enter the kingdom of God without being born of water and Spirit. What is born of flesh is flesh and what is born of spirit is spirit" (3:5). The Lord was talking about the sacrament of Baptism, about the pouring of water and the coming of the Holy Spirit to take away Original Sin and give us sanctifying grace, make us adopted children of God, introduce us into the family of God, which is the Church, and start us on our journey to heaven.

We are, in the words of St. Paul, "no longer strangers and sojourners, but you are fellow citizens with the holy ones and members of the household of God" (Ephesians 2:19).

Not long after that nocturnal meeting, the chief priests and Pharisees ridiculed the idea that Jesus could be the Messiah and said that no one in their religious circle believed such a thing about him. But Nicodemus spoke up, saying, "Does our law condemn a person before it first hears him and finds out what he is doing" (John 7:51)? They answered, "You are not from

Galilee also, are you? Look and see that no prophet arises from Galilee" (John 7:52). These Pharisees were apparently unaware that, while Jesus had grown up in Galilee, he had been born in Bethlehem of Judea, from where the prophet (cf. Micah 5:1) had said that the Messiah would come.

The last time we hear of Nicodemus is on Good Friday when he brought one hundred pounds of burial spices to anoint the body of Jesus before it was placed in the tomb (cf. John 19:39). He is also linked with another Pharisee and secret disciple of Jesus, Joseph of Arimathea. A man of wealth and status, Joseph was also not a part of the Sanhedrin's vendetta against Jesus (cf. Luke 23:51), and he courageously asked the Roman governor, Pontius Pilate, for permission to bury Jesus in a new tomb that Joseph had hewn out of rock near Golgotha (23:52).

Thomas

Ask someone about the expression "doubting Thomas," and they will identify it with the Apostle who said that he would not believe that Jesus had risen from the dead unless he could see and touch the Lord's wounds. Thomas was not present when Jesus appeared to the Apostles on Easter Sunday night and, when they told him the good news, he replied: "Unless I see the mark of the nails in his hands and put my finger into the nailmarks and put my hand into his side, I will not believe" (John 20:25).

One week later, Jesus appeared again to the Apostles, and this time Thomas was there. The Lord invited the skeptic to touch his wounds, saying, "Do not be unbelieving, but believe" (20:27). The Gospel of John does not say whether Thomas put his fingers into the wounds of Christ, only that the Apostle said, "My Lord and my God!" (20:28), words that millions of Catholics continue to repeat at Mass when the priest elevates the Host and chalice at the Consecration.

Of more importance to us today, however, are the next words of Jesus to Thomas: "Have you come to believe because you have seen me? Blessed are those who have not seen and have believed" (20:29). The Lord was talking about all those, like us, who would come to believe in him without being able, like Thomas, to see him in person. Indeed, we are blessed for our faith in Jesus.

But why include Thomas in a chapter on Bible heroes when he is best known as a doubter of the Lord? Because there are examples of the courage of Thomas apart from this one negative incident. For instance, he was brave enough on Easter Sunday night to be elsewhere in the city while the other Apostles were hiding in a locked room.

Recall, too, that shortly before the raising of Lazarus from the dead, the enemies of Christ were seeking to kill him. When he told the Apostles that he had to return to the Jerusalem area because his friend Lazarus was seriously ill, they tried to talk him out of going, saying, "Rabbi, the Jews were just trying to stone you, and you want to go back there" (John 11:8)? But Thomas spoke up and bravely said, "Let us also go to die with him" (11:16).

It was also Thomas who on another occasion asked Jesus, after the Lord had said he was going to prepare a place for them, "Master, we do not know where you are going; how can we know the way?" And Jesus replied: "I am the way and the truth and the life. No one comes to the Father except through me" (John 14:5-6).

So Thomas deserves more credit than is traditionally accorded to him.

Mary Magdalene

One of the closest and most loyal followers of Jesus was Mary Magdalene, the one out of whom he had cast seven demons (Luke 8:2). We know that she and many other Galilean women, including Joanna and Susanna, journeyed with Jesus and provided for him and the Apostles out of their own resources (Luke 8:2), that she was a witness of the Crucifixion (Matthew 27:56, Mark 15:40, John 19:25) and the burial of the Savior (Matthew 27:61 and Mark 15:47), and that she was the first person to whom Jesus appeared publicly after his Resurrection from the dead.

On that first Easter morning, Mary discovered that the tomb was empty and reported this stunning fact to Peter and John, who returned to the tomb with her. After they had left the site, Mary stayed behind, crying. She saw two angels there and, when they asked why she was weeping, Magdalene replied: "They have taken my Lord, and I don't know where they laid him" (John 20:13).

Jesus then appeared and asked why she was crying and for whom she was looking. Not recognizing him and thinking that he was the gardener, Mary answered: "Sir, if you carried him away, tell me where you laid him, and I will take him." The Lord then spoke her name, and Mary exclaimed, "Rabbouni," which means "Teacher" (John 20:15-16).

In her excitement, Magadalene must have embraced the Lord because he told her, "Stop holding on to me, for I have not yet ascended to the Father. But go to my brothers and tell them, 'I am going to my Father and your Father, to my God and your God' " (20:17). Mary raced back to the city to tell everyone the great news, but no one believed her (cf. Mark 16:11).

Modern-day fiction writers have sought to portray Magdalene in a romantic relationship with Jesus, with some even going so far as to contend that she was married to the Lord and that she fled to France after the Crucifixion with their child and started a royal dynasty there. This is sheer nonsense, of course, and there is nothing in Scripture or in any credible historical writings to support such a bizarre theory. But this lack of evidence hasn't prevented the theory from being promulgated in books and films and from confusing Christians who ought to know better the life of the One whom they call Lord and Savior.

There is also the perception that Magdalene had been a prostitute before she met Jesus, but there is nothing in Scripture to support that characterization either. The rumor apparently stems from the fact that the first mention of the woman from Magdala occurs in Luke 8:2, just two verses after the story of the sinful woman who bathed Jesus' feet with her tears, dried them with her hair, and then anointed them with an ointment that she carried in an alabaster jar.

That woman was publicly known in the city as a sinner, and presumably her sin was prostitution, but there is nothing in Scripture that would equate her with Magdalene. The Catholic Church has long recognized Mary Magdalene as a great saint, naming many churches after her and celebrating a feast day in her honor on July 22nd.

Priscilla (Prisca) and Aquila

A missionary colleague of St. Paul, Priscilla was married to Aquila, a Jewish tentmaker. They were living in Rome when the Emperor Claudius expelled all Jews from the city, and they moved to Corinth, where they met Paul, who was also a tentmaker. The Apostle to the Gentiles stayed with them for more than a year while they practiced their common trade.

According to the Acts of the Apostles (18:18), the trio left Corinth and sailed to Ephesus, where Priscilla and Aquila founded a house church after Paul had moved on to Antioch (cf. 1 Corinthians 16:19). They took under their wing a Jew from Alexandria named Apollos, who was an authority on the Scriptures. "He had been instructed in the Way of the Lord and, with ardent spirit, spoke and taught accurately about Jesus," it says in Acts, "although he knew only the baptism of John [the Baptist]. He began to speak boldly in the synagogue; but when Priscilla and Aquila heard him, they took him aside and explained to him the Way [of God] more accurately" (18:25-26).

There is also evidence that they returned to Rome, for Paul, in one of his letters (cf. Romans 16:3-4), said: "Greet Prisca and Aquila, my co-workers in Christ Jesus, who risked their necks for my life, to whom not only I am grateful but also all the churches of the Gentiles."

<u>WORDS TO REMEMBER</u>

* almsgiving   * born again
* Baptism   * witness

Samuel anoints David.

Chapter 11

A Unified Kingdom: Saul and David

> "I have made a covenant with my chosen one;
> I have sworn to David my servant:
> I will make your dynasty stand forever
> and establish your throne through all ages."
> — Psalm 89:4-5

Aleksander Solzhenitsyn, the famous Russian novelist who wrote eloquently about the horrors of labor camps in the former Soviet Union, told of an incident in his own life when he had lost all hope of ever being free again. He was so desperate that he had decided to make a run for it and let the guards shoot him and put an end to his suffering.

During a work break one morning, Solzhenitsyn sat under a tree alone so that no one else would get hurt in his escape attempt. He was just about to get to his feet and make his final dash when a man he had never seen before, and never saw again, came over and sat down next to him.

"I have never before or since had conveyed to me the love that I saw in that man's eyes," Solzhenitsyn recalled. "We looked at each other for at least thirty or forty seconds, and then my friend picked up a stick and in the sand drew a cross, praise God! I realized then that the Lord was speaking to me through the eyes of that man and saying, 'I have need for you.'"

The circumstances were not as dramatic when the Lord told Samuel that he had need for him, but Samuel would play a huge role in helping to establish a monarchy in Israel. That Samuel was destined for a special role in salvation history became clear in the manner of his birth.

His mother Hannah, following in the path of other Old Testament wives who were barren (Sarah, Rebekah, Rachel), beseeched God for a son and promised that she would dedicate him to the Lord as a Nazarite, drinking neither wine nor liquor nor letting

a razor touch his head. The Lord heard her prayerful plea, and
Hannah bore a son whom she named Samuel.

Once the child had been weaned, Hannah brought him to the
temple of the Lord in Shiloh and presented him to Eli the priest.
Hannah then sang a hymn of thanksgiving that resembles in
some verses the Magnificat of the Virgin Mary (cf. Luke 1:46-55).
For example, these opening lines:

> "My heart exults in the LORD,
> my horn is exalted in my God.
> I have swallowed up my enemies;
> I rejoice in my victory.
> There is no Holy One like the LORD;
> there is no Rock like our God" (1 Samuel 2:1-2).

The Lord later blessed Hannah with five more children, and
she saw Samuel once each year when she brought him clothes
and she and her husband Elkanah offered sacrifices to God.

God Calls Samuel

While growing up in the household of Eli, Samuel witnessed
Eli's disappointment over the wickedness of his two sons, whom
he had hoped would succeed him. But a man of God appeared to
Eli and told him that the Lord would strike down his two sons on
the same day and raise up "a faithful priest who shall do what I
have in heart and mind" (1 Samuel 2:35).

One night not long after that, as Eli and Samuel were sleeping in the temple where the Ark was kept, Samuel heard a voice
calling him. He thought the voice was that of Eli, but Eli told
him to go back to sleep and the next time he heard the voice to
respond, "Speak, LORD, for your servant is listening" (3:9).

Samuel did as he was told, and the Lord said that he was
going to condemn the family of Eli once and for all because of
the blasphemous actions of his sons. When Samuel reluctantly
revealed the Lord's words to Eli the next morning, the priest
said, "He is the LORD. He will do what he judges best" (3:18).
Would that all priests, and laity, would adopt this attitude that
the Lord knows best what should be done!

As Samuel grew older, he was widely recognized as a true
prophet of the Lord, and the Lord did not permit any of his words
to go without effect. This was at a time when the Israelites were

under attack by the Philistines, who had captured the Ark but then returned it. The Lord heard the prayer of Samuel and threw the Philistines into such confusion that the Israelites routed them in battle and chased them from their territory.

Establishment of the Monarchy

The time of the Judges was nearing its end, and the people demanded of Samuel that he appoint a king to judge them. Samuel warned the people that they were making a mistake. He said that a king would conscript their sons into the military and their daughters into domestic work, that he would take the best of all their crops and herds, along with their male and female servants, and that he would turn them all into his slaves.

But the people persisted in their demand and, when Samuel asked God about it, the Lord replied: "Grant the people's every request. It is not you they reject, they are rejecting me as their king. As they have treated me constantly from the day I brought them up from Egypt to this day, deserting me and worshiping strange gods, so do they treat you too" (8:7-8).

A short time later, God revealed to Samuel that, on the following day, he would send him a man from the land of Benjamin, whom he was to anoint as "commander of my people Israel. He shall save my people from the clutches of the Philistines, for I have witnessed their misery and accepted their cry for help" (9:16).

When Samuel caught sight the next day of a handsome young man named Saul, and heard the Lord say that this was the man chosen to govern his people, he took him aside to give him the message from God. Taking a flask from his pocket, Samuel poured oil on Saul's head and kissed him, saying: "The LORD anoints you commander over his heritage. You are to govern the LORD's people Israel, and to save them from the grasp of their enemies roundabout" (10:1).

Anointing with Oil

Over the centuries, olive oil has been used for many things: cooking, heating, lighting, and healing aching limbs. But it has also been widely used in religious ceremonies to symbolize spiritual healing or, in the case of Saul, to mark him as someone chosen by God for some special work.

In the Catholic Church, anointing with oil is a sign of the presence of the Holy Spirit and an important part of four sacraments: Baptism, Confirmation, Holy Orders, and Anointing of the Sick. The oils used in all the parishes in a diocese are blessed by the bishop every year during Holy Week, and each parish sends a representative to the bishop's church, usually known as a "cathedral," to bring the holy oils back to the parish.

Those being welcomed into the Church at Baptism are anointed with the Oil of Catechumens and the Oil of Chrism, symbolizing cleansing and strengthening and giving them a share in the priestly, prophetic, and kingly mission of Christ.

At Confirmation, the Oil of Chrism, a mixture of olive oil and a perfumed substance known as balm or balsam, is placed on the candidate's forehead to signify a strengthening of that person's faith. The confirmand is "sealed with the gift of the Holy Spirit" and has imprinted on the soul an indelible spiritual character that marks that person as one empowered to be a witness for Christ in the world.

The seven gifts imparted by the Holy Spirit at Confirmation are wisdom, understanding, knowledge, counsel or right judgment, fortitude or courage, piety or reverence, and fear of the Lord or wonder and awe in God's presence.

The word "chrism," by the way, comes from the same Greek word for Christ and it means "anoint." Thus, when Jesus is called "the Christ" (in Hebrew *messiah*), it means that he is the one specially anointed by God's Spirit.

Chrism is also used when a man is ordained a priest to signify his deeper configuration and special consecration to Christ, the eternal High Priest, and the assistance of the Spirit in making his ministry fruitful.

Finally, the Oil of the Sick is used to anoint those who are seriously ill or in danger of death so as to heal them spiritually and sometimes physically. Thus, the priest says to the person being anointed: "Through this holy anointing may the Lord in his love and mercy help you with the grace of the Holy Spirit. May the Lord who frees you from sin save you and raise you up" (Code of Canon Law, n. 847.1).

The Reign of Saul

Samuel later presented Saul to all the tribes of Israel as the king they had requested and, after Saul had led them in defeating the Ammonites, he was accepted as king. He ruled well for a period of time, leading successful military campaigns against the Philistines, but problems arose when he backed away from his religious obligations. He was supposed to let Samuel offer a sacrifice to God before going into battle, but he offered up the holocaust himself, earning the condemnation of Samuel, who prophesied that, because Saul had broken the Lord's command, his kingdom would not endure very long and the Lord would seek out "a man after his own heart" (1 Samuel 13:14).

When Saul on another occasion disobeyed the order of the Lord to wipe out the Amalekites completely, even all of their animals, and spared the Amalekite king and the best of his sheep, oxen, and lambs, Samuel reproved him again, saying that "obedience is better than sacrifice" (15:22). Saul asked for forgiveness, but Samuel told him that he would soon lose his kingship over Israel.

The Advent of David

Having rejected Saul as commander of Israel, God sent Samuel to Bethlehem to anoint one of Jesse's eight sons to succeed Saul. Seven of the sons were brought before Samuel for consideration, and he found them very impressive men, but the Lord told him not to judge from appearance or lofty stature. "Not as man sees does God see," said the Lord, "because man sees the appearance but the LORD looks into the heart" (16:7).

Have you any other sons, Samuel asked Jesse after rejecting seven of them. Yes, said Jesse, and he sent for his youngest son, who was tending sheep. When David arrived, Samuel saw a handsome youth who made a splendid appearance. "There — anoint him, for this is he!" said the Lord, and, as Samuel poured oil on David's head, the spirit of the Lord rushed upon him (cf. 16:12).

Meanwhile, Saul was in a terrible mood and was tormented by an evil spirit, so his aides looked for a man who was skilled with a harp to soothe the king in his melancholy. They had heard that one of Jesse's sons was a proficient harpist, so they sought him out and enlisted David in the service of Saul.

Saul became very fond of David and made him his armorbearer and, one day, reluctantly agreed to let the youth fight against a Philistine giant named Goliath. With God's help, David was able to knock Goliath to the ground with a stone from his sling, and then he seized the giant's sword and cut his head off.

The loss of their most-feared warrior shook the Philistines, and they fled from the battlefield.

David's victory over Goliath caused Saul to put him in charge of many soldiers, and David's fame as a warrior grew as he led the Israelites to more triumphs over their enemies. As he and Saul returned from a successful military campaign, the women played tambourines and danced, shouting and singing (18:7):

"Saul has slain his thousands,
and David his ten thousands."

This made Saul very angry and resentful and from that time on he was insanely jealous of David and tried more than once to kill him, but the Lord protected the young man. When Saul would tell his son Jonathan of his intention to kill David, Jonathan would inform David of the threat, as would his sister Michal, who was married to David, and the future king would escape to safety.

One time when Saul and his soldiers were pursuing David, Saul entered a cave unaware that David and his men were hiding in the deeper recesses of the cave. David was able to sneak up on the king and could have slain him, but instead he only cut off an end of Saul's cloak before Saul left the cave and walked away. David stepped out of the cave and called to Saul. He showed the king the piece of cloak he had cut and told him that was proof that he harbored no ill will against him.

When Saul heard David's words, he was very remorseful and thanked him for sparing his life. He said he knew that David would one day be king of Israel and asked David to swear an oath that "you will not destroy my descendants and that you will not blot out my name and family" (24:22). David agreed and Saul departed.

Not long after that, the Philistines mustered another army to battle the Israelites and Saul became so afraid that he consulted a fortune-teller, the witch of Endor, and asked her to conjure up the spirit of the late Samuel. Saul then asked Samuel why the Lord had abandoned him, and Samuel reminded him of his earlier disobedience. He also told Saul that, by the next day, the king and his sons, and the whole army of Israel, would be delivered into the hands of the Philistines.

And so it happened that the Philistines pursued the king and killed his three sons. When Saul was pierced through the stomach by an arrow during a raging battle, he asked his armor-bearer to run him through with a sword. The man refused, so Saul fell on his own sword, bringing an end to the life of the first king of Israel.

David Anointed King

After a period of mourning for Saul and his sons, David went up to Hebron and was anointed king of the Judahites. Some years later, after lengthy fighting between the houses of David and Saul, with David's forces growing stronger and Saul's family weaker, all the tribes of Israel came to Hebron and anointed David king of all Israel. He was thirty years old at the time and would reign over Israel for forty years, seven in Hebron and thirty-three in Jerusalem.

After David, with the Lord's help, had defeated the Philistines, he decided to bring the Ark of God to Jerusalem. He entered the city not in the robes of a king but in the vestments of a Levite priest, leaping and dancing before the Lord and then offering holocausts and peace offerings. He also distributed bread to all the people, recalling the king-priest Melchizedek and looking ahead to the King-Priest Jesus.

His wife Michal scolded him for conducting himself in such fashion before slave girls and commoners, but David replied: "I was dancing before the LORD. As the LORD lives, who preferred me to your father and his whole family when he appointed me commander of the LORD's people, Israel, not only will I make merry before the LORD, but I will demean myself even more. I will be lowly in your esteem, but in the esteem of the slave girls you spoke of I will be honored" (2 Samuel 6:21-22).

In bringing the Ark to Jerusalem, David made that city not only the political capital of Israel, but also its religious capital. But one day he told the prophet Nathan that the Ark should dwell in a house, not in a tent. Nathan spoke to the Lord about this, and God told him to tell David that the Almighty would build David into a temple and that one of his heirs (Solomon) would construct the physical temple.

After that temple is built by David's heir, said the Lord, "I will make his royal throne firm forever. I will be a father to him, and he shall be a son to me. And if he does wrong, I will correct him with the rod of men and with human chastisements; but I will not withdraw my favor from him as I withdrew it from your predecessor Saul, whom I removed from my presence. Your house and your kingdom shall endure forever before me; your throne shall stand firm forever" (2 Samuel 7:13-16).

In gratitude for this promise of a covenant that would last forever, one that would exceed those established with Noah, Abraham, and Moses, David praised the Lord and said: "Lord GOD, you are God and your words are truth; you have made this generous promise to your servant. Do, then, bless the house of your servant that it may be before you forever; for you, Lord GOD, have promised, and by your blessing the house of your servant shall be blessed forever" (7:28-29).

The Sins of David

As so often happens in life, just when we think that things could not be going along more smoothly, something goes terribly amiss. St. Paul warned against this kind of overconfidence when he cautioned: "Therefore whoever thinks he is standing secure should take care not to fall" (1 Corinthians 10:12). And so it was that David, while walking on the roof of his palace one night, saw a beautiful woman bathing across the way, and he lusted after her.

He had his aides bring him the woman, whose name was Bathsheba, they had sexual intercourse, and not long after that she informed David that she was pregnant. To make matters worse, when the king learned that Bathsheba's husband, Uriah, was in the military, he ordered Uriah's commanding officer to place him at the front lines, where the fighting was fiercest, and Uriah was killed in battle. After a period of mourning for her husband, Bathsheba moved into David's palace, became his wife, and bore him a son who died in infancy because the Lord was displeased at what David had done.

Nathan's Parable

In an effort to get David to repent of the terrible sins he had committed, God sent Nathan with instructions to tell him a story. Nathan asked the king to judge the case of two men in a certain town, one of whom was rich, and the other poor. The rich man had great herds of sheep, while the poor man had only one little lamb, who was like a member of his family. When a visitor came to the rich man's house, instead of killing one of his own lambs to make a meal for the visitor, the rich man took the poor man's ewe to provide food for his guest.

David was furious with the rich man and said that "the man who has done this merits death!" (2 Samuel 12:5). "You are the man!" said Nathan, reminding the king of all that God had done for him and asking, "Why have you spurned the LORD and done evil in his sight? You have cut down Uriah the Hittite with the sword; you took his wife as your own, and him you killed with the sword of the Ammonites" (12:7, 9).

Nathan conveyed the message of the Lord that evil would come to David's house and that his sinful actions would be made known to all Israel. David confessed his sin to the Lord and changed his ways, and Nathan told him that God had forgiven him and that he would not die. However, the prophet said that the child the king had conceived with Bathsheba would die, and so he did, despite a week of prayers and fasting by David.

The king consoled his wife and she soon conceived another child, whom they named Solomon. But in a penitential psalm (51:3-5, 11-12, 14, 19) that is attributed to him, David expressed his sorrow for sin:

> Have mercy on me, God, in your goodness;
> in your abundant compassion blot out my offense.
> Wash away all my guilt;/ from my sin cleanse me.
> For I know my offense;/ my sin is always before me....
> Turn away your face from my sins;
> blot out all my guilt.
> A clean heart create for me, God;
> renew in me a steadfast spirit....
> Restore my joy in your salvation;
> sustain in me a willing spirit....
> My sacrifice, God, is a broken spirit;
> God, do not spurn a broken, humbled heart.

The Cycle of Sin

But the evil that Nathan had prophesied did come to David's house through the sinful actions of his sons, Amnon and Absalom, including Amnon's rape of his sister Tamar and Absalom's role in putting Amnon to death. Later, Absalom conspired to become king, but his forces were defeated by David's army. Absalom died after his hair had caught in the branches of a tree while he was passing under it. As he hung suspended there, Joab, the same

138 / CATHOLICISM AND SCRIPTURE

army commander who had put Uriah in a position to be killed, executed him, even though David had wanted his son spared.

This series of events demonstrates again the way in which one sin leads to another. David's lust led to adultery and to killing, which spawned rape, conspiracy, and murder involving his sons. The same is true today, as lust leads to fornication and adultery and then to murder of a spouse or a lover, or to murder of a child by abortion. How important it is to say no to that first temptation to sin lest the cycle of sin spiral out of control.

The End of David's Reign

As David's kingship was coming to an end, there was a man named Adonijah who sought to take his place, and he was supported by Joab and Abiathar the priest. But Nathan asked Bathsheba to persuade David to name Solomon as king and the ailing monarch granted her wish. In his final instructions to his son, David told Solomon to "take courage and be a man. Keep the mandate of the LORD, your God, following his ways and observing his statutes, commands, ordinances, and decrees as they are written in the law of Moses, that you may succeed in whatever you do, wherever you turn" (1 Kings 2:2-3).

If you do this, David told Solomon, "the LORD may fulfill the promise he made on my behalf when he said, 'If your sons so conduct themselves that they remain faithful to me with their whole heart and with their whole soul, you shall always have someone of your line on the throne of Israel' " (2:2-4).

David was laid to rest in the City of David, having ruled Israel "with an iron rod" (Psalm 2:9) for forty years and having foreshadowed another King, who also came from Bethlehem and who would be "destined to rule all the nations with an iron rod" (Revelation 12:5). This King and Messiah, Jesus, called himself "son of David" (Mark 12:35), but he was far superior to David and his kingdom would have no end.

WORDS TO REMEMBER

* anointing
* oil of chrism
* oil of catechumens
* oil of the sick
* gifts of Holy Spirit

Chapter 12

A Divided Kingdom: Solomon and Others

> O God, give your judgment to the king;
> your justice to the son of kings;
> That he may govern your people with justice,
> your oppressed with right judgment.
>
> — Psalm 72:1-2

Two women who lived in the same house gave birth to sons at the same time. A few nights later, one of the women rolled over on her baby and smothered him. She switched babies with the other woman during the night and tried to convince that woman that the dead baby was hers.

Unable to resolve their dispute, the two women went to their king, who was noted for his wisdom. The king listened to both sides of the case and then told one of his aides to get him a sword. He told the aide to cut the living child in two and give one-half to one woman and one-half to the other.

The woman whose child it was pleaded with the king not to kill her son, but to give him to the other woman. The other, however, said to go ahead and divide the baby in two. When the king heard this, he said, "Give the first one the living child! By no means kill it, for she is the mother" (1 Kings 3:27).

The king in this story (cf. 1 Kings 3:16-28), of course, was Solomon, and his decision in the case of the two women is one thing that often comes to mind when the name of Solomon is raised. His reputation is enhanced by his authorship of many of the wise sayings in the Book of Proverbs.

The purpose of the Proverbs, according to the first chapter of that book, was so that "men may appreciate wisdom and discipline,/ may understand words of intelligence;/ May receive training in wise conduct,/ in what is right, just and honest;/ That resourcefulness may be imparted to the simple,/ to the young man knowledge and discretion" (1:2-4).

Some Proverbs of Solomon

Ill-gotten treasures profit nothing,
but virtue saves from death (10:2).

Hatred stirs up disputes,
but love covers all offenses (10:12).

The depraved in heart are an abomination to the LORD,
but those who walk blamelessly are his delight (11:20).

Lying lips are an abomination to the LORD,
but those who are truthful are his delight (12:22).

He who walks uprightly fears the LORD,
but he who is devious in his ways spurns him (14:2).

He sins who despises the hungry;
but happy is he who is kind to the poor (14:21).

A mild answer calms wrath,
but a harsh word stirs up anger (15:1).

The eyes of the LORD are in every place,
keeping watch on the evil and the good (15:3).

The fear of the LORD is training for wisdom,
and humility goes before honors (15:33).

Pride goes before disaster,
and a haughty spirit before a fall (16:18).

He who has compassion on the
poor lends to the LORD,
and he will repay him for his good deed (19:17).

Many are the plans in a man's heart,
but it is the decision of the LORD that endures (19:21).

A good name is more desirable than great riches,
and high esteem, than gold and silver (22:1).

Solomon's Request

Not long after Solomon was firmly seated on the throne of his father David, the LORD appeared to him in a dream and told him to ask for anything he wanted. "I am a mere youth, not knowing at all how to act," the king replied. "I serve you in the midst of the people whom you have chosen, a people so vast that it cannot be numbered or counted. Give your servant, therefore, an understanding heart to judge your people and to distinguish right from wrong. For who is able to govern this vast people of yours?" (1 Kings 3:7-9).

The LORD was pleased with this request and told Solomon: "Because you have asked for this — not for a long life for yourself, nor for riches, nor for the life of your enemies, but for understanding so that you may know what is right — I do as you requested. I give you a heart so wise and understanding that there has never been anyone like you up to now, and after you there will come no one to equal you" (3:11-12).

In addition to this, God continued, "I give you what you have not asked for, such riches and glory that among kings there is not your like. And if you follow me by keeping my statutes and commandments, as your father David did, I will give you a long life" (3:13-14).

When he awoke from the dream, Solomon went to Jerusalem and offered holocausts and peace offerings before the Ark of the Covenant of the Lord, and then gave a banquet for all his servants.

The Wealth and Wisdom of Solomon

Solomon quickly benefited from the wisdom and exceptional understanding and knowledge God had given him, and his kingdom grew rapidly in wealth and fame. His wealth was enormous (cf. 10:14-29), and his fame and reputed wisdom brought him visitors from other countries.

On one occasion, the Queen of Sheba arrived in Jerusalem to test Solomon's wisdom on a variety of subjects. King Solomon explained everything that she asked about, "and there remained nothing hidden from him that he could not explain to her" (10:3). The queen, a wealthy woman herself, was rendered "breathless" by the opulence she observed and said that the reports she had heard about Solomon "were not telling me the half. Your wisdom and prosperity surpass the report I heard .... Blessed be the LORD, your God, whom it has pleased to place you on the throne of Israel" (10:7, 9).

Some years later, Jesus would recall the visit of the Queen of Sheba and would compare the wisdom of Solomon to his own greater wisdom. With the scribes and Pharisees demanding a sign that would prove his divinity, Jesus said that only "an evil and unfaithful generation seeks a sign," and he reminded those seekers that "at the judgment the queen of the south will arise with this generation and condemn it, because she came from the ends of the earth to hear the wisdom of Solomon; and there is something greater than Solomon here" (Matthew 12:39, 42).

Building the Temple

After centuries of nomadic living and no permanent place for the Ark of the Covenant, Solomon fulfilled the promise of God that he would be the one to build a permanent place of worship for the Lord in Jerusalem. He hired skilled architects and builders, brought in materials from all over the world, and conscripted more than 30,000 workers to erect this magnificent edifice, which took seven years to finish and was lavishly decorated.

The building was 90 feet long by 30 feet wide and 45 feet high and had three major sections: the vestibule at the front, the Holy Place in the middle, and the innermost sanctuary known as the Holy of Holies. The Ark was kept in this latter room under two large cherubim made of cedar, each 15 feet high with a wingspread of 15 feet, so that they filled the room.

At the dedication of the Temple, King Solomon said to the Lord, "I have truly built you a princely house, a dwelling where you may abide forever" (8:13). He praised God for fulfilling all the promises he had made to the Israelites and asked God to keep his further promise that someone from the line of David would always sit on the throne of Israel.

When the Lord appeared to Solomon later, he said that he had heard the king's prayer of petition, had consecrated the Temple, and would establish "your throne of sovereignty over Israel forever" (9:5). He warned Solomon, however, that if he and his people failed to keep the commandments and statutes set before them, and venerated and worshiped strange gods, "I will cut off Israel from the land I gave them and repudiate the temple I have consecrated to my honor. Israel shall become a proverb and a byword among all nations, and this temple shall become a heap of ruins" (9:7-8).

The Temple of Solomon was destroyed by the Babylonians in 587 B.C. and replaced in 515 B.C. by the Temple of Zerubbabel, which stood until a new one was constructed by Herod the Great, beginning in 19 B.C. This was the temple that Jesus often visited during his time on earth and, in A.D. 70, it was destroyed by the Romans, just as Jesus had predicted forty years earlier when he told his Apostles: "Do you see these great buildings? There will not be one stone left upon another that will not be thrown down" (Mark 13:2).

A Different Kind of Temple

There would be no need for another temple, Jesus indicated, since his body would be the new temple, the Church, which would become God's earthly dwelling place. After driving the money-changers out of the Temple, Jesus told the Pharisees, "Destroy this temple and in three days I will raise it up." They thought that he was talking about the Temple of Herod, which had taken 46 years to build, but John said that Christ "was speaking about the temple of his body" (John 2:19, 21).

St. Paul identified the Church and its members with the new temple, saying that "you are no longer strangers and sojourners, but you are fellow citizens with the holy ones and members of the household of God, built upon the foundation of the apostles and prophets, with Christ Jesus himself as the capstone. Through him the whole structure is held together and grows into a temple sacred in the Lord; in him you also are being built together into a dwelling place of God in the Spirit" (Ephesians 2:19-22).

Paul also urged us to avoid immorality because the human body is "a temple of the holy Spirit" that we have received from God and that does not belong to us. He said that "you have been purchased at a price. Therefore glorify God in your body" (1 Corinthians 6:19-20).

In the heavenly city to come, there will be no temple either, "for its temple is the Lord God almighty and the Lamb. The city had no need of sun or moon to shine on it, for the glory of the Lord gave it light, and its lamp was the Lamb" (Revelation 21:22-23). No longer will there be a symbolic presence of God in a building, or his real presence in his Church; in the life to come, God will dwell among his people in all his glory.

The Sins of Solomon

Despite all the wonderful gifts of wisdom and understanding and prosperity with which Solomon had been blessed, he soon turned his back on the Lord and broke the laws that Moses had promulgated in the Book of Deuteronomy (cf. 17:14-20). Moses had said that a good king should not have a great number of horses or a great number of wives, nor should he accumulate vast amounts of gold and silver.

But Solomon increased his number of horses and the size of his army, he brought to Israel hundreds of foreign women of princely rank in an effort to establish alliances with other nations, and he piled up huge quantities of gold and silver. His foreign wives turned his heart away from the Lord and toward strange gods, and he even built shrines to these false gods.

The Lord, therefore, became angry with Solomon and said that, because he had not kept God's commandments and statutes, he would deprive him of his kingdom, though not in his lifetime "for the sake of your father David" (11:12). God raised up enemies against Solomon both inside and outside Israel and forecast the division of the country, with ten tribes breaking away from Solomon and his son Rehoboam, but with two remaining so that "my servant David may always have a lamp before me in Jerusalem, the city in which I choose to be honored" (11:36).

The fall of the kingdom was not a case of God going back on his promise to David that his kingdom would last forever, but rather God was delaying the fulfillment of his promise temporarily because Israel had been unfaithful to him.

Modern-day Solomons

At Confirmation, we receive the gifts of wisdom, understanding, and knowledge, the same gifts that Solomon possessed. Wisdom means to see things as God sees them, to see them as they really are. It means putting first things first, setting priorities, giving God first place in our lives, then people, and finally things. When we put people and things ahead of God, as Solomon did, then we are going down the wrong road.

Remember the warning of Jesus: "Whoever loves father or mother more than me is not worthy of me, and whoever loves son or daughter more than me is not worthy of me" (Matthew 10:37). Of course we are supposed to love parents and children, but we are not supposed to put their desires ahead of what God expects of us and them.

Thus, it would be wrong for a parent to counsel a daughter to get an abortion, or for a divorced son to demand that his parents support his decision to marry outside the Church. Loving one's family members does not mean going along with their immoral choices; it means encouraging them to follow the law of God, however difficult that might be.

Understanding means having a kind heart and a willingness to listen to others. It means to know the good qualities and the bad qualities of another person, and to be ready to challenge them, to encourage them, and to forgive them. All of us want others to understand us, our needs and concerns; we should be just as willing to offer others an understanding heart.

Knowledge means the ability to absorb information about a lot of things, particularly the things of God, and to put this information to good use. One can use acquired knowledge for good, such as feeding the hungry, helping the homeless, instructing the ignorant, or counseling the doubtful. One can also use knowledge for evil, such as planning a terrorist attack or stealing someone's identity.

The gifts of the Holy Spirit are in one sense like any gifts we receive. We can put them to good use or we can hide them away and forget about them. How are you using the spiritual gifts that you received at Confirmation, particularly the gifts of wisdom, understanding, and knowledge?

The Division of the Kingdom

After nearly a century of power and splendor under Kings David and Solomon, civil war came to Israel. Solomon had planted the seeds of rebellion with his oppression of the people to complete his building projects. These projects were continued by his son Rehoboam, who received two conflicting recommendations for the future. One group, the elders who had been in his father's service, suggested that he lighten the burden on the people. The other group, the ambitious young men who had grown up with him, urged him to make the load on the people even heavier.

So after three days of consultations, Rehoboam told the people: "My father put on you a heavy yoke, but I will make it heavier. My father beat you with whips, but I will beat you with scorpions" (1 Kings 12:14).

THE KINGS OF ISRAEL*

Saul (1030-1010)
David (1010-970)
Solomon (970-931)

Northern Kingdom (Israel)	Southern Kingdom (Judah)
Jeroboam I (931-910)	Rehoboam (931-913)
Nadab (910-909)	Abijah (913-911)
Baasha (909-886)	Asa (911-870)
Elah (886-885)	Jehoshaphat (870-848)
Zimri (885)	Jehoram (848-841)
Omri (885-874)	Ahaziah (841)
Ahab (874-853)	Athaliah (841-835)
Ahaziah (853-852)	Jehoash (Joash) (835-796)
Jehoram (852-841)	Amaziah (796-781)
Jehu (841-814)	Uzziah (781-740)
Jehoahaz (814-798)	Jotham (740-736)
Jehoash (Joash) (798-783)	Ahaz (736-716)
Jeroboam II (783-743)	Hezekiah (716-687)
Zechariah (743)	Manasseh (687-642)
Shallum (743)	Amon (642-640)
Menahem (743-738)	Josiah (640-609)
Pekahiah (738-737)	Jehoahaz (609)
Pekah (737-732)	Jehoiakim (609-598)
Hoshea (732-724)	Jehoiachin (598-597)
	Zedekiah (597-587)
(Fall of Samaria in 721)	
	(Fall of Jerusalem in 587)

* *This listing of the kings of Israel is taken from* The Consuming
Fire *by Rev. Michael Duggan, pp. 204-205.*

Soon the people rose up against Rehoboam, and he had to flee from Shechem back to Jerusalem. Meanwhile, Jeroboam returned from exile in Egypt and established a rival kingdom in Shechem. Fearing that his people would travel to Jerusalem to offer sacrifices at the Temple of the Lord there, and become loyal again to Rehoboam, Jeroboam made two calves of gold, setting up one in Bethel and one in Dan, and said to the people: "You have been going up to Jerusalem long enough. Here is your God, O Israel, who brought you up from the land of Egypt" (12:28).

As disaster had struck the Israelities the last time they had fashioned a golden calf, it happened again. The kingdom was eventually divided in two, with 10 tribes in the Northern Kingdom of Israel, and two tribes in the Southern Kingdom of Judah. There were nine successive family dynasties in the North with 19 kings, and one family dynasty in the South with 20 kings. There was no link to David in the North since Jeroboam was not of the royal family, but the lineage of David, from which Jesus would come, continued in the South.

One statement appears frequently in the accounts of the kings of Israel: they did evil in the sight of the Lord. Not many of those who ascended to the throne either in Israel or in Judah were admirable men. One exception was Josiah (640-609), who was installed as king at the age of eight and attempted to restore the kingdom of David and to eliminate all foreign cults. Jeremiah the prophet credited Josiah with doing "what was right and just," dispensing "justice to the weak and the poor" (Jeremiah 22:15-16).

With the land of Israel in a state of political and religious turmoil during the period of the kings, and with ruin and exile on the horizon, the stage had been set for the prophets whom God would send to call his people back to holiness.

WORDS TO REMEMBER

* Proverbs	* Temple	* Holy of Holies
* wisdom	* understanding	* knowledge

Elijah goes to heaven in a fiery chariot.

Chapter 13

Enter the Prophets

"Do not touch my anointed,
to my prophets do no harm."
— Psalm 105:15

He was a humble and obscure priest when he was named Archbishop of San Salvador in 1977. He did not seek the limelight, but his country was involved in a civil war, and Oscar Romero was obliged to speak out for peace and justice for the people of El Salvador. In the movie *Romero*, there is a scene where the Archbishop goes to a small village to rescue the Blessed Sacrament from a church occupied by soldiers.

As Romero approached the altar, a soldier with a machine gun opened fire on the tabernacle, scattering the Hosts on the floor. The Archbishop got down on his knees, picked up the Hosts while bullets screamed over his head, and then walked out of the church without saying a word to the soldiers or the villagers gathered in front of the church. He got into his car with his driver, and they drove away from the town square.

A minute or so later, however, the car returned. Romero got out, put on his vestments, and with the villagers behind him, walked back into the church through the soldiers and reclaimed the place of worship for the people.

His frequent clashes with the military government over the next few years earned him the enmity of supporters of the regime. On March 24, 1980, while celebrating Mass in a hospital chapel, Oscar Romero raised the chalice and began the familiar words, "This is the cup of my blood, the blood of the new and everlasting covenant. It will be shed for you and for all ...." Suddenly, shots were fired from the back of the chapel by a lone assassin, and the Archbishop of San Salvador fell dead.

He died while carrying out the most important action of his priesthood, bringing Christ down from heaven to earth in the Holy Sacrifice of the Mass. He died as a peacemaker and promoter of justice. He died as a prophet who tried to call the government and people of El Salvador to holiness, to the love of God and neighbor that Jesus had said were the two greatest commandments. And like other prophets who had gone before him, Oscar Romero was willing to give up his life in this apostolate.

Characteristics of the Prophets

Jesus warned against false prophets, those who "will perform signs and wonders in order to mislead, if that were possible, the elect" (Mark 13:22), so how are we to recognize true prophets? Here are some characteristics of the authentic prophets of the Old Testament:

- They were called by God and got their authority from God.
- They recognized the divine influence in their lives.
- They sometimes foretold the future, but their primary role was to speak for God, to make his message known to the world.
- They were not always willing to accept their role and were sometimes afraid.
- They came from all walks of life: Elisha was a farmer, Amos a shepherd, Isaiah a nobleman, Jeremiah and Ezekiel were priests.
- They differed from the false prophets by their holiness of life, their adherence to the law of Moses, and sometimes by their ability to predict the future and to perform miracles.
- They were needed to keep Israel from turning away completely from the one, true God.
- They were, in the words of Peter F. Ellis, C.SS.R (*The Men and the Message of the Old Testament*), "extraordinary preachers, men who came rarely, preached dramatically, on subjects of fundamental religious importance, at times of religious crisis."

Elijah the Prophet

It was during the reign of King Ahab (874-853) in the Northern Kingdom that Elijah appeared on the scene. Ahab had married a pagan woman named Jezebel, one of the wickedest women in the Bible, and had erected altars to her Canaanite god Baal. She supported 450 prophets of Baal and sought to kill all of Yahweh's prophets, especially Elijah after he had stirred up a revolt that led to the extermination of the prophets of Baal.

In an effort to bring Ahab back to Yahweh, Elijah predicted a three-year drought and then hid out east of the Jordan River, where ravens brought him bread and meat every day, just as God had provided the same food to the Israelites in the desert. He then moved on to Zarephath, where he multiplied flour and oil for a poor widow and later brought the woman's child back to life after an illness had caused his death.

The Prophets of Baal

Elijah returned to famine-wracked Samaria after three years and proposed to Ahab a contest with the prophets of Baal to see who could bring rain down on the earth. The king ordered all the pagan prophets to assemble at Mount Carmel, where Elijah oversaw the construction of two altars, with wood and a young bull placed on each. "You shall call on the name of your gods, and I will call on the name of the LORD," said Elijah. "The God who answers with fire is God" (1 Kings 18:24). All agreed to the terms, and the prophets of Baal went first.

All morning the pagan prophets danced around the altar and shouted to their god, "Answer us, Baal!" But there was no answer. When their frenzied actions, including slashing themselves with swords and spears until the blood gushed over them, produced no results by noon, Elijah needled them, telling them to shout even louder for their god might be asleep or retired or away on a journey. But still nothing happened to the holocaust they had prepared.

So Elijah built another altar to replace the one that had been partially destroyed, setting it on 12 stones representing the Tribes of Israel, arranging the wood, and cutting up a young bull and placing the pieces on the wood. He had four large jars of water poured over the altar, soaking the wood, and then called on the God of Abraham, Isaac, and Jacob to prove that he was the only God in Israel and that Elijah was his prophet.

Fire then came down from heaven and consumed the altar, the wood, and the holocaust. When the people saw this miracle, they prostrated themselves on the ground and said, "The LORD is God! The LORD is God!" (18:39). Elijah ordered that all the prophets of Baal be seized, and they were executed. He then told Ahab, who had witnessed this spectacular occurrence, to leave the mountain quickly because a heavy rainstorm was coming, the first in three years.

A Whisper from God

When Ahab told Jezebel that her prophets had been executed, she vowed to have Elijah killed, so he fled for his life to Mount Horeb and took shelter in a cave. The Lord appeared to him and told him to go outside and stand on the mountain, for he would be passing by. Elijah did as the Lord said, and soon there was a strong and violent wind crushing the rocks on the mountain, but the Lord was not in the wind.

Then there was an earthquake, but the Lord was not in the earthquake. After that came fire, but the Lord was not in the fire. Finally, there was a tiny, whispering sound, and Elijah hid his face in his cloak and stood at the entrance of the cave. "Why are you here?" God asked Elijah, and the prophet replied that he had been "most zealous for the LORD, the God of hosts. But the Israelites have forsaken your covenant, torn down your altars, and put your prophets to the sword. I alone am left, and they seek to take my life" (1 Kings 19:13-14).

God told Elijah to go back near Damascus and anoint Hazael king of Aram and Jehu king of Israel and Elisha as his successor. The prophet did as he was told and met with Elisha as he was plowing a field. Elisha left his work and followed Elijah. Some time later, as the two men went on to Jericho, they stopped at the Jordan River. Elijah rolled up his mantle and struck the water. It divided in two and the men walked across on dry ground.

When they reached the other side, Elijah told Elisha to ask for anything that he could do for him, and Elisha asked for "a double portion of your spirit" (2 Kings 2:9). Elijah granted the request and, as they walked along, a flaming chariot came between them and Elijah went up to heaven in a whirlwind. Elisha picked up his mentor's mantle, struck the water of the river with it, and crossed over on dry land as the waters parted.

A Type of Christ

In the life of Elijah, we can see foreshadowings of Christ. Both multiplied food, both were rejected by their people, both were threatened with death, and both were taken up into heaven at the end of their lives. The miraculous ascent of Elijah led those in the time of Christ to think that the prophet would come back again, and some thought that he had come back either as Jesus or as John the Baptist.

Jesus clarified the matter, after he had met on the mountain with Moses and Elijah, by saying that Elijah had come back, but in the person of the Baptist (cf. Matthew 11:14).

There is much we can learn from Elijah: his faithfulness and perseverance in carrying out the Lord's wishes, even at the risk of his life, and his intimacy with God, as demonstrated by the Lord coming to him in a gentle breeze, not in violent and noisy events. Are we able to hear God whispering to us today, surrounded as we are with constant chatter, loud music, noisy television programs, and frantic videos?

Do we try to set aside some quiet time each day to pray and listen to what God might be telling us? God has a plan for each one of us, some piece of the puzzle of salvation history that only we can fit into place. But if God's voice is drowned out by the cacophony of voices around us, how can we perform the prophetic role God has in mind for us? Let us imitate Elijah and be open to the tiny, whispering sound of God in our daily life.

Elisha the Prophet

During more than 60 years as God's mouthpiece in the Northern Kingdom, Elisha performed many miracles similar to those of Jesus. He told a barren woman that she would have a child and, when the child became seriously ill and died, Elisha brought him back to life (2 Kings 4:32-37); he multiplied loaves of bread to feed a hundred men (4:43); and he cured the Syrian army commander Naaman of leprosy by having him wash seven times in the Jordan River (cf. 5:1-14).

Jesus recalled this incident of a prophet curing a Gentile while speaking in the synagogue at Nazareth. It was his way of indicating that his ministry and message were not just to the people of Israel, but he infuriated those in the synagogue, who drove him out of town and attempted to throw him over a cliff. Jesus, however, passed through the midst of them and walked away unharmed (cf. Luke 4:30).

Later, Elisha sent his disciple to Ramoth-gilead to anoint Jehu king of Isrsael and to order Jehu to destroy the house of Ahab in order to avenge the murders of the prophets. Jehu then traveled to Jezreel and executed King Joram to put an end to "the many fornications and witchcrafts of your mother Jezebel" (9:22). He also had Jezebel thrown from the window of her palace, bringing an end to her evil reign. When the remaining members of the royal family and the priests of Baal had been destroyed, Elisha was able to restore the true religion in Israel for a time.

Reporting on these incidents does not mean that the use of murder and assassination to advance the plan of God is defensible from a moral point of view. It is not defensible and is condemned elsewhere in the Bible (cf. Hosea 1:4).

Amos the Prophet

A shepherd and dresser of sycamore trees 800 years before Christ, Amos was the first prophet to preach and write. He traveled from Judah to the Northern Kingdom and pronounced judgment on the foreign nations for their immorality (Amos 1, 2). This was followed by his prediction of divine retribution against the people of Israel for their crimes against the Lord who had brought them up from the land of Egypt (3:2).

He foretold, however, that the destruction of Israel would not be total and that a remnant would survive. In a vision, the Lord told him that "I will bring about the restoration of my people Israel;/ they shall rebuild and inhabit their ruined cities,/ Plant vineyards and drink the wine,/ set out gardens and eat the fruits./ I will plant them upon their own ground;/ never again shall they be plucked/ From the land I have given them,/ say I, the LORD, your God" (Amos 9:14-15).

His prophecies were recalled by Stephen (Acts 7:42-43) and by James (Acts 15:16-18).

Like Oscar Romero, Amos was known as a prophet of social justice. He condemned the rich for "Storing up in their castles/ what they have extorted and robbed" (3:10), the women of Bashan as "cows ... who oppress the weak/ and abuse the needy" (4:1), and those who had "trampled upon the weak/ and exacted of them levies of grain" (5:11). Only if they were to "seek good and not evil" (5:14) would the Lord allow them to live, said Amos.

Hosea the Prophet

The last of the prophets of the Northern Kingdom before its fall to the Assyrians in 721, Hosea (formerly Osee) is known as the prophet of divine love, the St. John of the Old Testament. He used the story of his own failed marriage to symbolize the relationship between God and his people Israel. Jesus would develop the same imagery in his parables of the wedding feast (Matthew 22:1-14) and the ten virgins (Matthew 25:1-13).

Hosea is God in the story, his adulteress wife Gomer is unfaithful Israel, and her lovers are the Baals with whom Israel was committing adultery. His willingness to forgive his unfaithful wife if she would repent and return to him mirrors God's willingness to forgive unfaithful Israel under the same conditions. But it will be necessary for God to chastise Israel by ending her material prosperity, sending her into exile to be purified, and only then taking her back as his faithful spouse.

In balancing God's love with his justice, Hosea corrects the belief that the God of the Old Testament is a God of vengeance. It is not a matter of God being loving in the New Testament and vengeful in the Old Testament (we will see examples of both in the life of Jesus and the early Church), but rather an emphasis on love sometimes and justice other times.

This was made clear in the Book of Deuteronomy when God said that "I, the LORD, your God, am a jealous God, inflicting punishments for their fathers' wickedness on the children of those who hate me, down to the third and fourth generation but bestowing mercy, down to the thousandth generation, on the children of those who love me and keep my commandments" (5:9-10).

In the life of Hosea we see many foreshadowings of Jesus, notably the prophet's imagery of the vine for Israel (10:1), anticipating the same image that Jesus used in Matthew 21:33-44 and John 15:1-8. Hosea denounced merely external religious observance, saying, "it is love that I desire, not sacrifice,/ and knowledge of God rather than holocausts" (6:6). Jesus would level the same charge of religious hypocrisy against the scribes and Pharisees in his "woe to you" diatribe in Matthew 23:13:36.

Micah the Prophet

Micah was a contemporary of Isaiah in Jerualem in the eighth century before Christ. His description of the social evils of the time — covetousness, theft, corruption, oppression, the breakdown of family life — parallels the evils of our own time. His solution to these problems is just as applicable today: "Only to do the right and to love goodness,/ and to walk humbly with your God" (Micah 6:8).

It is from Micah that we get the prophecy of a ruler in Israel who will come from Bethlehem of Judea and shepherd his people (5:1-3), a reference to Jesus. It was this prophecy that led the Magi to Bethlehem shortly after the birth of the Messiah (cf. Matthew 2:5-6). And it is Micah who prophesied that when this ruler comes, nations "shall beat their swords into plowshares,/ and their spears into pruning hooks;/ One nation shall not raise the sword against another,/ nor shall they train for war again,/ .... But we will walk in the name of/ the LORD,/ our God, forever and ever" (4:3-5).

Isaiah the Prophet

Sometimes called the prophet of holiness, Isaiah was sitting in the Temple in Jerusalem when he was called by the Lord. He was shown a vision of God sitting upon a lofty throne with seraphim hovering above him. The angels had six wings, two above them, two hiding their feet, and two veiling their faces so as not to look upon the divine majesty. The seraphim were crying out, "Holy, holy, holy is the LORD of hosts!... All the earth is filled with his glory" (Isaiah 6:3).

We say or sing virtually these same words just before the Eucharistic prayer at every Mass we attend.

This manifestation of God's glory unnerved Isaiah, who acknowledged his own unworthiness, saying, "Woe is me, I am doomed! For I am a man of unclean lips, living among a people of unclean lips; yet my eyes have seen the King, the LORD of hosts!" Then one of the seraphim took a burning coal from the altar and touched it to Isaiah's lips, saying that "your wickedness is removed, your sin purged" (6:5, 7).

The "burning coal" available to cleanse us from sin is the sacrament of Penance or Reconciliation. God first inspires in us a recognition of our sins and then a sense of sorrow for them. We are blessed, however, in that we can confess our sins to a priest, as Jesus commanded (cf. John 20:22-23), receive sound advice on how to avoid sins in the future, as well as the grace necessary to say no to sin, and know when we leave the confessional after hearing the priest's words of absolution, that our sins have truly been forgiven.

After the angel had purged Isaiah's sins, the Lord asked him, "Whom shall I send? Who will go for us?" And Isaiah replied: "Here I am ... send me!" (6:8). The prophet went out from the Temple and acted as God's voice to the people of the Southern Kingdom until, according to Hebrew legend, his martyrdom about the year 687 under King Manasseh, who had Isaiah placed in a hollow tree and sawed in half.

If God asked you, "Whom shall I send to spread my love and message to the world," would you have the courage to say, "Here I am; send me"? Does God need faithful and courageous messengers today? By your Baptism and Confirmation you were given the sacramental grace you need to become another Isaiah. Are you willing to act on that grace?

Did you ever stop to think that you might be the only face of Christ that some persons will ever see in their lifetime? What a challenge and a responsibility!

The Immanuel Prophecy

When Isaiah was instructed to tell King Ahaz not to fear enemy plots against him, the Lord invited Ahaz to ask for a sign. But Ahaz said that he would not ask for a sign, that he would not tempt the Lord. So Isaiah responded: "Listen, O house of David! Is it not enough for you to weary men, must you also weary my God? Therefore the Lord himself will give you this sign: the virgin shall be with child, and bear a son, and shall name him Immanuel" (7:13-14).

The Church has always followed the interpretation of Matthew (1:23), who found in this passage a prophecy of the virgin birth of Jesus. Thus, the *Catechism of the Catholic Church* says (n. 497) that "the Church sees here the fulfillment of the divine promise given through the prophet Isaiah: 'Behold, a virgin shall conceive and bear a son' " [*Isa* 7:14 in the LXX, quoted in *Mt* 1:23 (Gk.)].

The Sayings of Isaiah

Catholics who faithfully attend Mass every week, or especially every day, will hear many passages from Isaiah. There are words of hope for the most hardened sinners (1:18):

> Come now, let us set things right,
>   says the LORD:
> Though your sins be like scarlet,
>   they may become white as snow;
> Though they be crimson red,
>   they may become white as wool.

And for those considering abortion (49:15):

> Can a mother forget her infant,
> be without tenderness for the
> child of her womb?
> Even should she forget,
> I will never forget you.

And for the discouraged (54:10):

> Though the mountains leave their place
> and the hills be shaken,
> My love shall never leave you
> nor my covenant of peace be shaken,
> says the LORD, who has mercy on you.

And for those who try to figure out God's plans (55:8-9):

> For my thoughts are not your thoughts,
> nor are your ways my ways, says the LORD.
> As high as the heavens are above the earth,
> so high are my ways above your ways/
> and my thoughts above your thoughts.

The Servant Songs

But perhaps the most famous passages in the Book of Isaiah are those that refer to the suffering of Jesus. These "Servant Songs" can be found in chapters 42, 49, 50, 52, and 53 of Isaiah. It would be helpful to read all of these chapters in their entirety and see how many passages you can remember hearing, particularly during Lent and Holy Week. But just consider the following verses and try to imagine if they could possibly refer to any person other than Christ:

> Yet it was our infirmities that
> he bore,
> our sufferings that he endured,
> While we thought of him as stricken,
> as one smitten by God
> and afflicted.

But he was pierced for our offenses,
crushed for our sins,
Upon him was the chastisement
that makes us whole,
by his stripes we were healed (53:4-5).

Isaiah and Rabbi Zolli

In his book *Why I Became a Catholic*, Israel Zolli, the former chief rabbi of Rome, said that chapters 52 and 53 of Isaiah had led him into the Catholic Church in 1945. Zolli took the baptismal name Eugenio in honor of Pope Pius XII for all that the Holy Father had done to help the Jewish people during the Nazi Holocaust. In a visit with the Supreme Pontiff on July 25, 1944, then-Rabbi Zolli officially thanked Pius XII "for all he, personally and through the Catholics in Rome, had done in favor of the Jews, opening convents and monasteries, dispensing with papal cloister as stated in canon law, so that Jews could be received even in female monasteries and protected from the fury of the Nazis."

Zolli comments completely contradict the charges of recent decades that Pius XII did nothing to help the Jews during World War II. Another Jewish leader, former Israeli diplomat Pinchas Lapide, who authored the book *Three Popes and the Jews*, estimated that the Holy Father saved the lives of at least 860,000 Jews during those terrible years.

<u>WORDS TO REMEMBER</u>

* Immanuel   * Servant Songs

Ezekiel's vision of the valley of dry bones.

Chapter 14

Prophets of the Exile: Jeremiah and Ezekiel

> O God, the nations have invaded your heritage;
> they have defiled your holy temple,
> have laid Jerusalem in ruins.
> — Psalm 79:1

The hurricane had swirled out of the Caribbean and had cut a destructive path through many communities. In one town, a Catholic church was severely damaged. In front of the church, however, a statue of the Sacred Heart of Jesus remained standing, except that the outstretched hands were missing. The next morning, an enterprising parishioner had placed a sign in front of the statue. It read: "I have no hands but yours."

For more than a thousand years, God had remained faithful to the people of Israel, despite their idolatry and infidelity. The cycle of sin had been repeated over and over again, from sin to punishment to repentance to liberation, but God finally decided to let Israel's enemies triumph over her, even permitting them to send his people into exile in Babylon. First the people from the North in 721 and then those from the South in 597 and again in 587, when the Temple in Jerusalem was destroyed.

But the hands of God would continue to be those of the prophets, particularly Jeremiah and Ezekiel. Jeremiah tried, in the years leading up to the capture of Jerusalem, to warn the people about their coming fate, but they persecuted him and tried to kill him. His message is found not only in the Book of Jeremiah, but also in Lamentations.

Ezekiel came along after the fall of Jerusalem and preached among the exiles in Babylon, calling them to take responsibility for their actions and to use this period of exile to purify themselves for their eventual return to their homeland. His powerful visions, especially the dry bones that were brought to life, were to convey a message of hope to the people.

Jeremiah the Prophet

When Jeremiah first heard God's call during the reign of the good King Josiah (640-609), he told the Lord that he was too young to take on the burden of a prophet. The Lord responded that Jeremiah had always been destined to be a prophet: "Before I formed you in the womb I knew you,/ before you were born I dedicated you,/ a prophet to the nations I appointed you" (Jeremiah 1:5).

God told Jeremiah not to fear anything because he would be with him. Then he touched the new prophet's mouth with his hand and said, "See, I place my words in your mouth!/ This day I set you/ over nations and over kingdoms,/ To root up and to tear down,/ to destroy and to demolish,/ to build and to plant" (1:9-10). He said that he had made Jeremiah "a fortified city,/ A pillar of iron, a wall of brass,/ against the whole land" (1:18).

In chapter seven of the Book of Jeremiah, we find the sermon he delivered in the Temple. He told the people to reform their ways and their deeds completely and not merely to spout pious words, such as, "This is the temple of the LORD! The temple of the LORD! The temple of the LORD!" (7:4).

He accused the people of putting their trust in "deceitful words" while continuing to engage in all kinds of wickedness, such as stealing and murder, adultery and perjury, and burning incense before strange gods. The people thought that they had only to come to the Temple and recite certain magic words, and that would leave them free to commit all those abominations again, but Jeremiah told them otherwise.

These abuses in the Temple caused the Lord to ask, "Has this house which bears my name become in your eyes a den of thieves?" (7:11) Jesus would recall these words when he overturned the tables of the money-changers (cf. Matthew 21:13).

The Reforms of Josiah

During the reign of Josiah, a scroll from the Book of Deuter-onomy had been found in the Temple and, after hearing it read, the king instituted a religious revival. He had the Temple repaired, ordered all the shrines and altars to false gods destroyed and their priests executed, and issued a command to resume observance of the feast of Passover. He also forbade all consultation of ghosts and spirits.

Before Josiah, says 2nd Kings, "there had been no king who turned to the LORD as he did, with his whole heart, his whole soul, and his whole strength, in accord with the entire law of Moses; nor could any after him compare with him" (23:25).

Josiah was able to institute these reforms because of the waning power of the Assyrians in Palestine. However, his attempt to restore the kingdom of David to Israel came to an end when he was killed in a battle with the Egyptians in 609. Both Egypt and Babylon were trying to take over the Assyrian empire, and Babylon was successful under Nebuchadnezzar, who would later preside over the destruction of Jerusalem.

Conspiracy Against Jeremiah

Meanwhile, Jeremiah continued to call the people to repentance and holiness and warned them of the coming catastrophe, but their response was to plot his assassination (cf. 11:9, 18), to have him scourged and placed in stocks at one of the gates of the city (cf. 20:2), and to put him on trial and threaten his execution (cf. 26:11).

But Jeremiah spoke out at his trial, saying that putting him to death would mean the shedding of innocent blood since he was just telling them what the Lord wanted them to do. The princes and people at the trial were persuaded by his words and said: "This man does not deserve death; it is in the name of the LORD, our God, that he speaks to us" (26:16). So they set him free for the time being.

The Potter's Vessel

On one occasion, God told Jeremiah to visit the house of a potter and to watch the man shape the vessels he was making. If a vessel turned out badly, the potter would start over again until he had worked the clay into the object he wanted. Comparing the potter's work with Israel, God asked, "Can I not do to you, house of Israel, as this potter has done? ... Indeed, like clay in the hand of the potter, so are you in my hand, house of Israel. Sometimes I threaten to uproot and tear down and destroy a nation or a kingdom. But if that nation which I have threatened turns from its evil, I also repent of the evil which I threatened to do" (18:6-8).

Like the vessel in the hands of the potter, so are we "earthen vessels" in the hands of the Lord. "For we are his handiwork," said St. Paul, "created in Christ Jesus for the good works that God has prepared in advance, that we should live in them" (Ephesians 2:10).

God knew that his warnings through Jeremiah would go unheeded. He predicted that the people would continue to follow their own immoral course, that each person would vow to "behave according to the stubbornness of his evil heart!" (18:12).

The situation in Jeremiah's time is not unlike today, except for the imminent threat of exile to a foreign land. The same kinds of moral evils that he condemned are very prevalent in the 21st century. Modern-day prophets, like Pope John Paul II, tried to show people the awful consequences of sin and its contribution to what the Holy Father called a "culture of death," but these prophets have been mostly ignored, as Jeremiah was.

In the weeks after the death of John Paul in 2005, it was difficult to find anyone who did not express admiration for the Pontiff, but it was not difficult to find persons, even Catholics, who said that, while they liked the Holy Father personally, they didn't agree with some of the things he said. This was usually a reference to his opposition to abortion, contraception, euthanasia, embryonic stem cell research, same-sex unions, and women priests.

That these were all core teachings of the Catholic Church that the Pope had no authority, nor any wish, to change seemed to have eluded those who dissented from these teachings. Had John Paul reversed course on any of these matters, he would have been guilty of conforming the Church to the culture, instead of the other way around. He found, as Jeremiah and his colleagues had discovered, that those who stubbornly adhere to moral evils don't want to be told to repent and believe in the Gospel. But the duty of a true prophet is to shout that unpopular message from the rooftops anyway (cf. Matthew 10:27).

A Type of Christ

It has been said of Jeremiah that no man did more for his nation and was treated worse. The same could later be said of Jesus, who resembled Jeremiah in many ways. Both men embraced celibacy, were rejected by the people in their hometowns, and were eventually put to death by those to whom they preached. Both predicted the fall of Jerusalem and the destruction of the Temple; in fact, what happened to Jeremiah, Jerusalem, the

Temple, and the Babylonians parallels what happened to Jesus, Jerusalem, the Temple, and the Romans.

Jeremiah's Final Days

The prophet's good relations with King Josiah were not duplicated with King Jehoiakim (609-598), who was denounced by Jeremiah for treating the poor and the weak unjustly, for shedding innocent blood, and for "practicing oppression and extortion" (22:17). The prophet had compiled all his sermons in a scroll which his scribe Baruch was to read publicly to the people. However, when Jehoiakim heard of it, he had the scroll destroyed.

His continued predictions of defeat at the hands of the Babylonians did not endear Jeremiah with King Zedekiah (597-587) or his aides, who believed that the predictions undermined the will of the people to resist. When he left Jerusalem briefly just before the fall of the city, Jeremiah was arrested and charged with desertion. He later was placed in a cistern to starve to death, but was released.

After the fall of Jerusalem, Jeremiah was treated well by the Babylonians because they thought his predictions of their victory meant that he was on their side. They offered him the choice of living in Babylon or Judah, and he chose Judah. When some members of the Jewish community asked his advice on whether to stay or go to Egypt, Jeremiah told them to stay.

But the community forced him and Baruch to accompany them to Egypt, where he incurred the enmity of the Egyptians by predicting that they would be overcome by the Babylonians. He also rebuked his own people for worshiping the pagan "queen of heaven," and legend has it that he was stoned to death by the Jews in Egypt.

A Prophet of Hope

Despite his many prophecies of doom, Jeremiah also offered words of hope to his people. He wrote that "the days are coming, says the LORD, when I will make a new covenant with the house of Israel and the house of Judah. It will not be like the covenant I made with their fathers the day I took them by the hand and led them forth from the land of Egypt; for they broke my covenant and I had to show myself their master, says the LORD."

He said that "this is the covenant which I will make with the house of Israel after those days, says the LORD. I will place my law within them, and write it upon their hearts; I will be their God, and they shall be my people. No longer will they have need to teach their friends and their kinsmen how to know the LORD. All, from least to greatest, shall know me, says the LORD, for I will forgive their evildoing and remember their sin no more" (31:31, 33-34).

Ezekiel the Prophet

Having gone to Babylon with the first group of exiles in 597, the priest Ezekiel preached to the Israelites about the coming destruction of Jerusalem for ten years. God had chosen him to be "a watchman for the house of Israel" (Ezekiel 3:17) and to speak to these obstinate and rebellious people about the consequences of their apostasy and infidelity. He told Ezekiel not to fear them when they contradicted him and rejected him.

At the time of his calling, Ezekiel was told by God to eat a scroll covered with writing on the front and back. He said that the scroll "was as sweet as honey in my mouth" (3:3), and that the Lord commanded him to speak the words on the scroll to the exiles, whether they listened to him or resisted what he was saying, because this was God's warning to them. The following words from the Almighty ought to serve as a warning to those of the present generation, too.

"If I say to the wicked man, You shall surely die," the Lord told Ezekiel, "and you do not warn him or speak out to dissuade him from his wicked conduct so that he may live: that wicked man shall die for his sin, but I will hold you responsible for his death. If, on the other hand, you have warned the wicked man, yet he has not turned away from his evil nor from his wicked conduct, then he shall die for his sin, but you shall save your life" (3:18-19).

Furthermore, the Lord continued, "if a virtuous man turns away from virtue and does wrong when I place a stumbling block before him, he shall die. He shall die for his sin, and his virtuous deeds shall not be remembered; but I will hold you responsible for his death if you did not warn him. When, on the other hand, you have warned a virtuous man not to sin, and he has in fact not sinned, he shall surely live because of the warning, and you shall save your own life" (3:20-21)
.

Responsibility for Others

Compare these words of God to the modern-day attitude of tolerance and indifference to the sins of others. How many times are we told not to be judgmental, to let each person live the way he wants to live? Some of those who argue in this fashion even quote the words of Jesus about not judging others lest we be judged ourselves. But was Christ saying that we should never call sin by its right name, or was he saying that we should not judge the motives of others since only God knows what is in a person's heart?

Jesus thought it important to condemn "evil thoughts, un-chastity, theft, murder, adultery, greed, malice, deceit, licentiousness, envy, blasphemy, arrogance, folly" (Mark 7:21-22), so are we not to call the sinfulness of these actions to the attention of those around us? Granted, those guilty of these sins won't appreciate hearing that what they are doing is wrong, but if we fail to warn them to desist from wicked conduct, then we are neither showing concern for the spiritual well-being and salvation of our neighbor, nor are we taking steps that, according to Ezekiel 3:18-19, are necessary to save the sinner and ourselves.

God told Ezekiel that he takes "no pleasure in the death of anyone who dies" (18:32), but that he has little patience with those who say that the Lord's ways are unfair. "Is it my way that is not fair, house of Israel," God asked, "or rather, is it not that your ways are not fair?" (18:29). He said that he will judge each person according to his own ways, but the best thing to do would be to "turn and be converted from all your crimes, that they may be no cause of guilt for you. Cast away from you all the crimes you have committed, and make for yourselves a new heart and a new spirit" (18:30-31).

Our responsibility for others, of course, is contingent upon the recognition — with the help of God's grace — of sin in our own lives. Remember the admonition of Jesus that we must "remove the wooden beam" from our own eye first, "then you will see clearly to remove the splinter from your brother's eye" (Matthew 7:3-5).

The Good Shepherd

One of the most enduring images of Jesus is that of the Good Shepherd who goes after his lost sheep (cf. Luke 15:1-7 and John

10:7-15). This same image appears in chapter 34 of the Book of Ezekiel. In a vision to Ezekiel, the Lord said that he would take his sheep back from their bad shepherds and "rescue them from every place where they were scattered when it was cloudy and dark .... The lost I will seek out, the strayed I will bring back, the injured I will bind up, the sick I will heal" (34:12-16).

After separating one sheep from another and judging between the good and the bad, the Lord said, "I will appoint one shepherd over them to pasture them, my servant David; he shall pasture them and be their shepherd. I, the LORD, will be their God, and my servant David shall be prince among them. I, the LORD, have spoken" (Ezekiel 34:23-24).

That the Father was talking about Jesus was made clear years later by Christ, when he proclaimed, "I am the good shepherd. A good shepherd lays down his life for the sheep. A hired man, who is not a shepherd and whose sheep are not his own, sees a wolf coming and leaves the sheep and runs away, and the wolf catches and scatters them. This is because he works for pay and has no concern for the sheep. I am the good shepherd, and I know mine and mine know me, just as the Father knows me and I know the Father; and I will lay down my life for the sheep" (John 10:11-15).

The Dry Bones Vision

After years of preaching gloom and doom, Ezekiel began to offer the exiles some hope of a return to their homeland. He told of walking across a plain that was covered with dry bones in every direction. "Can these bones come to life?" God asked the prophet, and Ezekiel replied that only the Lord knew the answer to that question. God then told him to prophesy over these bones and say, "Dry bones, hear the word of the LORD!" (37:3-4).

As he began prophesying, said Ezekiel, he heard the bones rattling as they joined together and took on sinews and flesh, but there was no life in them. So the Lord told him to prophesy to the spirit to breathe life into these bones and, when he had done so, "they came alive and stood upright, a vast army. Then he said to me: Son of man, these bones are the whole house of Israel. They have been saying, 'Our bones are dried up, our hope is lost, and we are cut off' " (37:10-11).

Ezekiel continued prophesying, saying, "Thus says the Lord GOD: O my people, I will open your graves and have you rise from them, and bring you back to the land of Israel. Then you shall know that I am the LORD, when I open your graves and have you rise from them, O my people! I will put my spirit in you that you may live, and I will settle you upon your land; thus you shall know that I am the LORD. I have promised, and I will do it, says the LORD" (37:12-14).

Promise of Our Resurrection

God always keeps his promises, and this promise to put life into dead bones was fulfilled in the Resurrection of Jesus, who had promised the same thing to Martha, the sister of Lazarus, when he said: "I am the resurrection and the life; whoever believes in me, even if he dies, will live, and everyone who lives and believes in me will never die" (John 11:25-26).

The same promise applies to us, too, as St. Paul made clear in chapter 15 of the First Letter to the Corinthians. If Christ did not rise from the dead, said Paul, then his preaching and our faith are empty and in vain. But since Christ did overcome death, he said, so will we. And on the last day our natural bodies will be raised as spiritual bodies, "for the trumpet will sound, the dead will be raised incorruptible, and we shall be changed. For that which is corruptible must clothe itself with incorruptibility, and that which is mortal must clothe itself with immortality" (15:52-53).

The Heavenly City

Another vision given to Ezekiel was that of the temple and the city of Jerusalem, which are also described in the Book of Revelation. Both Ezekiel (cf. 40:1-4) and John (Revelation 21:10) were taken to a high mountain and shown the city. But whereas Ezekiel described in great detail the exterior and interior of the temple that would be rebuilt in the earthly Jerusalem, John said that there would be no temple in the heavenly city, "for its temple is the Lord God almighty and the Lamb. The city had no need of sun or moon to shine on it, for the glory of God gave it light, and its lamp was the Lamb" (21:22-23).

Ezekiel also saw the waters of life flowing out from the temple and bringing new life to every sort of living creature (cf. 47:1-12). In his conversation with the Samaritan woman at the well, Jesus talked about living water that would flow out from him, saying that "whoever drinks the water I shall give will never thirst; the water I shall give will become in him a spring of water welling up to eternal life" (John 4:14).

The same "river of life-giving water, sparkling like crystal," will flow through the heavenly city, said John, with "the tree of life" growing on each side of the river. He said that "nothing accursed will be found there anymore. The throne of God and of the Lamb will be in it, and his servants will worship him. They will look upon his face, and his name will be on their foreheads. Night will be no more, nor will they need light from lamp or sun, for the Lord God shall give them light, and they shall reign forever and ever" (22:1-5).

A New Heart

In a foreshadowing of the sacrament of Baptism (cf. John 3:5), Ezekiel said that God had told him, "I will sprinkle clean water upon you to cleanse you from all your impurities, and from all your idols I will cleanse you" (36:25). He said that God also promised to give his people "a new heart and place a new spirit within you, taking from your bodies your stony hearts and giving you natural hearts" (36:26).

Too many persons today have hearts of stone, hearts that are hardened against God and against his love and his Commandments. But just as the Lord promised to give natural hearts to those in exile in Babylon, so he will give natural hearts to those who are in exile from our homeland with God in heaven. We need to unite our hearts to the heart of Jesus, which was pierced on the cross.

"The blood and water that flowed from the pierced side of the crucified Christ," says the *Catechism* (n. 1225), "are types of Baptism and the Eucharist, the sacraments of new life" [cf. *Jn* 19:34; *1 Jn* 5:6-8].

Chapter 15

Return from Exile
and the Maccabees

> When the LORD restored the fortunes of Zion,
> then we thought we were dreaming.
> Our mouths were filled with laughter,
> our tongues sang for joy.
> — Psalm 126:1-2

When Navy pilot Jeremiah Denton took off on a bombing mission over North Vietnam in the summer of 1965, he did not know that he would not taste freedom again for almost eight years. His aircraft was shot down during that mission, and he was captured by the Communists and subjected to brutal torture over the years in an attempt to get information from him. His book, appropriately titled *When Hell Was in Session*, provides the stark details of his captivity.

When he was finally granted freedom from his exile in North Vietnam in 1973, Admiral Denton attributed his survival to a strong faith in God. He said that "my principal battle with the North Vietnamese was a moral one, and prayer was my prime source of strength."

Denton told of one Easter that the captives observed by reciting a poem he had written entitled "The Great Sign." The poem was about a conversation that might have taken place on the first Holy Saturday among three of the women who would discover the empty tomb on Easter morning. The lines in the poem about praying with faith at the tomb of Christ, said Denton, "illustrated as well as anything the desperate hopefulness of the prisoners in our dark and lonely cells as we looked for a 'Great Sign.' "

It was also a strong faith in God, and the great signs described by Ezekiel, that created a spark of hope in the Israelites and enabled them to survive 40 years of exile in Babylon. They had been sent there by the Babylonian dictator Nebuchadnezzar, but the power structure had changed during the exile and now the more benevolent Persians ruled the world. It was King Cyrus (538-529) who made it possible for a remnant of some 42,000 Israelites to return to their homeland in 538 and to rebuild the Temple that Nebuchadnezzar had destroyed. It was the policy of the Persians at that time to permit those under their domination to continue their own religion and customs.

With only two tribes (Judah and Benjamin) coming out of Babylon after the exile, and the other ten vanishing from history, the two key figures in the restoration of Jerusalem and the rebuilding of the community were Ezra and Nehemiah. Ezra, "a scribe, well-versed in the law of Moses" (Ezra 7:6), was the religious leader of the restoration and sought to make the first five books of the Bible the basic rule of the community. Nehemiah was the organizer and administrator who introduced the necessary political reforms and rebuilt the walls of Jerusalem.

The Role of Cyrus

In the first year of his reign, King Cyrus was inspired by the Lord "to build him a house in Jerusalem, which is in Judah." He issued a proclamation saying that "whoever, therefore, among you belongs to any part of his people, let him go up, and may his God be with him! Let everyone who has survived, in whatever place he may have dwelt, be assisted by the people of that place with silver, gold, goods, and cattle, together with free-will offerings for the house of God in Jerusalem" (Ezra 1:2-4).

The proclamation of Cyrus was reminiscent of what happened in Egypt when Pharaoh finally agreed to let the people of Israel go and the Egyptians provided them with silver and gold and clothing (Exodus 12:35). Unlike Pharaoh, however, Cyrus did not change his mind and send soldiers after the Israelites to bring them back.

Rebuilding the Temple

Within a year of their return, the people, under the guidance of Jeshua and Zerrubbabel, constructed an altar to offer holocausts to the Lord and then laid the foundation of the new Temple. This was accompanied by joyful shouting and songs of praise for the Lord, "for he is good, for his kindness to Israel endures forever" (Ezra 3:11). The Samaritans, however, who were enemies of the tribes of Judah and Benjamin, sought to intimidate and discourage those who were building the Temple, and they thwarted their plans until the reign of King Darius I (521-485). Work resumed in 520 and was completed in 515. The people celebrated the completion of their house of worship with the sacrifice of hundreds of animals as a sin-offering for all Israel, set up classes of priests and Levites for service at the Temple, and kept the feast of Passover and Unleavened Bread for seven days, "for the LORD had filled them with joy by making the king of Assyria favorable to them, so that he gave them help in their work on the house of God, the God of Israel" (6:22).

When the whole people had been gathered at the Water Gate of the city, Ezra read to them from the law of Moses from dawn until midday. The people, who were listening intently, began to cry. "Do not be sad, and do not weep," Ezra told them, "... for today is holy to our LORD. Do not be saddened this day, for rejoicing in the LORD must be your strength" (Nehemiah 8:9-10). He prayed and acknowledged the guilt of the people and demanded holiness from them. They swore that they would do what he had demanded (cf. Ezra 10:1-5).

The Deeds of Nehemiah

While Ezra was a priest concerned with reformation in temple worship and spiritual matters, Nehemiah was a layman who was appointed by King Artaxerxes (464-423) to rebuild the walls of Jerusalem. Like Ezra, Nehemiah was also opposed by the Samaritans, who were led by the governor of Samaria, Sanballat. He resisted their opposition and completed the walls in 52 days, stationing gatekeepers at the doors in the walls and appointing watchmen from among the inhabitants of Jerusalem.

At the dedication ceremony of the wall of the city, there were thanksgiving hymns and the joyful music of cymbals, harps, and lyres. Great sacrifices were offered that day, the women and children joined in, "and the rejoicing at Jerusalem could be heard from afar off" (Nehemiah 12:43).

Nehemiah, who had gone back to Babylon for a while, returned to Jerusalem to discover that some officials were using the Temple for their own enrichment and that others were not carrying out the religious services that had been assigned to them. He took the magistrates to task for abandoning the house of God and had the Levites resume their stations.

Nehemiah also cracked down on the merchants who were selling their wares on the sabbath, demanding of them: "What is this evil thing that you are doing, profaning the sabbath day? Did not your fathers act in this same way, with the result that our God has brought all this evil upon us and upon this city? Would you add to the wrath against Israel by once more profaning the sabbath?" (13:17-18).

He ordered that the doors of the city be closed before the sabbath and not be reopened until the sabbath was over. Nehemiah also ordered an end to the marriage of Jews with foreign women, asking, "Did not Solomon, the king of Israel, sin because of them?" (13:26). He summed up his accomplishments by saying,"Thus I cleansed them of all foreign contamination. I established the various functions for the priests and Levites, so that each had his appointed task. I also provided for the procurement of wood at stated times and for the first fruits. Remember this in my favor, O my God!" (13:30-31).

The Maccabean Revolt

While the people of Israel were trying to get their house in order, world power changed hands again. The Persian Empire came to an end in 331 B.C. with the defeat of King Darius III by Alexander the Great, the Greek general who ruled the world until his death in 323. The Greek Empire was then divided into the Ptolemys and the Seleucids, and the Jews faced a new threat of extermination from Antiochus IV Epiphanes (175-164).

One of ten Seleucid kings, Antiochus sought to impose his Hellenistic culture on Israel. He plundered the Temple to build up his own depleted treasury and ordered his officers to suppress Jewish worship and religious practices, while at the same time promoting worship of Greek gods. He even had erected in the Temple an altar of Zeus Olympios, the "horrible abomination" referred to in Daniel 9:27 and 11:31.

Opposition to Antiochus was not long in coming, and it was spearheaded by the family of a man named Mattathias, particularly through his three sons, Judas, Jonathan, and Simon, and his grandson, John Hyrcanus. The name "Maccabee," which probably means "hammer," was applied only to Judas, the first leader of the revolt against the Seleucid kings, but the two books (1st Maccabees and 2nd Maccabees) describing the heroic exploits of this family go by that name.

When Mattathias saw the sacrileges that were being committed against the Temple and Jewish religious practice, he said, "Woe is me! Why was I born to see the ruin of my people and the ruin of the holy city, and to sit idle while it is given into the hands of enemies, and the sanctuary into the hands of strangers?" (1 Maccabees 2:7). He and his sons refused the king's order to offer sacrifice to pagan gods, and Mattathias killed a messenger of the king who was forcing them to sacrifice and tore down the pagan altar.

He traveled throughout Jerusalem, calling upon all those who were "zealous for the law" (2:27) and who stood by the covenant to follow him into the mountains, where they mounted a campaign to restore true worship in the land. When it came time for Mattathias to die, he called together his sons and told them to "avenge the wrongs of your people. Pay back the Gentiles what they deserve, and observe the precepts of the law" (2:67-68).

Judas Maccabeus

The leadership of the movement went from Mattathias to his son Judas, who was called Maccabeus and who waged several successful battles against the forces of Antiochus. Prior to one battle, in which his 10,000-man army faced a force of 65,000 soldiers and cavalry, Judas called upon the Lord for help.

Recalling that God had come to the assistance of David in his struggle against the Philistines, Judas asked the Lord to deliver this enemy into his hands. "Strike them with fear, weaken the boldness of their strength, and let them tremble at their own destruction," he prayed. "Strike them down by the sword of those who love you, that all who know your name may hymn your praise" (4:32-33).

His prayer was answered, and the enemy general Lysias fled to Antioch to recruit mercenaries so as to return to Judah with greater numbers at another time.

Having defeated their enemies for the time being, Judas and his brothers went up to Mount Zion and found the Temple desolate and desecrated. They tore down the pagan altar and built a new one, repaired the sanctuary and the interior of the Temple, and provided new sacred vessels and furnishings. When everything was ready, the altar was rededicated, and the people joyfully offered holocausts and sacrifices of deliverance and praise for eight days.

It was decreed that this purification of the Temple would be observed every year. Sometimes called the Feast of Lights, the celebration is known today as Hanukkah.

The Fighting Continues

When the Gentiles in the surrounding regions heard about the reconsecration of the Temple in Jerusalem, they were angry and vowed to persecute and massacre the Jews. Judas assembled his forces again and put the armies of the enemy to flight. When this news reached Antiochus in Persia, he became frightened and took to his bed. He recalled the abomination he had inflicted in Jerusalem and said, "I know that this is why these evils have overtaken me; and now I am dying, in bitter grief, in a foreign land" (6:13). He succumbed a short time later.

General Lysias immediately installed the nine-year-old son of Antiochus as king, gave him the title Eupator, and waged war in his name. However, both of them were dead within two years, and the next man sent to destroy the Jews was named Nicanor. He deceitfully sent a message of peace to the Maccabees, saying, "Let there be no fight between me and you. I will come with a few men to meet you peaceably" (7:28).

Judas met peacefully with Nicanor the first time, but suspecting deceit, decided not to meet with him again. Realizing that his plan had been discovered, Nicanor launched one unsuccessful battle against Judas and then went up to Mount Zion and threatened to destroy the Temple if Judas and his army were not delivered up to him. Judas again called on the Lord for help and, when the two armies met in battle, the superior forces of Nicanor were crushed and he was killed in the fighting.

The Death of Judas

The region of Judah was quiet for a time and Judas, aware of the rising power of the Romans, sent an envoy to Rome to establish an alliance with them. Both sides agreed that if either one should be attacked, the other would come to their assistance.

Meanwhile, an army led by Bacchides and Alcimus invaded Judah once again. Judas, though his forces were depleted, decided to fight the enemy anyway, saying, "If our time has come, let us die bravely for our kinsmen and not leave a stain upon our glory!" (9:10). After a desperate struggle, Judas fell in the battle and his men fled. The man who was called the "savior of Israel!" (9:21) was succeeded by his brother Jonathan, who defeated Bacchides in battle and brought another period of quiet to Judah.

During the next few years, Jonathan was involved in alternating alliances and battles with the kings of Egypt and Syria and with officials in Rome and Sparta until he was tricked by a man named Trypho into dismissing most of his troops. As soon as he entered the city of Ptolemais accompanied by a thousand men, Jonathan and all of his men were killed, and his brother Simon became leader of the Maccabees.

The cycle of battles and alliances continued under Simon until he instructed his oldest sons, John and Judas, to take his place and fight for their nation. But while John was pursuing an enemy force, Ptolemy, who had been appointed governor of Jericho, invited Simon, Mattathias, and Judas to a banquet in Jericho and, when they had had too much to drink, he had them killed in the banquet hall.

When John Hyrcanus heard what had happened to his father and brothers, and that Ptolemy had sent men to kill him, he had those men arrested and put to death. He was the ruler and high priest in Judah from 134 B.C. until his death in 104.

Second Maccabees

The Second Book of Maccabees is not a continuation of the first book, but rather a supplementary account of some of the events related earlier. It is notable for two things: the inspiring stories of martyrdom aimed at strengthening the resolve of the Jewish people, and evidence of the practice of offering prayers for the dead.

The martyrdom of Eleazar has already been mentioned in chapter 10, which lists him as one of the heroes of the Old Testament. His story is followed in 2nd Maccabees by the incredible account of a mother and her seven sons who suffered excruciating torture and death for refusing to eat pork and break the Jewish dietary laws.

One by one, the mother watched as her sons were burned and scalped, had their tongues cut out and their limbs amputated before they died. She encouraged them to remain faithful to God and promised them that their Creator "in his mercy, will give you back both breath and life, because you now disregard yourselves for the sake of his law" (2 Maccabees 7:23). After encouraging her last child not to be afraid of the executioner, but to look forward to meeting her and his brothers again in the next life, the mother suffered her own brutal death.

The Existence of Purgatory

After one of the battles fought by Judas, he and his men went to gather up the bodies of those who had been slain. They discovered that some of the dead were wearing pagan amulets, which was forbidden by Jewish law. Judas and his men prayed that the sinful deeds of their fallen comrades might be blotted out, and Judas took up a collection, amounting to 2,000 silver drachmas, which he sent to Jerusalem to provide for a sacrifice to atone for their sin.

"In doing this," said the author of 2nd Maccabees, "he acted in a very excellent and noble way, inasmuch as he had the resurrection of the dead in view; for if he were not expecting the fallen to rise again, it would have been useless and foolish to pray for them in death. But if he did this with a view to the splendid reward that awaits those who had gone to rest in godliness, it was a holy and pious thought. Thus he made atonement for the dead that they might be freed from this sin" (12:43-46).

The belief of Judas that expiation could be made for the sins of otherwise good men resembles Catholic belief in Purgatory, and the passage from 2nd Maccabees is often heard at funeral Masses. However, Protestants and Jews do not accept the Books of Maccabees as the inspired word of God and, consequently, do not agree with Catholic teaching on the existence of Purgatory, where those who have died with all mortal sins forgiven, but with some temporal punishment still attached to those sins, can undergo a process of purification before entering heaven.

But there are passages in the New Testament as well that support a belief in a cleansing fire for certain lesser faults. For example, there is Jesus' statement that "every sin and blasphemy will be forgiven people, but blasphemy against the Spirit will not be forgiven. And whoever speaks a word against the Son of Man will be forgiven; but whoever speaks against the holy Spirit will not be forgiven, either in this age or in the age to come" (Matthew 12:31-32).

There is also a passage from 1st Corinthians where St. Paul talked about fire purifying gold and silver (a reference to our good works) while it burns away wood, hay, and straw (our imperfect works). When our lives are examined on the day of judgment, said Paul, fire "will test the quality of each one's work. If the work stands that someone built upon the foundation [of Jesus Christ], that person will receive a wage. But if someone's work is burned up, that one will suffer loss; the person will be saved, but only as through fire" (3:13-15).

Thus, the purgatorial fire burns away all the imperfections acquired in this life and prepares us for entry into the new and heavenly Jerusalem, where nothing profane or unclean can enter (cf. Revelation 21:27 and *Catechism*, nn. 1030-1032).

The doctrine of Purgatory is also grounded upon the ancient practice of the Church and was formulated especially at the Councils of Florence and Trent. "From the beginning," the *Catechism* says (n. 1032), "the Church has honored the memory of the dead and offered prayers in suffrage for them, above all the Eucharistic sacrifice, so that, thus purified, they may attain the beatific vision of God" [cf. Council of Lyons II (1274): DS 856].

What greater service can we do for our deceased brothers and sisters than to undertake almsgiving, indulgences, and works of penance for those who have gone before us?

The Book of Daniel

Written during the terrible persecution of Antiochus IV Epiphanes, the Book of Daniel contains visions and exploits by the book's main character, as well as short stories that teach a moral lesson and a beautiful canticle of praise (Daniel 3:52-90). The best-known incident is probably Daniel's rescue from the lion's den after the king had reluctantly cast him into the pit for having been caught praying to God. Daniel thanked the Lord afterwards for having sent an angel to close the mouths of the hungry lions, and the king ordered that those who had accused Daniel be fed to the lions themselves (cf. 6:2:25).

There is also the account of Shadrach, Meshach, and Abednego, who were cast into a fiery furnace by King Nebuch-adnezzar for refusing to worship a golden statue. Even if God does not save us from the white-hot furnace, the trio told the king, "we will not serve your god or worship the golden statue which you set up" (3:18). The men were thrown into the furnace, but were helped by an angel to emerge from the flames unharmed, causing Nebuchadnezzar to proclaim that there was no God but the God of Shadrach, Meshach, and Abednego (cf. 3:96).

Vision of the Four Beasts

In a terrifying dream one night, Daniel had a vision of four immense beasts emerging from the sea, and these beasts have traditionally been interpreted to represent the kingdoms of the Babylonians, Medes, Persians, and Greeks — all of which would eventually be destroyed. He also saw a vision of the throne of God ("the Ancient One") in heaven, where "thousands upon thousands were ministering to him,/ and myriads upon myriads attended him" (7:9-10).

As his visions continued, said Daniel, he saw "one like a son of man coming,/ on the clouds of heaven;/ When he reached the Ancient One/ and was presented before him,/ He received dominion, glory, and kingship;/ nations and peoples of every language serve him./ His dominion is an/ everlasting dominion/ that shall not be taken away,/ his kingship shall not/ be destroyed" (7:13-14).

In his trial before the Sanhedrin in the early morning hours of Good Friday, Jesus was asked if he were the Messiah. He echoed Daniel when he replied: "I am;/ and 'you will see the Son of Man/ seated at the right hand of the Power/ and coming with the clouds of heaven'" (Mark 14:62). The high priest recognized what Jesus was claiming and accused him of blasphemy, and the Sanhedrin sentenced him to die for making this claim.

In other visions, Daniel used numbers of weeks and years to describe the period during which Israel would be persecuted. The numbers are not to be taken literally, but the message is that God will eventually triumph over all the forces of evil. "At that time," Daniel said, "there shall arise/ Michael, the great prince,/ guardian of your people;/ it shall be a time unsurpassed in distress/ since nations began until that time./ At that time your people shall escape,/ everyone who is found written in the book./ Many of those who sleep/ in the dust of the earth shall awake;/ some shall live forever,/ others shall be an everlasting horror and disgrace./ But the wise shall shine brightly/ like the splendor of the firmament,/ And those who lead the many to justice/ shall be like the stars forever" (12:1-3).

WORDS TO REMEMBER

* Hanukkah   * Purgatory   * Son of Man

Chapter 16

Villains in the Bible

Put the wicked to shame;
reduce them to silence in Sheol.
— Psalm 31:18

Just as there are many good people in the Bible, so too there are many wicked people. Some of the latter have already been mentioned, or will be mentioned, in connection with certain events in salvation history, but this chapter will provide more information about some of the most notorious villains in Scripture.

Satan

At the root of all the villainy in salvation history is that rebellious angel known as Satan or the devil, who brought sin into the world by tempting Adam and Eve to disobey God. He appealed to their pride by falsely telling them that eating the forbidden fruit would make them "like gods" (Genesis 3:5). Thus, Jesus would later describe Satan as "a liar and the father of lies" (John 8:44), and he would come to earth "to destroy the works of the devil" (1 John 3:8).

Satan entered human history as the tempter of our first parents, and he appeared again as a tempter at the beginning of Jesus' public life, trying unsuccessfully to divert Christ from his mission of salvation. Jesus had been praying and fasting for 40 days in the desert when the devil approached him. Apparently, Satan was not sure who Jesus was, since he prefaced each of the three temptations with the words, "If you are the Son of God...."

In reading about these temptations in chapter 4 of Matthew and chapter 4 of Luke, notice that Jesus' quotations are all from the Book of Deuteronomy (8:3, 6:16, 6:13), and that the devil himself can quote Scripture, which may account for Paul's warning to beware of false apostles since "even Satan masquerades as an angel of light" (2 Corinthians 11:14).

As the Author of Scripture, Jesus can also quote Bible passages. So when the devil commanded the Lord to turn the stones into bread to assuage his hunger, Christ replied that " 'one does not live by bread alone,/ but by every word that comes forth/ from the mouth of God' " (Matthew 4:4).

The devil then took Jesus to the top of the Temple and told him to jump off, "for it is written:/ 'He will command his angels concerning you'/ and 'with their hands they will support you,/ lest you dash your foot against a stone' " (Matthew 4:6). Christ answered the temptation by saying, "Again it is written, 'You shall not put the Lord, your God, to the test' " (4:7).

Finally, Satan appealed to the temptation for power, showing Jesus all the kingdoms of the world in all their magnificence and promising to give him all of these "if you will prostrate yourself and worship me." But Christ replied: "Get away, Satan! It is written:/ 'The Lord, your God, shall you worship/ and him alone shall you serve' " (Matthew 4:9-10).

Matthew said that the devil then left Jesus, and angels came and ministered to him, but Luke added that, "when the devil had finished every temptation, he departed from him for a time" (Luke 4:13). Although Satan is not specifically mentioned during Christ's Agony in the Garden of Gethsemane, it seems likely that the tempter was there, trying once again to divert Jesus from his mission.

The temptations of Jesus in the desert remind us of the temptations of the Israelites in the desert, but unlike Israel, which gave in to temptations to abandon the one, true God, Jesus rebuffed Satan's attempts to turn him away from God and to focus attention on himself by displays of miraculous power. Jesus will later use miracles to establish his credentials as the God-man, but he will exercise his divine power at the proper time and for good reasons, not merely to show off at the instigation of his ancient enemy.

The Role of Satan Today

It is fashionable today to deny the existence of Satan, to see him as only the creation of producers of scary movies in Hollywood (cf. all the films about diabolical possession and exorcism). But we know from the New Testament about the power of Satan to influence persons and events. Thus, the devil entered into the heart of Judas and persuaded him to betray Jesus (Luke 22:3 and John 13:2), which is why the Lord warned the disciples that "Satan has demanded to sift all of you like wheat" (Luke 22:31).

Satan is the one who sows the weeds of wickedness in the field of the world (cf. Matthew 13:39), he is the one who takes away the word of God from some persons so that they may not believe and be saved (cf. Luke 8:12), he is the one who tempts us against truth, righteousness, peace, and faith (cf. Ephesians 6:11-17), and he is the one who prowls around the world "like a roaring lion looking for [someone] to devour" (1 Peter 5:8).

And yet the Evil One is subject to the power of God, his time on earth is short (Revelation 12:12), and he will eventually be subdued and cast "into the eternal fire prepared for the devil and his angels" (Matthew 25:41). If we draw near to God and resist the devil, said James, "he will flee from you" (4:7), and if we are "wise as to what is good, and simple as to what is evil," said Paul, "then the God of peace will quickly crush Satan under your feet" (Romans 16:19-20).

At a general audience on November 15, 1972, Pope Paul VI described the devil as "a living, spiritual being, perverted and perverting. A terrible reality. Mysterious and frightening .... He is the enemy number one, a tempter par excellence. So we know that this dark and disturbing spirit really exists, and that he still acts with treacherous cunning; he is the secret enemy that sows errors and misfortunes in human history."

Paul VI was echoed on August 13, 1986 by Pope John Paul II, who said that "the action of Satan consists primarily in tempting men to evil, by influencing their imaginations and highest faculties, to turn them away from the law of God."

But while Satan is powerful, he is still only a creature and is subject to the greater power of the Creator. He can influence our decisions, but he cannot force us to do anything against our will. We can resist him by fervently saying the Lord's Prayer and asking the Father to "deliver us from evil," which really means from "the Evil One, the angel who opposes God. The devil (*dia-bo-los*) is the one who 'throws himself across' God's plan and his work of salvation accomplished in Christ" (*Catechism*, n. 2851).

Jesus won victory over Satan on Good Friday, and he will cast him into hell forever at the Second Coming. Until then, we pray with the priest at every Mass these words:

> Deliver us, Lord, from every evil,
> and grant us peace in our day.

In your mercy keep us free from sin
and protect us from all anxiety
as we await in joyful hope
for the coming of our Savior, Jesus Christ.

Jezebel

Sometimes referred to as the wickedest woman in the Bible, Jezebel was the wife of King Ahab (874-853), whom she persuaded to worship Baal and erect an altar to the pagan god at the temple that Ahab had built in Samaria. The malign influence of Jezebel undoubtedly was a major reason why the author of 1st Kings could say that Ahab "did more to anger the LORD, the God of Israel, than any of the kings of Israel before him" (16:33).

As mentioned earlier in chapter 13, Elijah outperformed the prophets of Baal on Mount Carmel and had them all executed after the Lord had sent down fire to consume the holocaust Elijah had prepared. When Jezebel learned of this, she put out a death warrant against Elijah, who then fled for his life to the mountain of Horeb, where the Lord instructed him to anoint Jehu king of Israel and Elisha as a prophet to succeed him.

Meanwhile, King Ahab wanted to acquire a vineyard next to his palace and he offered money to the owner, a man named Naboth. However, Naboth refused the king's offer and said that he would not part with his "ancestral heritage" (1 Kings 21:4).

When Ahab told Jezebel what had happened, she scolded him for his timidity and promised to get the vineyard for him. The queen wrote letters in Ahab's name to the elders who lived in the same city as Naboth and told them to get "two scoundrels" to accuse Naboth of having cursed God and the king. The elders did as they were instructed and then led Naboth outside the city and stoned him to death.

When Naboth's fate had been reported to Jezebel, she told Ahab to go and take possession of the vineyard. But God instructed Elijah to express his displeasure to Ahab over what had happened to Naboth, and to tell the king that "in the place where the dogs licked up the blood of Naboth, the dogs shall lick up your blood, too" (21:19). This threat caused Ahab to repent, and God told Elijah to tell the king that the Lord would not bring evil on his house at this time.

However, God also predicted that dogs would devour the body of Jezebel in the streets of Jezreel. Some time later, as King Jehu rode into Jezreel, he saw Jezebel looking down from her window, and he ordered some men to throw her onto the street. Jehu rode over her dead body and later ordered the burial of that "accursed woman." But when his men went to bury Jezebel, they found that dogs had eaten away all her flesh (cf. 2 Kings 9:35-36), just as the Lord had predicted.

Nebuchadnezzar

A former Babylonian general who succeeded his father as king, Nebuchadnezzar reigned for 43 years (605-562) and is noted for his administrative skills and prowess as a builder. He repaired the walls of Babylon, constructed the Ishtar Gate, rebuilt the temple of Marduk, and erected the "hanging gardens of Babylon," one of the seven wonders of the ancient world. At the time of his death, Babylon had reached the zenith of world power.

It is Nebuchadnezzar's role in the history of Israel, however, that brings him to our attention. For in both 597 and 587, he had the people of Jerusalem bound in ropes and chains and forced-marched some 600 miles to Babylon (modern-day Iraq), where they were put to work on the construction projects of Nebuchadnezzar and on the plantations of wealthy landowners. While their treatment may not have been as harsh as that of their ancestors in Egypt, the Israelites were certainly treated as slaves.

After King Jehoiachin surrendered in 597, says the Second Book of Kings (cf. 24:8-16)), Nebuchadnezzar's forces carried off all the treasures of the Temple, deported some 10,000 officers and men of the army, and also deported Jeohiachin, along with his mother, his wives, and his functionaries. Zedekiah was appointed to take Jehoiachin's place, but when he rebelled against the occupying forces ten years later, he was made to watch as his two sons were executed, and then he was blinded and taken captive to Babylon, where presumably he died.

Once Zedekiah had been deposed as the last king of Judah, Nebuchadnezzar's army burned down the Temple, the king's palace, and every building in Jerusalem. Then they tore down the walls of the city and sent the remaining citizens into exile.

Herod the Great

An astute and very ambitious politician who attached himself to whichever clique was in power in Rome, Herod got himself appointed King of Judea (37-4 B.C.). He was called king of the Jews, although he was only partly Jewish and not a faithful observer of Jewish religious practices. He was also a master-builder, rebuilding cities destroyed by an earthquake in 31 B.C., constructing magnificent palaces in various parts of the land, and rebuilding the Temple in Jerusalem.

On the negative side, Herod was a power-mad tyrant who committed unspeakable cruelties during his brutal reign. He is certain to have put to death hundreds of persons. He murdered many members of his own dysfunctional household, including uncles and brothers-in-law, his first wife Mariamne, her mother, and two of their sons.

As the end of his life neared, Herod wanted to make sure that his passing was accompanied with tears instead of rejoicing. So he summoned many prominent Jews to Jericho and gave orders to have all of them slaughtered after his death. Thus, there were tears at his funeral, although they were from families of the victims of the slaughter.

Shortly before he died, Herod showed another example of why he is known as one of the bloodiest men in history when he ordered the murder of all boys under the age of two in the region of Bethlehem. The Magi and his own chief priests had informed him that the Messiah, the "newborn king of the Jews," was to be born in Bethlehem, and Herod wanted to eliminate any threat to his throne (cf. Matthew 2:1-18).

Herodias

Married to Herod Antipas (4 B.C.-40 A.D.), son and successor of Herod the Great as tetrarch but not as king, Herodias had been married to Philip, the half-brother of Antipas, when Antipas came to Rome for a visit. She soon took up with him, although he was already married, and, with a young daughter named Salome, moved from Rome to the palatial fortress at Machaerus on the eastern shore of the Dead Sea.

It wasn't long before her adulterous union was known to the Jews of Galilee, and before it was publicly denounced by John the Baptist. Nor was it long afterwards that Herod had John arrested and imprisoned at Machaerus because he had been publicly telling the tetrarch that "it is not lawful for you to have your brother's wife" (Mark 6:18).

It is interesting to note that, while Herod "feared John, knowing him to be a righteous and holy man," he also liked to listen to him speak (cf. Mark 6:20). Apparently, the truth in John's words was able to reach the heart of even someone as sinful as Herod. In fact, the king was so impressed with John that, when the fame of Jesus became widespread, Herod thought that the Baptist had come back from the dead (cf. Mark 6:16).

John had been imprisoned at Machaerus for about ten months when Herodias threw a birthday party for the king and had her daughter Salome perform a dance for him. The dance so delighted Herod that he told the girl to ask anything of him, even half of his kingdom, and he would grant it. She went to her mother for advice, and Herodias told her to say, "Give me here on a platter the head of John the Baptist" (Matthew 14:8).

Antipas was very distressed at this request, but his pride would not let him break the promise made in front of all the guests at the dinner. So he dispatched an executioner to John's prison cell and had the Baptist's head cut off. The bloody head was delivered on a platter first to Salome and then to her mother, who had long borne a grudge against John and at last achieved her goal of having him killed.

According to historians, the ambition of Herodias backfired a few years later when she persuaded Antipas to go to Rome and ask for the same royal honors that had been accorded to her brother Agrippa. Agrippa brought charges of disloyalty against Antipas, which he could not refute, and he and Herodias were exiled to Gaul (modern-day France).

Caiaphas

The high priest in Jerusalem from A.D. 18-36, Caiaphas was the son-in-law of Annas, who was the chief plotter in the campaign to kill Jesus. The religious leaders in Jerusalem were jealous of the popularity of Jesus, angry at his charges of hypocrisy against them, and fearful that his followers could cause trouble that might bring down upon them all the might of Rome, whose soldiers already occupied the country.

Following the raising of Lazarus from the dead, the Pharisees saw a pressing need to get rid of Jesus immediately, and they convened the Sanhedrin, the 71-member national-religious court of Israel. "What are we going to do?" one member asked. "This man is performing many signs. If we leave him alone, all will believe in him, and the Romans will come and take away both our land and our nation" (John 11:47-48). Caiaphas proposed the solution to the problem of Jesus, saying that it would be better for Jesus to die than for the whole nation to perish.

John the Evangelist saw the words of Caiaphas as prophetic in that he did not say them "on his own, but since he was high priest for that year, he prophesied that Jesus was going to die for the nation, and not only for the nation, but also to gather into one the dispersed children of God. So from that day on they planned to kill him" (John 11:51-54).

Some time later, after his arrest in the Garden of Geth-se-mane, Jesus was brought to the house of Annas and Caiaphas, where he underwent two interrogation sessions in the early morning hours in an effort to find a charge to use against him. The Lord had been arrested late at night so that his followers would not know of his incarceration and start a riot.

But the two sessions were not productive and, when Jesus was put on trial before the Sanhedrin at dawn on Good Friday, strong testimony against him was still lacking. So almost in desperation, Caiaphas confronted Jesus directly and, in a completely illegal maneuver under the Sanhedrin's own rules, demanded that Jesus testify against himself.

"I order you," said Caiaphas, "to tell us under oath before the living God whether you are the Messiah, the Son of God" (Matthew 26:63). Jesus answered, "I am;/ and 'you will see the Son of Man/ seated at the right hand of the Power/ and coming with the clouds of heaven'" (Mark 14:62). At that, the high priest tore his garments and asked what further proof was needed. He said that Jesus had committed the crime of blasphemy by claiming to be God, and the Sanhedrin sentenced him to death.

The last time we hear of Caiaphas in Scripture is when Peter and John are brought before the Sanhedrin (Acts 4:5-22), questioned about what power or name had enabled them to cure a crippled beggar, and then ordered not to speak or teach again in the name of Jesus. To which the Apostles replied: "It is impossible for us not to speak about what we have seen and heard" (Acts 4:20).

Pontius Pilate

The Roman procurator or governor of Judea from A.D. 27-35, Pontius Pilate was the military commander of the region, the man who levied taxes on the people, and the dispenser of

Roman justice in his own court, where he had the authority to pass a death sentence. He was, according to Jewish historian Flavius Josephus and Jewish philosopher Philo of Alexandria, an insolent, cruel, vindictive, violent, and stubborn tyrant. Pilate's task was to keep peace in Judea, but he had already antagonized the Jews by displaying Roman standards with the emperor's image in the holy city, thus violating Jewish laws against idolatry, and by using sacred money from the Temple treasury to build an aqueduct that would bring water into the city. In both instances, Pilate had Jewish protesters beaten and even killed.

Then on that Good Friday morning long ago, the procurator was thrust into a serious conflict over religious matters between Jesus and the Sanhedrin. The Sanhedrists had sentenced Jesus to die for blasphemy, but they lacked the power to put him to death; that power belonged only to the Roman governor. So they marched Jesus to the fortress Antonia, where Pilate was staying, and asked him to judge the case.

Because the Sanhedrists knew that Pilate would not be interested in religious crimes, they falsely accused Jesus of political crimes, such as subverting the nation, failing to pay taxes, and claiming to be a king. It is doubtful whether the procurator had ever heard of Jesus, and he was probably suspicious of the charges, but the possibility of him being a kingly rival to the emperor in Rome got Pilate's attention.

After he had taken Jesus away from his accusers, the governor wanted to know only one thing: Was Jesus a king? The Lord's reply to the question was the statement that "my kingdom does not belong to this world" (John 18:36). In other words, Jesus' kingdom was a spiritual one, not a political or worldly one.

Pilate found Jesus' statement convincing, took him back before his accusers, and said, "I find this man not guilty" (Luke 23:4)), which should have ended the matter right there. But the enemies of Christ were adamant and accused him of stirring up trouble ever since he had come there from Galilee. The procurator saw a way out of the dilemma by sending Jesus to Herod Antipas, the tetrarch in charge of Galilee, who was in Jerusalem at the time.

That did not work out the way that Pilate intended since Herod's mockery of Christ and his demand for miracles, which Jesus refused to perform, led him to return Christ to Pilate.

The governor, knowing that Jesus was innocent of the charges, tried two things to appease the crowd. First, he gave them a choice between releasing Jesus or a dangerous murderer named Barabbas, and he was surprised to hear the mob shout for Barabbas to go free. When he asked them what he should do with Jesus, and what evil he had committed, they only shouted, "Let him be crucified!" (Matthew 27:23).

Pilate was still reluctant to have Jesus executed, so he decided to have him scourged instead, then perhaps the crowd's blood-lust would be satisfied. But not even the brutal whipping of the Lord, so vividly portrayed in the Mel Gibson movie *The Passion of the Christ*, could placate the crowd, for when Pilate brought the horribly wounded Christ out before them and said, "Behold, your king!" (John 19:14), there was no cry for mercy for the accused.

The people shouted instead that "if you release him, you are not a Friend of Caesar. Everyone who makes himself a king opposes Caesar" (John 19:12). Imagine, people who hated the current Caesarean emperor because he was oppressing their country were now taking his side over that of Jesus! So Pilate caved in and ordered the crucifixion of Christ after publicly washing his hands in a basin of water and saying, "I am innocent of this man's blood" (Matthew 27:24).

Pontius Pilate is a villain because he had the power to prevent the execution of a man he believed to be innocent, but was afraid of the crowd. There is a little of Pontius Pilate in all of us when we are afraid to do the right thing because of what others might say or do. He would make a perfect role model for those politicians who say that they are "personally opposed" to the killing of unborn babies by abortion, but who either take no steps to stop the killing or who vote for laws that continue the carnage.

Judas

One of the 12 Apostles chosen by Jesus, Judas is infamous because he betrayed the Lord for 30 pieces of silver (as predicted in Zechariah 11:12), but there were other signs of Judas' estrangement from Christ before the events of Holy Week. For instance, after Jesus had given his "Bread of Life" discourse a year or so earlier, and some followers of his walked away from him because they could not accept his teaching that his body was real food and his blood real drink, the Lord asked the Twelve if they wanted to leave him, too.

No, Simon Peter answered and then asked, "Master, to whom shall we go? You have the words of eternal life. We have come to believe and are convinced that you are the Holy One of God" (John 6:68-69). To which Christ responded, "Did I not choose you twelve? Yet is not one of you a devil?" (John 6:70). The evangelist explained that Jesus was "referring to Judas, son of Simon the Iscariot; it was he who would betray him, one of the Twelve" (John 6:71).

Then there was the anointing of Jesus in Bethany a few days before his death. Mary, the sister of Lazarus and Martha, took some costly perfumed oil, spread it on the feet of the Lord, and then dried his feet with her hair. One of the Apostles, only John identifies him as Judas, complained about this waste of oil and said that it could have been sold and the money given to the poor. "He said this," John told us, "not because he cared about the poor but because he was a thief and held the money bag and used to steal the contributions" (John 12:6).

Another sign that Judas had moved away from the Lord came at the Last Supper when Jesus startled the Twelve by saying, "Amen, I say to you, one of you will betray me." Each of the Apostles said, "Surely, it is not I, Lord?" But Judas said, "Surely, it is not I, Rabbi?" (Matthew 26:21-22, 25). He no longer recognized Jesus as Lord, but merely as a teacher.

Christ then told Judas to go quickly and complete the conspiratorial plan into which he had entered and, when he had left the Last Supper, said John, "it was night" (John 13:30). It is always night when we turn our backs on the Lord.

Judas then met with Caiaphas and the other conspirators, told them that Jesus would be in the Garden of Gethsemane shortly, and arranged a signal by which the soldiers and guards would be able to recognize Christ. When the soldiers arrived in the garden in the early morning hours of Good Friday, Judas went up to Jesus and gave the promised sign by kissing him on the cheek.

Jesus, still trying to reach out to Judas, called him "Friend" (Matthew 26:50) and asked him, "Judas, are you betraying the Son of Man with a kiss?" (Luke 22:48). The question went unanswered and the soldiers arrested Jesus and took him back to the city for the interrogations and trials that would lead to his death on the cross.

The motive for the actions of Judas is usually thought to be greed, a love of money that exceeded his love for the Son of God, and there certainly is something to that. But how can we explain the subsequent effort by Judas to give the money back? When the betrayer saw that Jesus had been condemned, said Matthew, Judas "deeply regretted" his actions, returned the 30 pieces of silver to the chief priests and elders, and said, "I have sinned in betraying innocent blood" (Matthew 27:3-4). His plea fell on deaf ears, so Judas threw the money on the floor and went out and hanged himself.

His greatest sin was not the betrayal of Christ, or even taking his own life, but rather the despair that so engulfed him that he would not seek forgiveness from the One whom he had seen extend forgiveness to so many persons. So is Judas in hell? Only God knows the answer to that. Yes, Jesus had said that it would have been better for him "if he had never been born" (Matthew 26:24), but we don't know if that meant eternal damnation.

Perhaps Judas, who had spent so much time in the company of the Lord, had the presence of mind to beg for forgiveness just before he died. But we won't know until the next life the fate of the man whose name is synonymous with treachery.

<u>WORDS TO REMEMBER</u>

* Sanhedrin   * blasphemy

Sermon on the Mount.

Chapter 17

The Coming
of the Messiah

The stone the builders rejected
has become the cornerstone.
By the LORD has this been done;
it is wonderful in our eyes.
— Psalm 118:22-23

There was a wealthy man who loved to collect rare works of art and, over the years, he had accumulated the works of many famous artists. He and his only son spent hours together discussing and admiring their treasures.

When war broke out in the Persian Gulf in 1991, the son joined the military and went off to fight in the war. He was very courageous and died in battle while rescuing another soldier. The father was notified of his son's death and grieved deeply.

Some months later, a young fellow came to the man's door carrying a large package. "You don't know me, sir," the fellow said, "but I am the soldier for whom your son gave his life. He was carrying me to safety when a bullet struck him in the heart."

The soldier went on to say that he and the man's son often spoke about the father's love for art. "I know this isn't much," he said, holding the package out to the father, "and I'm not a good artist, but I think your son would have wanted you to have this."

The father opened the package and was stunned to see a portrait of his son that the young man had painted. He stared in awe at the way the personality of his son had been captured, thanked the soldier profusely, and offered to pay him for the painting. "Oh, no, sir," the soldier said. "I could never repay what your son did for me. This is a gift."

The father hung the portrait over his mantel and, every time visitors came to his home, he took them to see the painting of his son before showing them any of the great works of art he had collected over the years.

When the father died not long after that, there was an auction of his paintings. Many rich people gathered for the auction, excited over the opportunity to purchase some of the masterpieces on display. On the platform sat the soldier's portrait of the man's son and, when the auctioneer pounded his gavel, he said, "We will start the bidding with this picture of the son."

There was silence at first, but then someone said, "We want to see the famous paintings. Skip this one." But the auctioneer persisted, "What will you bid for this painting? Do I hear $100? $200?" Another person yelled, "We didn't come here to see that painting. Get on with the real auction."

But the auctioneer continued, "The son, the son, who will take the son?" Finally, from the back of the room, someone said, "I'll give $10 for that painting." It was the man's longtime gardener. He had very little money, but he knew how much the father loved his son and the painting of him.

"We have $10," the auctioneer said. "Who will bid $20?" Someone shouted, "Give it to him for $10, and let's get to the masterpieces." The auctioneer replied, "$10 is the bid. Won't someone bid $20?" The crowd was becoming angry since they didn't want the painting of the son. So the auctioneer pounded his gavel again and said, "Going once. Going twice. SOLD for $10."

A man sitting in the second row said, "Good, now let's get on with the real auction." But the auctioneer laid down his gavel and said, "I'm sorry, the auction is over. When I was called to conduct this auction, I was told of a secret stipulation in the owner's will that I could not reveal until now."

He said the owner had stipulated that only the painting of his son would be auctioned and that whoever bought that painting would inherit all the other paintings and the entire estate. It was the owner's wish, the auctioneer said, that "the man who took the son would get everything."

The moral of the story is that God so loved the world that he gave his only Son, so that everyone who believes in him might not perish, but might have eternal life. And it has been true for 2,000 years, that whoever takes the Son gets everything!

Jesus' Opinion Poll

While walking with the Apostles one day near the region of Caesarea Philippi, Jesus asked them who people thought he was. The disciples replied that some thought he was John the Baptist, and others Elijah, Jeremiah, or one of the prophets. "But who do you say that I am?" Jesus asked, and Simon Peter answered, "You are the Messiah, the Son of the living God" (Matthew 16:15-16). That question about the identity of Jesus has been asked countless times ever since. Was Jesus just *a* prophet, or was he *the* Prophet? Was he just another religious leader, like Buddha, Confucius, or Mohammed, or was he the long-awaited Messiah? The answer to these questions is important. For if Jesus was just an ordinary man, there isn't much reason to pay attention to what he said. But if Jesus is God, as he said he was, then we had better listen to him if we want to get to heaven.

The *Catechism* (n. 460) teaches that " 'the only-begotten Son of God, wanting to make us sharers in his divinity, assumed our nature, so that he, made man, might make men gods' " [St. Thomas Aquinas, *Opusc.* 57:1-4].

Human Testimony About Jesus

We have just seen that Simon Peter believed that Jesus was the Messiah, the Son of the living God. But was this view shared by other contemporaries of the Lord? The answer is yes. For example, John the Baptist was the first to call Jesus "the Lamb of God, who takes away the sin of the world" (John 1:29). John told his followers that Jesus was "the one of whom I said, 'A man is coming after me who ranks ahead of me because he existed before me' " (John 1:30).

Andrew was a disciple of the Baptist, but when he heard John identify Jesus as the "Son of God" (John 1:34), he spent a day with Christ and then went and told his brother, Simon Peter, "We have found the Messiah" (John 1:41). He later introduced Peter to Jesus.

The following day, Jesus met Philip and told him to "follow me" (John 1:43). Philip in turn recruited Nathanael, telling him, "We have found the one about whom Moses wrote in the law, and also the prophets, Jesus son of Joseph, from Nazareth" (John 1:45). When Jesus later saw Nathanael coming toward him, he said, "Here is a true Israelite. There is no duplicity in him" (John 1:47).

When Nathanael asked the Lord how he knew him, Christ replied: "Before Philip called you, I saw you under the fig tree." To which Nathanael responded: "Rabbi, you are the Son of God; you are the King of Israel." Jesus promised Nathanael that he would see even greater things than this, such as the sky opening "and the angels of God ascending and descending on the Son of Man" (John 1:48-51).

The Samaritan Woman

Not long after that, Jesus was traveling from Galilee to Judea and, while passing through Samaria, he stopped at Jacob's well about noon and sent the Apostles into town to buy food. When a Samaritan woman came to draw water from the well, Jesus asked her for a drink. She was startled by the request, first because Jews and Samaritans were enemies and second because it was unseemly for a man to talk with a woman in public.

During their conversation, Jesus moved the topic from the water in the well to the "living water" that he would provide. He said that "everyone who drinks this water will be thirsty again; but whoever drinks the water I shall give will never thirst; the water I shall give will become in him a spring of water welling up to eternal life" (John 4:13-14).

Christ then told the woman to go call her husband and bring him back. When the woman said that she did not have a husband, Jesus told her that she had had five husbands, and that the man she was then living with was not her husband.

"Sir, I can see that you are a prophet" (John 4:19), the woman replied, but then changed the subject to whether it was better to worship God in Jerusalem or on Mt. Gerizim in Samaria, where a temple had been built in the fourth century B.C. to rival the one on Mt. Zion in Jerusalem.

When Jesus said that the hour was already here "when true worshipers will worship the Father in Spirit and truth," the woman said, "I know that the Messiah is coming, the one called the Anointed; when he comes, he will tell us everything." Jesus answered her: "I am he, the one who is speaking with you" (John 4:23-26).

The woman ran off to the town to tell the people about the possibility that Jesus was the Messiah. Her testimony led many of her neighbors to believe in Jesus, and they invited him to remain with them. He stayed there for two days, and many more came to believe in him. They told the woman, "We no longer believe because of your word; for we have heard for ourselves, and we know that this is truly the savior of the world" (John 4:42).

Good Man or God?

Hardly anyone will give you an argument if you say that Jesus was a good man. But if you say that he was *just a good man*, and nothing more than that, you will not find support for that theory in the four Gospels. For the Gospels make very clear that Jesus claimed to be God. Think, for example, of his comments to the Samaritan woman. Or his statement at the synagogue in Nazareth, when he read passages from Isaiah 61:1-2 about one who had been anointed by "the Spirit of the Lord," and told his listeners that he was the anointed one referred to by Isaiah (cf. Luke 4:21).

Or perhaps most convincingly when he was on trial for his life and he knew that proclaiming his divinity would mean his death. The high priest Caiaphas had brought in witnesses to testify against Jesus, but their testimony did not agree. So in desperation Caiaphas demanded that Christ testify against himself, something that was forbidden by the Sanhedrin's own rules.

"Are you the Messiah, the son of the Blessed One?" asked Caiaphas. To which Jesus replied: "I am;

and 'you will see the Son of Man
seated at the right hand of
the Power
and coming with the clouds
of heaven'" (Mark 14:61-62).

Such a claim to be God was "blasphemy," said Caiphas, who then asked the Sanhedrin for its verdict. The members responded by condemning Jesus to death.

Caiaphas and his colleagues recognized that Jesus was alluding to Daniel 7:13, which talked about "One like a son of man coming,/ on the clouds of heaven." They also knew that the Lord's use of the words "I am" was another indication of his identification with the Father, who had told Moses centuries earlier that his name was "I AM" (Exodus 3:14).

If Jesus said he was God, and he was not, then he could not be a good man, for good men don't tell lies. Furthermore, if Jesus was not God, and lied about it, knowing that such a lie would result in his execution, then he must have been crazy, and a crazy person cannot be a good man. We are faced then, as the late English apologist C.S. Lewis once wrote, with only three plausibilities about the identity of Jesus: He was either a liar (or worse), a lunatic, or the Lord.

Those who study the Gospels, "which occupy a central place because Christ Jesus is their center" (*Catechism*, n. 139), will not find any evidence that Jesus was either a liar or a lunatic. What they will find is that he was a person of outstanding character and exemplary virtue, a wise and compassionate spiritual leader. He was, in fact, the perfect man.

Divine Testimony About Jesus

But Christ was more than true man; he was also true God, the "chosen Son" (Luke 9:35) of the Father. His divinity can be demonstrated by the Old Testament prophecies he fulfilled, the prophecies of the future that he himself made, and the spectacular miracles that he performed.

Of all the persons who ever lived, Jesus of Nazareth is the only one whose biography was written hundreds of years before he was born. He and only he fulfilled perfectly scores of Old Testament prophecies about the Messiah who was to come. For example, he was descended from the house of David (Isaiah 11:1), born in Bethlehem (Micah 5:1) of a virgin mother (Isaiah 7:14), worshiped by kings bearing gifts (Psalm 72:10), betrayed (Psalm 41:10) for thirty pieces of silver (Zechariah 11:12-13), and "pierced for our offenses,/ crushed for our sins" (Isaiah 53:5).

Secondly, Jesus was able to predict future events accurately, such as his Scourging and Crucifixion (Matthew 20:19), the betrayal by Judas (John 13:21-27), the triple denial by Peter (Matthew 26:34), his Resurrection from the dead (Luke 9:22), and the destruction of Jerusalem (Luke 21:24), which occurred in A.D. 70. He had said that such predictions would be clear evidence that he was a divine messenger from God: "From now on I am telling you before it happens, so that when it happens you may believe that I AM" (John 13:19).

Since miracles are by definition beyond the power of science and nature, and can only be explained by the power of God, the fact that Jesus performed dozens of them during his brief public life demonstrates that he is God. He called these miracles his divine credentials, saying that "these works that I perform testify on my behalf that the Father has sent me" (John 5:36).

These spectacular works included changing water into wine, curing the blind and the lame, walking on water and calming the sea, feeding thousands with a few loaves of bread and some fish, exorcising demons, and bringing the dead back to life, including Jesus' friend Lazarus. The enemies of the Lord, a title that indicates divine sovereignty (cf. *Catechism*, n. 455), could not deny the miraculous nature of his actions because many of the miracles were witnessed by crowds of people. What these foes did instead was either to attribute the miracles to the devil or to denounce Jesus for performing them on the Sabbath. For example, the raising of Lazarus, which should have persuaded eyewitnesses to believe in Christ, prompted some of them instead to initiate a plot to kill him (John 11:53)! "If we leave him alone," said the chief priests, "all will believe in him, and the Romans will come and take away both our land and our nation" (John 11:48).

So the Gospels offer us much convincing evidence to back up Jesus' claim to be God, which of course is why they were written. As the Apostle explained: "Now Jesus did many other signs in the presence of [his] disciples that are not written in this book. But these are written that you may [come to] believe that Jesus is the Messiah, the Son of God, and that through this belief you may have life in his name" (John 20:30-31).

That same Apostle had earlier recorded a question asked by his colleague, Thomas, as to how the followers of Christ could know the way to heaven. Jesus replied: "I am the way and the truth and the life. No one comes to the Father except through me" (John 14:6). Let us consider how Jesus is the way and the truth and the life.

Jesus the Way

There are some people today who are fond of portraying Jesus as just a nice man who went around telling people to be good to each other, but who never made any difficult demands of anyone. This false portrait of Jesus usually makes an appearance when the Catholic Church reaffirms a moral teaching about such evils as abortion, fornication, adultery, homosexual behavior, or invalid marriages. "Jesus would never be judgmental about such things," we are told. "He wants us to be happy."

The answer to this wishful thinking, of course, is that Jesus first and foremost wants us to be good, and that means to live up to the moral code that he proclaimed while on earth. When a rich young man asked Christ what had to be done to get to heaven,

Jesus replied: "Keep the commandments." When the young man asked which ones, the Lord said:

> " 'You shall not kill; you shall not commit adultery; you shall not steal; you shall not bear false witness; honor your father and your mother'; and 'you shall love your neighbor as yourself' " (Matthew 19:16, 18-19).

Following Jesus is not easy, but it can be done if we follow a Person, not a set of rules. So when faced with keeping the Commandments, we can take heart in these gentle words of the Lord:

> Come to me, all of you who labor and are burdened, and I will give you rest. Take my yoke upon you and learn from me, for I am meek and humble of heart; and you will find rest for yourselves. For my yoke is easy, and my burden light" (Matthew 11:28-30).

Jesus said that he had come to earth not to abolish "the law or the prophets," but to fulfill them. He said that "until heaven and earth pass away, not the smallest letter or the smallest part of a letter will pass from the law, until all things have taken place. Therefore, whoever breaks one of the least of these commandments and teaches others to do so will be called least in the kingdom of heaven. But whoever obeys and teaches these commandments will be called greatest in the kingdom of heaven" (Matthew 5:17-19).

Christ knew that his teachings would pose great difficulty for many people, but he didn't soften them. He condemned "evil thoughts, unchastity, theft, murder, adultery, greed, malice, deceit, licentiousness, envy, blasphemy, arrogance, folly" as sins that come from within and defile a person (Mark 7:21-23).

He said that "whoever does not take up his cross and follow after me is not worthy of me," and that he had not come to earth to bring peace, "but the sword. For I have come to set

> a man 'against his father,
> a daughter against her mother,
> and a daughter-in-law against
> her mother-in-law;
> and one's enemies will be those
> of his household' (Matthew 10:34-38).

Jesus said that "everyone who acknowledges me before others I will acknowledge before my heavenly Father. But whoever denies me before others, I will deny before my heavenly Father" (Matthew 10:32-33). These hard sayings of the Lord are either largely unknown or ignored today, so it is important to proclaim and live them in order to experience true and lasting happiness.

The Beatitudes

At the beginning of the Sermon on the Mount, Jesus spelled out his definition of happiness in the eight Beatitudes (cf. Matthew 5:3-10). His definition, however, contradicted the attitudes of his own time, and it goes against the grain of the modern world as well. Imagine praising those who are poor in spirit, mournful, meek, hungry for righteousness, merciful, clean of heart, makers of peace, and objects of persecution!

The world of today, which puts such stock in money, ambition, prestige, sensual pleasure, aggressive behavior, and ridicule of others' beliefs, holds in contempt those who would live the Beatitudes. Modern critics, like those at the time of Christ, fail to recognize the revolutionary nature of this blueprint for the ethical reform of society. They say that such a lifestyle demands too much and offers too little reward here and now.

But the Lord knew better when he proposed this way of living. "God knows your hearts," Jesus told the Pharisees, "for what is of human esteem is an abomination in the sight of God" (Luke 16:15). Or as another translation of this verse puts it: "What man thinks important, God holds in contempt."

True happiness involves sacrifice and suffering. It does not take the easy road of instant gratification, but rather the hard road of toil and tribulation. It means abandoning the values of the world and following those of Christ. St. Augustine struggled to find happiness in material and sensual pleasures before he finally reached this conclusion about God: "You have made us for yourself, and our heart is restless until it rests in you."

The *Catechism* also reminds us that "man is made to live in communion with God in whom he finds happiness" (n. 45).

Sermon on the Plain

While Matthew has Jesus stating eight Beatitudes, Luke has him mentioning only four — those having to do with the poor, the hungry, the weeping, and the hated and persecuted, but Christ promises the same great reward in heaven for those who can live them (cf. Luke 6:20-23).

The other significant difference in this sermon of Jesus on the plain is the contrasting of the beatitudes with four "woes" (Luke 6:24-26):

> But woe to you who are rich,
> for you have received your consolation.
> But woe to you who are filled now,
> for you will be hungry.
> Woe to you who laugh now,
> for you will grieve and weep.
> Woe to you when all speak well of you,
> for their ancestors treated
> the false prophets in this way.

The key to this passage from Luke is verse 24, where Jesus tells the rich that if they concentrate all their efforts in piling up wealth, that is all the reward they will ever get. There will be no reward for them in heaven. But those who concentrate all their efforts, not on accumulating material things but on fidelity to Christ, even though it may cause them pain and heartache, will experience a joy in heaven that will wipe away all tears. In the words of St. Paul: "For this momentary light affliction is producing for us an eternal weight of glory beyond all comparison" (2 Corinthians 4:17).

Jesus' first words at the start of his public life were, "Repent, and believe in the gospel" (Mark 1:15). So it is not enough just to say that you believe in Jesus; the other side of the coin is to demonstrate the sincerity of that belief by following the way that he marked out for us. He made clear the nature of a true disciple when he said, "Not everyone who says to me, 'Lord, Lord,' will enter the kingdom of heaven, but only the one who does the will of my Father in heaven" (Matthew 7:21).

Jesus the Truth

At his trial before the Roman governor Pontius Pilate, Jesus declared that he had come into the world "to testify to the truth. Everyone who belongs to the truth listens to my voice" (John 18:37). He had previously told the Pharisees that they could not bear to hear the truth because "you belong to your father the devil and you willingly carry out your father's desires. He was a murderer from the beginning and does not stand in truth, because there is no truth in him. When he tells a lie, he speaks in character, because he is a liar and the father of lies. But because I speak the truth, you do not believe me" (John 8:44-45).

To those who did believe in him, Jesus said, "If you remain in my word, you will truly be my disciples, and you will know the truth, and the truth will set you free" (John 8:31-32). He later promised that this truth would always be accessible to his followers through the Holy Spirit, "the Spirit of truth," who "will guide you to all truth" (John 16:13). That same truth would also be accessible through the Church that Jesus founded, the Catholic Church, the Body of Christ, which St. Paul called "the pillar and foundation of truth" (1 Timothy 3:15).

In addition to the truths already mentioned, there are other truths taught by Jesus, through whom, as the *Catechism* says (n. 2466), "the whole of God's truth has been made manifest."

(1) He taught us about the Blessed Trinity — the loving union of three divine Persons, Father, Son, and Holy Spirit, in one God — at the time of his Baptism by John in the Jordan (cf. Mark 1:9-11) and in his final instructions to the Apostles to go out into the whole world and baptize everyone "in the name of the Father, and of the Son, and of the holy Spirit" (Matthew 28:19).

"The mystery of the Most Holy Trinity," says the *Catechism*, "is the central mystery of the Christian faith and of Christian life. God alone can make it known to us by revealing himself as Father, Son, and Holy Spirit" (n. 261).

(2) He taught us about the importance of prayer, telling us to "ask and it will be given to you; seek and you will find; knock and the door will be opened to you" (Matthew 7:7).

(3) He taught us the most perfect prayer of all — the Our Father (cf. Matthew 6:9-13). "We can invoke God as 'Father' because the Son of God made man has revealed him to us" (*Catechism*, n. 2798). This Father in heaven, whose name is holy, whose kingdom will come, and whose will must be done on earth as it is in heaven, will give us all that we need each day, forgive our sins provided that we forgive those who have sinned against us, help us in time of temptation, and deliver us from evil.

(4) He taught us to follow the Church that he built on Peter (the name means "rock") because that Church would never fail and because Peter and his successors would always have the

authority to teach and make laws in the name of Jesus (cf. Matthew 16:18-19 and John 21:15-17).

(5) He taught us that he is the "true vine," that we are the branches, and that apart from him we can do nothing (cf. John 15:1-5).

(6) He taught us not to be concerned about material things, saying that the same God who cares for the birds and the flowers cares even more for us. He said that we should "seek first the kingdom [of God] and his righteousness, and all these things will be given to you besides" (Matthew 6:33).

(7) He taught us that he is the Good Shepherd who seeks out those who are lost in sin and even lays down his life for the sheep. He also said that he is the gate for the sheep and that "whoever enters through me will be saved" (John 10:9).

(8) He taught us that he will come again on the Day of Judgment "with power and great glory" (Matthew 24:30) and "will repay everyone according to his conduct" (Matthew 16:27). He said that we must be watchful and prepared, "for at an hour you do not expect, the Son of Man will come" (Luke 12:40).

(9) He taught us about the existence of hell (cf. Matthew 5:22, 29; 13:42, 50; Mark 9:43-48; Luke 16:19-31), and warned that those who failed to help their needy brothers and sisters would be cast "into the eternal fire prepared for the devil and his angels" (Matthew 25:41).

(10) He taught us about the resurrection of the dead (Matthew 22:23-32) and said, "I am the resurrection and the life; whoever believes in me, even if he dies, will live, and everyone who lives and believes in me will never die" (John 11:25-26).

Jesus taught not only through words, but through his whole life. Quoting from Pope John Paul II, the *Catechism* says (n. 561) that "the whole of Christ's life was a continual teaching: his silences, his miracles, his gestures, his prayer, his love for people, his special affection for the little and the poor, his acceptance of the total sacrifice on the Cross for the redemption of the world, and his Resurrection are the actualization of his word and the fulfillment of Revelation" [John Paul II, *CT* 9).

Jesus the Life

In his parable about the Good Shepherd, Jesus said that he had come to earth so that we "might have life and have it more abundantly" (John 10:10). St. John echoed these words when he said that "God gave us eternal life, and this life is in his Son. Whoever possesses the Son has life; whoever does not possess the Son of God does not have life" (1 John 5:11-12).

Christ, therefore, is the source of our spiritual life. He is, as he told the Samaritan woman, "a spring of water welling up to eternal life" (John 4:14), and it is through the Seven Sacraments, and the Holy Sacrifice of the Mass, that we share in his divine life. "The sacraments," said the *Catechism of the Catholic Church*, "are efficacious signs of grace, instituted by Christ and entrusted to the Church, by which divine life is dispensed to us" (n. 1131).

The Sacraments, as St. Thomas Aquinas noted, parallel the stages of our natural life and are available to us at all the important moments of life from birth to death. Thus, Baptism, which opens the door to all the other Sacraments, frees us from sin, gives us new birth as children of God, initiates us as members of the Church, and makes us sharers in the mission of Christ.

Confirmation strengthens our relationship with God, Penance provides the opportunity to seek forgiveness for our sins, and the Holy Eucharist gives us the spiritual nourishment necessary to be a faithful follower of Christ. Holy Orders and Matrimony are sacraments at the service of communion, assisting those entering the priesthood or the married life, and the Anointing of the Sick is available to offer spiritual, and sometimes physical, healing to those who are in danger of death from sickness or old age.

Each of these Sacraments was instituted by Christ (cf. *Catechism*, n. 1114) and is rooted in the New Testament. "No one can enter the kingdom of God without being born of water and Spirit" (John 3:5), Jesus told Nicodemus in a reference to Baptism, and the Lord later commissioned the Apostles to baptize all nations "in the name of the Father, and of the Son, and of the holy Spirit" (Matthew 28:19).

Peter and John, while visiting the Christian community in Samaria, found that the people there "had only been baptized in the name of the Lord Jesus" and had not yet received Confirmation, so "they laid hands on them and they received the holy Spirit" (Acts 8:16-17).

In his appearance to the Apostles on the first Easter Sunday, Jesus "breathed on them and said to them, 'Receive the holy Spirit. Whose sins you forgive are forgiven them, and whose sins you retain are retained'" (John 20:22-23). Note that in instituting the sacrament of Penance or Reconciliation, Jesus did not say,

"Whose sins *I* forgive," but rather, "Whose sins *you* forgive." He also indicated that a priest could hardly forgive, or not forgive, someone's sins unless the penitent first confessed those sins to the priest.

At the Last Supper on Holy Thursday, Jesus gave us the Holy Eucharist by changing bread and wine into his Body and Blood, saying, "Take and eat; this is my body .... Drink from it, all of you, for this is my blood of the covenant, which will be shed on behalf of many for the forgiveness of sins" (Matthew 26:26-28; cf. Luke 22:17-20 and 1 Corinthians 11:23-26).

Also at the Last Supper, Jesus made the Apostles his first priests when he told them to offer up the bread and wine "in memory of me" (Luke 22:19; 1 Corinthians 11:24-25). The sacrament of Holy Orders was conferred in the early Church when, for example, Paul and Barnabas visited cities and "appointed presbyters [priests] for them in each church" (Acts 14:23).

God the Father had established marriage as a covenant in the beginning (cf. Genesis 2:24), and Jesus raised Matrimony to the level of a sacrament, repeating what the Father had said in Genesis: "Have you not read that from the beginning the Creator 'made them male and female' and said, 'For this reason a man shall leave his father and mother and be joined to his wife, and the two shall become one flesh'? So they are no longer two, but one flesh. Therefore, what God has joined together, no human being must separate" (Matthew 19:4-6).

The Anointing of the Sick can be found in the Gospels, where the Apostles "anointed with oil many who were sick and cured them" (Mark 6:13), and in the letter of James: "Is anyone among you sick? He should summon the presbyters [priests] of the church, and they should pray over him and anoint [him] with oil in the name of the Lord, and the prayer of faith will save the sick person, and the Lord will raise him up. If he has committed any sins, he will be forgiven" (James 5:14-15).

The Bread of Life

"Just as the Father raises the dead and gives life," said Jesus, "so also does the Son give life to whomever he wishes" (John 5:21). And that life, Christ explained later, comes from receiving his own Body and Blood. "I am the bread of life," he said. "Your ancestors ate the manna in the desert, but they died; this is the bread that comes down from heaven so that one may eat it and not die. I am the living bread that came down from heaven; whoever eats this bread will live forever; and the bread that I give is my flesh for the life of the world" (John 6:48-51).

The divine life of the God-man himself is available to us through all the Sacraments, but especially through the Holy Eucharist. For as Jesus said, "Whoever eats my flesh and drinks my blood has eternal life, and I will raise him on the last day" (John 6:54). It is difficult to imagine anyone who is aware of this promise of Christ staying away from Holy Mass and refusing the opportunity to share in the Bread of Life.

In the Fullness of Time

After Adam and Eve had sinned, it would have been easy for God to wash his hands of humanity. But instead he showed his great love for us by sending his only Son, in "the fullness of time" (Galatians 4:4), to ransom us from our sins. This Jesus, said St. Paul (Philippians 2:6-11),

> Who, though he was in the form of God,
> did not regard equality with God
> something to be grasped.
> Rather, he emptied himself,
> taking the form of a slave,
> coming in human likeness;
> and found human in appearance,
> he humbled himself,
> becoming obedient to death,
> even death on a cross.
> Because of this, God greatly exalted him
> and bestowed on him the name
> that is above every name,
> that at the name of Jesus
> every knee should bend,
> of those in heaven and on earth
> and under the earth,
> and every tongue confess that
> Jesus Christ is Lord,
> to the glory of God the Father.

Before becoming Pope Benedict XVI, Joseph Cardinal Ratzinger said of Jesus' unique role in the economy of salvation:

Christ is totally different from all the founders of other religions, and he cannot be reduced to a Buddha, a Socrates, or a Confucius. He is really the bridge between heaven and earth, the light of truth who has appeared to us.

After taking the chair of Peter, Pope Benedict said: "One thing is clear: without God things cannot go well, and because only in Christ has God shown us his face ... without Christ there is no ultimate hope." In other words, the Holy Father might have added, "Whoever takes the Son gets everything."

WORDS TO REMEMBER

* Messiah   * Samaritan   * parables
* prophecies   * miracles   * Sacraments
* Beatitudes   * Trinity

Nativity of Jesus.

Chapter 18

The Joyful Mysteries of Christ's Life

You formed my inmost being;
you knit me in my mother's womb.
— Psalm 139:13

A medical doctor and mother of three children, Gianna Beretta Molla knew the problems she faced when a fibrous tumor was discovered in her ovary during her fourth pregnancy. She had two choices: surgery that would remove the tumor but that might take the life of her unborn child, or surgery that would remove the tumor in such a way as to save the pregnancy but that would put her life at risk. She never hesitated in opting for the second type of surgery.

Shortly before her due date, Gianna told the doctor, "If you have to choose, there should be no doubt. Choose — I demand it — the life of the baby. Save the baby." For her, "choice" did not mean what it means to some women today, i.e., ending the life of a child, but rather, freely choosing to do what was good and loving by bringing another child of God into the world.

On April 21, 1962, a healthy Gianna Emanuela Molla was born, but a week later her mother succumbed to multiple complications from carrying the child to term. The daughter, who is now a physician herself, brought up the Offertory gifts to Pope John Paul II when her mother was beatified in 1994.

On May 16, 2004, the same Holy Father canonized Gianna Beretta Molla for her heroic sanctity and gave the world a role model for women and for mothers. St. Gianna had wanted as a young woman to be a missionary in Brazil, but God had other plans for her.

Interestingly, one of the two miracles that led to her canonization involved a Brazilian woman who was able to get through a difficult pregnancy through the intercession of St. Gianna. The saint may not have been able to travel to Brazil physically, but her spiritual presence was certainly felt there.

Some 2,000 years ago, another woman faced an unusual pregnancy, not unusual in that there were health problems, but rather in the unique manner in which the Child was conceived. The circumstances surrounding the Virgin Mary and her Child, from his conception until he reached the age of twelve, are recounted in what we have come to know as the Joyful Mysteries of the rosary. In this and subsequent chapters, the overview of the life of Christ that appeared in the previous chapter will be supplemented by a discussion of twenty specific events in the lives of the Blessed Mother and her Son.

The Annunciation

As the child of practicing Jewish parents, whom tradition tells us were named Anne and Joachim, Mary was surely familiar with Bible prophecies about the Messiah. Yet no familiarity with the Old Testament could have prepared this teenage girl for the momentous request conveyed to her by the angel Gabriel.

After hailing Mary as "favored one!" Gabriel told her that "you will conceive in your womb and bear a son, and you shall name him Jesus. He will be great and will be called Son of the Most High, and the Lord God will give him the throne of David his father, and he will rule over the house of Jacob forever, and of his kingdom there will be no end" (Luke 1:28, 31-33).

Mary, who was betrothed to a man named Joseph, wondered how this could happen since she had vowed not to have marital relations with her husband. The angel said to her in reply: "The holy Spirit will come upon you, and the power of the Most High will overshadow you. Therefore the child to be born will be called holy, the Son of God" (1:35).

By way of giving her a sign that this would all come to pass, Gabriel told Mary that her relative Elizabeth "has also conceived a son in her old age, and this is the sixth month for her who was called barren; for nothing will be impossible for God." Mary found this announcement persuasive and said, "Behold, I am the handmaid of the Lord. May it be done to me according to your word" (1:36-38). At that moment, which is called the Incarnation, the Second Person of the Blessed Trinity took on human flesh and initiated the process of redemption.

Mary has often been referred to as the "new Eve" because she said yes to God, while the first Eve had said no. She is also called the "Ark of the Covenant" because she carried in her womb the true "Bread of Life," Jesus himself, while the original ark carried the miraculous bread or manna which God had sent from heaven to feed the Israelites in the desert.

The conception of Jesus without a human father is sometimes confused with the Immaculate Conception of Mary. What the latter doctrine means, however, is that Mary, from the first moment of her conception in the womb of St. Anne, was free from Original Sin. It was only fitting that the woman given the privilege of carrying the sinless Son of God in her womb should be sinless herself.

Furthermore, if Mary were "full of grace," as some translations (and the Hail Mary prayer) have Gabriel saying, then she must have been free from all taint of sin since being full of grace means being full of God's divine life, which excludes any sin.

As for Mary's reference to God as "my savior" (Luke 1:47), which implies the need to be saved from one's sins (the name Jesus means "God saves"), the Church teaches that the Blessed Virgin was redeemed from all sin at the moment of her conception (cf. *Catechism*, n. 491), and "by the grace of God Mary remained free of every personal sin her whole life long" (n. 493).

The Visitation

Immediately upon learning that an elderly relative was six months' pregnant (recalling the elderly and barren women of the Old Testament whom God had blessed with children), Mary showed her love and compassion by hastening into the hill country and greeting Elizabeth. When Elizabeth heard Mary's voice, the child in her womb, who would come to be known as John the Baptist, became very active as he recognized the presence of his cousin, whom he would years later call the "Lamb of God."

Elizabeth, filled with the Holy Spirit, cried out, "Most blessed are you among women, and blessed is the fruit of your womb. And how does this happen to me, that the mother of my Lord should come to me? For at the moment the sound of your greeting reached my ears, the infant in my womb leaped for joy. Blessed are you who believed that what was spoken to you by the Lord would be fulfilled" (Luke 1:39-45).

After hearing the divinely inspired words of Elizabeth (recalling those of Hannah in 1 Samuel 2:1-10), Mary responded with the beautiful canticle sometimes called "The Magnificat." Here are the opening lines of that canticle (Luke 1:46-49):

> My soul proclaims the greatness of the Lord;
> my spirit rejoices in God my savior.
> For he has looked upon his handmaid's lowliness;
> behold, from now on will all ages call me blessed.
> The Mighty One has done great things for me,
> and holy is his name.

When Mary returned to Nazareth, she was three months' pregnant, and her husband Joseph, being "a righteous man" but not being willing to expose her to the shame of an accusation of adultery, "decided to divorce her quietly" (Matthew 1:19). Although some commentators have suggested that Mary was an "unwed mother," that is not true. Betrothal under Jewish law was the legal or true marriage of a couple, but they did not live together until after a certain period of time. And why would Joseph consider divorcing Mary unless they were already married?

In any case, an angel put Joseph's mind at rest by coming to him in a dream and telling him, "Joseph, son of David, do not be afraid to take Mary your wife into your home. For it is through the holy Spirit that this child has been conceived in her. She will bear a son and you are to name him Jesus, because he will save his people from their sins" (1:20-21).

All this took place, said the evangelist, to fulfull what the Lord had said through the prophet Isaiah (cf. 7:14):

> " 'Behold, the virgin shall be with child and bear a son,
> and they shall name him Emmanuel,'

which means 'God is with us' " (Matthew 1:23).

Jesus was the only Child of Mary, although some people take the reference to the "brothers" and "sisters" of Jesus (cf. Mark 6:3) to mean that Mary had other children. That is not true. The "brothers" and "sisters" of Jesus were not blood relations of the Lord, but rather cousins or other relatives. We know, for example, that the James and Joses mentioned in Mark 6:3 as Jesus' brothers were in fact the sons of another Mary, the wife of Clopas and a relative of the Blessed Mother (cf. John 19:25), which would make James and Joses Jesus' cousins.

The belief of Catholics today (cf. *Catechism*, nn. 499-501) is the same as that of St. Augustine in the fifth century, when he described Mary as "a virgin who conceives, a virgin who gives birth, a virgin with child, a virgin delivered of child — a virgin ever virgin."

The Birth of Jesus

Of all the events in the New Testament, perhaps none is as familiar to us as the Birth of Jesus in Bethlehem. He should have been born in Nazareth, where Mary and Joseph were living as the time of the birth drew near, but a secular ruler, the Roman emperor Caesar Augustus, had ordered a census of the region of the world that was under his domination. The census required that each person should register in the town where his family originated, so Joseph and Mary had to travel to Bethlehem, a journey of about 90 miles.

While the Persian king Cyrus had wittingly facilitated God's plan by liberating the Jews from exile in Babylon (cf. Isaiah 44:28), Augustus unwittingly helped to fulfill the prophecy of Micah (5:1) that the Messiah would be born in Bethlehem. The name Bethlehem, by the way, means "house of bread." How fitting that the one who would call himself the "Bread of Life" should be born there.

When the couple from Nazareth arrived in the City of David, there was no lodging available for them, so they had to stay in a cave where animals were kept. The manger where the newborn Child was placed was a feedbox for the animals. Shortly after the birth of Christ, the angel of the Lord appeared to a group of shepherds keeping night watch nearby over their flocks.

"Do not be afraid," the angel told the frightened shepherds, "for behold, I proclaim to you good news of great joy that will be for all the people. For today in the city of David a savior has been born for you who is Messiah and Lord. And this will be a sign for you: you will find an infant wrapped in swaddling clothes and lying in a manger" (Luke 2:10-12).

Suddenly, the shepherds heard a multitude of angels, prasing God and saying: "Glory to God in the highest/ and on earth peace to those on whom his favor rests" (2:14).

Notice that St. Luke doesn't leave any doubt about the identity of the Child. He calls him "savior," "Messiah," and "Lord."

After the angels had departed, the shepherds hastened into Bethlehem and found Mary and Joseph and the Infant lying in the manger. They made known the message that the angel had conveyed to them, and those who heard the message were amazed at what the shepherds said. After visiting with the Child and his parents, the shepherds returned to the fields, "glorifying and praising God for all they had heard and seen, just as it had been told to them" (2:20).

Meanwhile, a trio of visitors from the East, described either as kings or Magi, arrived in Jerusalem and asked for information about a "newborn king of the Jews" (Matthew 2:2), whose star they had seen in the sky and had followed for a long distance. When King Herod heard of their request, he summoned all his chief priests and scribes and inquired of them where the Messiah was to be born. They told Herod "in Bethlehem of Judea" (2:5), citing the prophecy of Micah (5:1).

Herod then met secretly with the Magi, ascertained when the star had appeared to them, and told them to go to Bethlehem and search for the Child. "When you have found him," he said, "bring me word, that I too may go and do him homage" (2:8).

After their audience with Herod, the three kings followed the star to Bethlehem and, when they reached the house where Mary and Joseph were now staying, they entered and "prostrated themselves and did him homage. Then they opened their treasures and offered him gifts of gold, frankincense, and myrrh. And having been warned in a dream not to return to Herod, they departed for their country by another way" (2:11-12).

The symbolism of the gifts is important. Gold symbolized Christ's royal kingship, frankincense his divinity, and myrrh, which is a burial ointment, his Passion and Death. Even at the Birth of Christ there was the shadow of the cross.

It wasn't long before King Herod realized that the Magi were not coming back to report to him, so to eliminate the newborn King he ordered his soldiers to kill every male child two years of age and under in the region of Bethlehem. This massacre of the Holy Innocents, which the Church observes on December 28th, fulfilled what was said through Jeremiah the prophet: "A voice was heard in Ramah,/ sobbing and loud lamentation;/ Rachel weeping for her children,/ and she would not be consoled,/ since they were no more" (Jeremiah 31:15 and Matthew 2:18).

The threat to the life of Jesus was revealed to Joseph in a dream, and he was told to take Mary and the Child into Egypt and to stay there until the danger was over. Joseph did as the angel had told him and, after Herod had died, the angel appeared to him again and told him to return to the land of Israel.

In imitation of Moses, who had led the children of Israel out of Egypt, and in fulfillment of the prophecy of Hosea 11:1 ("Out of Egypt I called my son"), Joseph brought his wife and foster Son back to Israel, and they settled in the town of Nazareth.

The Presentation in the Temple

Eight days after his birth, Joseph and Mary had given Jesus the name assigned him by the angel and had had him circumcised as a sign of the covenant between God and Abraham (cf. Genesis 17:10-14). The requirements of that covenant were removed at the Council of Jerusalem around A.D. 49 (cf. Acts 15:28), and St. Paul also mentioned the no-longer-binding nature of the pact. "For in Christ Jesus," he said, "neither circumcision nor uncircumcision counts for anything, but only faith working through love" (Galatians 5:6).

Forty days after his birth, Mary and Joseph had taken the Child to the Temple in Jerusalem to present him to the Lord, according to the law of Moses, and to undergo the rite of purification. A woman was considered legally impure for forty days after the birth of a son and was required (cf. Leviticus 12:2-8) to offer a sacrifice of, in Mary's case, a pair of turtledoves or two young pigeons, as an expiation for sin.

The parents of a first-born son were also expected to consecrate him to God (cf. Exodus 13:1), since the child that first opened his mother's womb was considered to belong to the Lord. The law required (cf. Numbers 3:47-48) that the parents redeem their son by paying five shekels to a member of the priestly family in the Temple, but that requirement is not mentioned in connection with the presentation of Jesus.

In the Temple during the Presentation of the Christ Child were two elderly and devout Jews, Simeon and Anna, who had long been praying for the coming of the Messiah. The Holy Spirit had revealed to Simeon that he would not die before he had seen the Messiah of the Lord and, when he saw Jesus that day, he took the Child into his arms and said (Luke 2:29-32):

"Now, Master, you may let your servant go
in peace, according to your word,
for my eyes have seen your salvation,
which you prepared in sight of all the peoples,
a light for revelation to the Gentiles,
and glory for your people Israel."

Mary and Joseph were amazed at Simeon's words about Jesus, but probably even more amazed at what he said to the Blessed Mother: "Behold, this child is destined for the fall and rise of many in Israel, and to be a sign that will be contradicted (and you yourself a sword will pierce) so that the thoughts of many hearts may be revealed" (2:34-35).

This prediction of Simeon was the first of seven sorrows that the Church has traditionally associated with Mary. The others are the flight into Egypt to escape the murderous wrath of King Herod, the three-day separation from Jesus when he was twelve years old, the meeting with her Son on the road to Calvary, the crucifixion and death of our Lord, the placing of his body in Mary's arms after it was taken down from the cross, and his burial in the tomb provided by Joseph of Arimathea.

Also in the Temple that day was an 84-year-old widow named Anna, a prophetess who had worshiped there day and night with fasting and prayer for many years. Coming forward after the presentation of the Child, "she gave thanks to God and spoke about the child to all who were awaiting the redemption of Jerusalem" (2:38).

The Finding in the Temple

Little is known about the life of Jesus from the time of the presentation and subsequent flight into and return from Egypt until he began his public life around the age of thirty, except that he lived in Nazareth, where he "grew and became strong, filled with wisdom; and the favor of God was upon him" (Luke 2:40). The one incident revealed to us during those hidden years occurred when Jesus was twelve years old.

His parents, as was their custom as devout Jews, had gone up to Jerusalem for the feast of the Passover and, when the days of the festival were completed, they began the return trip home, thinking that Jesus was elsewhere in the caravan with relatives or friends. But after a day of not catching sight of him, Mary and Joseph hurried back to the city and spent three days searchng for their son.

They finally located him in the Temple, where he was sitting in the midst of the religious teachers, listening to them and asking them questions. The teachers were astounded at his understanding of what they were discussing and at the answers he gave to their questions. His parents were also astonished when they saw him, and Mary asked him, "Son, why have you done this to us? Your father and I have been looking for you with great anxiety" (Luke 2:48).

But Jesus replied, "Why were you looking for me? Did you not know that I must be in my Father's house?" (Luke 2:49). They did not understand what he was saying, but he left the Temple and returned with them to Nazareth, where he was "obedient to them; and his mother kept all these things in her heart. And Jesus advanced [in] wisdom and age and favor before God and man" (2:31-32).

How Often Are We Found in the "Temple"?

Most of us were presented in the "temple," our local parish church, at the time of our baptism, but how much time do we now spend in God's house? Surely, we are there every weekend for Mass, but do we participate in Eucharistic adoration weekly or monthly? Do we stop in the church during the day to spend some time with the Lord, perhaps saying the rosary or the Stations of the Cross, or reading from the Bible, or just meditating?

Jesus thought it important to be in his Father's house. Shouldn't that also be important to us? Here is a little bit of verse to remind us to spend time with God: "Whenever I go by a church, I always stop to visit. So when they carry my casket down the aisle, God won't ask, 'Who is it?' "

Jesus' Knowledge

There are some people today who contend that Jesus only gradually became aware of his divine nature and mission and perhaps wasn't fully aware of what he was about until after the resurrection. That contention does not square with what the Church teaches about the knowledge of Jesus.

For example, the *Catechism* (n. 474) says that "by its union to the divine wisdom in the person of the Word incarnate, Christ enjoyed in his human knowledge the fullness of understanding of the eternal plans he had come to reveal" [cf. *Mk* 8:31; 9:31; 10:33-34; 14:18-20, 26-30]. "What he admitted to not knowing in this area, he elsewhere declared himself not sent to reveal" [cf. *Mk* 13-32; *Acts* 1:7]. A glance at these scriptural citations will show that Jesus was very much aware of his mission.

Pope John Paul II went so far as to say that Jesus first proclaimed his Messiahship publicly in the Temple at the age of twelve, when he told Mary and Joseph that he had to be in his Father's house. This proclamation, said the Holy Father, was our Lord's "manifestation of his awareness that he was the 'Son of God' and thus of his duty to be 'in his Father's house,' the Temple, to 'take care of his Father's business' (according to another translation of the Gospel phrase). Thus, Jesus publicly declared, perhaps for the first time, his Messiahship and his divine identity."

<u>WORDS TO REMEMBER</u>

* Annunciation   * Visitation   * Incarnation
          * Immaculate Conception   * Magnificat
* betrothal   * Emmanuel   * Magi

Jesus is baptized by John.

Chapter 19

The Luminous Mysteries of Christ's Life

The Lord is my light and my salvation;
whom do I fear?
— Psalm 27:1

There is a story of a teenage boy who was confined to a wheelchair, but managed to eke out a living with a small convenience stand in Grand Central Station in New York City. Late one Christmas Eve, as the commuters were hurrying to catch their trains, two men came running down the concourse.

The first man came around the corner too fast and crashed into the boy's stand, scattering newspapers, magazines, and other items across the floor. He picked himself up, cursed at the boy, and raced off to the train.

When the second man came around the corner and saw what had happened, he stopped, although he, too, was in a hurry. He helped the boy pick up the things on the floor, made sure that he was all right, gave him a $20 bill to cover any damages, and wished him a Merry Christmas.

As the second man started down the concourse, the boy shouted after him, "Mister, are you Jesus Christ?"

The man paused for a moment, turned around, and said, "No, son, I'm not. But I try to do what he would do if he were here now."

For hundreds of years, Catholics prayed the rosary while meditating on the joyful, sorrowful, and glorious events in the life of our Lord. But these mysteries encompassed only the early and final years Christ was on earth. They did not cover some important events that occurred during the nearly three years of his public life.

In 2002, Pope John Paul II sought to fill that gap through an apostolic letter entitled "The Rosary of the Virgin Mary" (*Rosarium Virginis Mariae*). In that letter, the Holy Father proposed five "mysteries of light" that would include significant moments in the life of the one who said, "I am the light of the world" (John 8:12).

These "mysteries of light" are (1) the Baptism of Jesus in the Jordan, (2) his Self-manifestation at the Wedding in Cana, (3) his Proclamation of the Kingdom of God, (4) his Transfiguration on the Mountain, and (5) his Institution of the Holy Eucharist at the Last Supper.

Praying the rosary while meditating on these Luminous Mysteries will help us to follow Jesus more closely, that is, to do what he would do if he were here now.

The Baptism of Jesus in the Jordan

Some thirty years had elapsed since the Visitation of Mary to Elizabeth, when her unborn child, John, leaped for joy at the presence of his unborn cousin, Jesus. It was at that moment, says St. Luke, that John was "filled with the holy Spirit" (1:15). The angel Gabriel had told John's father, Zechariah, that his son would be "great in the sight of [the] Lord," that he would "drink neither wine nor strong drink" in imitation of Samson (Judges 13:4-5) and Samuel (1 Samuel 1:11), and that he would "turn many of the children of Israel to the Lord their God" (1:15-16).

One can see why Pope John Paul led the Mysteries of Light with the one involving John since the Gospels tell us that the Baptist had come "to testify to the light, so that all might believe through him. He was not the light, but came to testify to the light. The true light, which enlightens everyone, was coming into the world" (John 1:7-9).

John became the last and greatest of the prophets of Israel because he was the precursor of the Messiah. Wearing clothing of camel's hair with a leather belt, and feeding himself on a diet of locusts and wild honey, he must have been a commanding presence and a powerful preacher, for many came from all over the region to repent of their sins and to be baptized by him.

But when asked if he himself were the Messiah, John responded by recalling the words of the prophet Isaiah (40:3) and saying that he was

"A voice of one crying out in the desert:
'Prepare the way of the Lord,
make straight his paths'" (Mark 1:3).

He said that "I am baptizing you with water, for repentance, but the one who is coming after me is mightier than I. I am not worthy to carry his sandals. He will baptize you with the holy Spirit and fire. His winnowing fan is in his hand. He will clear the threshing floor and gather his wheat into the barn, but the chaff he will burn with unquenchable fire" (Matthew 3:11-12).

A winnowing fan was a pitchfork shaped like a shovel with which the threshed wheat was thrown into the air when the wind was blowing. The kernels of wheat fell to the ground, while the light chaff blew away and was later gathered and burned. The image was used to describe the fate of unrepentant sinners on judgment day.

One day while John was baptizing, Jesus came to the Jordan and asked to be baptized. John protested at first, saying that "I need to be baptized by you, and yet you are coming to me?" Jesus said in reply, "Allow it now, for thus it is fitting for us to fulfill all righteousness" (Matthew 3:13-15).

After John had baptized the Lord, Jesus came up from the water, the heavens were opened for him, and John saw "the Spirit of God descending like a dove [and] coming upon him. And a voice came from the heavens, saying, 'This is my beloved Son, with whom I am well pleased' " (Matthew 3:16-17). John would later testify that this experience convinced him that Jesus "is the Son of God" (John 1:34).

The presence of the Father and the Son and the Holy Spirit was a manifestation of the Trinity and of Jesus as the Messiah of Israel and Son of God. Though the sinless Christ had no need of baptism, says the *Catechism of the Catholic Church* (n. 536), he requested it of John to inaugurate his mission as "God's suffering Servant," to allow himself "to be numbered among sinners," and to be "the Lamb of God, who takes away the sin of the world" [*Jn* 1:29; cf. *Isa* 53:12], and to submit himself "entirely to his Father's will" [*Mt* 3:15; cf. 26:39].

Furthermore, says the same paragraph of the *Catechism*, we find the Father "proclaiming his entire delight in his Son" [cf. *Lk* 3:22; *Isa* 42:1], the Holy Spirit coming to rest on him as a sign that "Jesus will be the source of the Spirit for all mankind," and the heavens that had been closed by Adam's sin opening up as Jesus sanctified the waters of the Jordan and foreshadowed the sanctifying waters of our own baptism.

Just as the Baptism of Jesus anticipated his Death and Resurrection, so our baptism buries us with Christ so as to rise

222 / CATHOLICISM AND SCRIPTURE

with him and to be glorified with him. As St. Hilary of Poitiers explained (cf. *Catechism*, n. 537):

"Everything that happened to Christ lets us know that, after the bath of water, the Holy Spirit swoops down upon us from high heaven and that, adopted by the Father's voice, we become sons of God" [*In Matth.* 2, 5: PL 9, 927].

Before leaving this mystery of the rosary, a final word about the humility and courage of John the Baptist. Try to imagine someone today with as large a following as John had stepping aside and letting another person take over his movement. Instead of competing with Jesus, John compared himself to the best man at a wedding in relation to the bridegroom and said of Jesus: "He must increase; I must decrease" (John 3:30).

No wonder Jesus said of John: "I tell you, among those born of women, no one is greater than John; yet the least in the kingdom of God is greater than he" (Luke 7:28). This is not a putdown of John, but rather it is Jesus' way of saying that while John's greatness was due to his announcement of the coming kingdom, those who actually belong to the kingdom are even more privileged than John.

The courage of the Baptist has already been discussed in chapter sixteen in connection with his beheading at the hand of King Herod and his wife Herodias. John knew what his fate would be if he criticized the royal couple for their adulterous relationship, but he was faithful to his calling to state the truth. He was not only a herald of the light that was coming into the world, he was himself a light who, like the great prophets who went before him, was not afraid to proclaim the message of God.

The Wedding Feast at Cana

Not long after his baptism by John and his recruitment of twelve disciples, Jesus and his friends attended a wedding in the town of Cana (cf. John 2:1-11). His mother was also there and, apparently, was close enough to the bride and groom to know that the wine had run out. Anyone who has ever attended a wedding reception knows what a social disaster that would be. This may have been even more true in the region around Cana, where the people were not well off and a successful wedding banquet, involving considerable expense, was a major event.

When the Blessed Virgin learned of the problem, she went immediately to Jesus and said to him, "They have no wine." To which Jesus replied, "Woman, how does your concern affect me? My hour has not yet come" (John 2:3-4).

Notice, first of all, that Jesus did not call Mary "Mother," but rather "woman." This was not a sign of disrespect, but an acknowledgement of Mary's key role in salvation history. The use of the word "woman" connects Mary with the woman of Genesis 3:15, whose offspring (Jesus) will defeat Satan. Christ will use the same form of address on Calvary (cf. John 19:26) to show that Mary is the mother of all humankind, and John will repeat the word in the Book of Revelation, when he describes his vision of "a woman clothed with the sun, with the moon under her feet, and on her head a crown of twelve stars" (12:1).

While the reference to "woman" in Revelation can be understood as referring to Israel, with the twelve stars representing the Tribes of Israel, that does not rule out a secondary understanding of the woman as Mary.

Thus, the *Catechism* (n. 1138) sees a connection with "the all-holy Mother of God (the Woman)," and speaks in paragraph 2853 of Satan pursuing the woman (cf. Revelation 12:13-16), but having "no hold on her: the new Eve, 'full of grace' of the Holy Spirit, is preserved from sin and the corruption of death (the Immaculate Conception and the Assumption of the Most Holy Mother of God, Mary, ever virgin)."

The second thing to notice is Jesus' reference to his "hour" not having yet come. He was talking about the hour of his death on the cross (cf. Matthew 26:45, Luke 22:53, John 12:27), the hour when he would "pass from this world to the Father" (John 13:1). Jesus was understandably reluctant to perform the miracle requested by Mary because he knew it would initiate a chain of events that would lead inexorably to Good Friday.

The Blessed Virgin was not put off by her Son's hesitation, and she did not shake her fist at him and tell him to obey her. Knowing her Son better than anyone, Mary went to the waiters and said in regard to Jesus, "Do whatever he tells you" (John 2:5). Those are the last words we hear from the Blessed Mother in the New Testament, but what a powerful message they send.

Imagine what a great world this would be if everyone did what Jesus told them to do! Things like keep the Commandments, live the Beatitudes, pray constantly, perform works of mercy for others, and receive him in the Eucharist.

When the waiters approached Jesus for instructions, he told them to fill six stone jars, each holding twenty to thirty gallons, with water. They filled the jars to the brim, and Jesus told them to draw out some of the liquid and take it to the headwaiter. When the headwaiter tasted it, without knowing where it had come from, he called the bridegroom over and said to him: "Everyone serves good wine first, and then when people have drunk freely, an inferior one; but you have kept the good wine until now" (John 2:10).

As a result of this first of his miracles, says the Evangelist, Jesus had "revealed his glory, and his disciples began to believe in him" (2:11). So the changing of water into wine was not just to help out friends at a wedding; it was the sign that Jesus had begun his mission of salvation, and that his mother would be an instrumental part of that mission.

The Proclamation of the Kingdom

During his brief public life, Jesus spoke of many things, as we have seen, but one constant theme was the coming of his kingdom. His very first words in the Gospel of Mark were: "This is the time of fulfillment. The kingdom of God is at hand. Repent, and believe in the gospel" (1:15). Notice the twofold command: Repent first and then believe in the gospel. It is not enough just to believe in the Gospel; one must also repent of one's sins.

Jesus was a powerful and persuasive speaker, so much so that when the chief priests and Pharisees sent guards to arrest him, the guards returned empty-handed. When they were asked why they had not apprehended Christ, the guards replied: "Never before has anyone spoken like this one" (John 7:46).

Although Jesus often spoke plainly, on some occasions he tried to get his message across to the crowds that followed him through the use of parables, stories with a moral lesson. Some of his stories have become part of our modern lexicon, and it is not unusual to see in the media references to such parables as those of the "Good Samaritan" or the "Prodigal Son."

There are many parables of Jesus worthy of discussion and application to our lives, such as those dealing with workers in the vineyard (Matthew 20:1-16), faithful and unfaithful servants (Matthew 24:45-51), wise and foolish virgins (Matthew 25:1-13), failure to use one's talents well (Matthew 25:14-30), the rich fool (Luke 12:16-21), the lost sheep (Luke 15:1-7), the rich man and

Lazarus (Luke 16:19-31), the persistent widow (Luke 18:1-8), and the Pharisee and the tax collector (Luke 18:9-14).

But our focus here is on those parables about the kingdom of God, many of which can be found in chapter 13 of Matthew's Gospel. In proclaiming the kingdom, Jesus compared it to a sower going out to plant seed, to the devil sowing weeds among the wheat, and to a mustard seed, yeast in a batch of dough, a treasure buried in a field, a pearl of great price, and a net that catches all kinds of fish.

In the parable of the sower, Jesus compared the seed which falls on both arid and fertile soil with the word of God, which falls on both arid and fertile hearts. He said that Satan would sow the weeds of error among the wheat of truth, but that God would let both grow together until the final harvest at the end of the world, lest pulling up the weeds now might also uproot the wheat along with them.

He said that his kingdom would start out tiny like a mustard seed, or small like yeast, but that it would eventually grow and spread throughout the world. He said that recognizing his kingdom and becoming part of it was like finding a treasure buried in a field, and then doing everything possible to buy that field so as not to lose the treasure. And he said that his kingdom, like a net full of fish, would attract all kinds of people, the righteous and the wicked, but that he would dispatch his angels to separate the good from the bad at the end of the world, sending the good to heaven and the bad to "the fiery furnace, where there will be wailing and grinding of teeth" (Matthew 13:50).

When the disciples asked Jesus why he usually spoke to the people in parables, the Lord replied that knowledge of the mysteries of heaven had been granted to the disciples, but not to the people outside because their hearts were not disposed to hear the truth. He said that Isaiah's prophecy (Isaiah 6:9-10) was fulfilled in them:

'Gross is the heart of this people,
they will hardly hear with their ears,
they have closed their eyes,
lest they see with their eyes
and hear with their ears
and understand with their heart and be converted,
and I heal them' (Matthew 13:15).

As Jesus told Pontius Pilate (cf. John 18:36), his kingdom is not of this world. But the Church gathered around Christ is "the seed and beginning of that kingdom" [*LG* 5], says the *Catechism of the Catholic Church* (n. 541). We are all called to enter that kingdom by giving everything we have (cf. Matthew 13:44-45; 22:1-14) and by becoming a fervent disciple of Christ.

"The Kingdom of God," says the *Catechism* (n. 2816), "has been coming since the Last Supper and, in the Eucharist, it is in our midst." It will not attain its final glory until Jesus hands the kingdom over to his Father. Until then, we must fervently proclaim that petition in the Lord's Prayer: "Thy kingdom come!"

The Transfiguration

Peter, James, and John were given a foretaste of the kingdom and of the glory of God when Jesus one day took them up a high mountain and was transfigured before their eyes. It wasn't a case of the bright sun shining on him, but rather his glory radiating from within. "While he was praying," St. Luke tells us, "his face changed in appearance and his clothing became dazzling white" (9:29). The radiant face of Jesus was reminiscent of the radiant face of Moses when he came down from Mount Sinai after conversing with God (cf. Exodus 34:29-35).

The Transfiguration of Jesus came about a week after his first prediction of his Passion and was his way of providing the apostolic trio with a sign of hope, with a demonstration that his horrible suffering and death would end in glory. Appearing in conversation with the Lord on the mountain were Moses and Elijah, representing the Old Testament law and the prophets. They were discussing what Jesus "was going to accomplish in Jerusalem" (Luke 9:31).

Peter offered to erect three tents, "one for you, one for Moses, and one for Elijah" (9:33). He was hoping to prolong the glorious occasion, but while he was speaking a cloud cast a shadow over them, and then from the cloud came a voice that said, "This is my chosen Son; listen to him" (9:35). Jesus was then alone, and Peter, James, and John walked down the mountain and back to a hostile world desperately in need of redemption.

At the Baptism of Jesus, the voice of the Father had expressed the pleasure he felt toward his beloved Son. Now he goes one step beyond that and commands us to listen to Jesus, just as Mary had told us to do whatever Jesus tells us. The only way that we can know what Christ expects of us is by immersing ourselves in the Gospels and familiarizing ourselves with the message that the Lord has communicated to us in his life and in his teachings.

Another lesson from the Transfiguration has to do with the condition of our risen bodies in heaven. Will they be glorified like the body of Jesus on the mountain? The *Catechism* says (n. 999) that just as Christ did not return to an earthly life after his Resurrection from the dead, "so, in him, 'all of them will rise again with their own bodies which they now bear,' but Christ 'will change our lowly body to be like his glorious body,' into a 'spiritual body' " [Lateran Council IV (1215): DS 801; *Phil* 3:21; *1 Cor* 15:44].

The Institution of the Eucharist

Jesus is an historical figure, someone who lived on earth a long time ago, but he is not merely someone from the past. He assured that he would always be present to us by giving us himself in the Holy Eucharist. On the night before he died, he changed bread and wine into his Body and Blood and gave the Apostles, his first priests, the power to do the same, commanding them to "do this in memory of me" (Luke 22:19).

And so for two thousand years, as Malachi prophesied (cf. 1:11), the sacrifice of Christ on Calvary has been re-presented in an unbloody manner on the altars of the world, and hundreds of millions have participated in the holy banquet that we call the Mass by receiving Jesus — Body and Blood, Soul and Divinity — in Holy Communion. He promised to be with us all days, until the end of the world (cf. Matthew 28:20), and he has kept that promise.

The Eucharist was foreshadowed in various places in the Old Testament, but particularly in the manna from heaven that God provided to the Israelites wandering in the desert (cf. Exodus 16:4-15). It was foreshadowed again in the New Testament in Jesus' multiplication of the loaves and fishes, the only one of his miracles that appears in all four Gospels.

Large crowds had been following Jesus and he saw that they were hungry. He asked Philip where enough food could be bought to feed the five thousand men, plus women and children, in the crowd. Jesus already knew what he planned to do; he was just testing Philip to see what his response would be. Philip said that even two hundred days' wages would not be enough to give each of them a tiny bit of food.

The Apostle Andrew discovered that a boy in the crowd had five loaves of bread and two fish, but asked, "What good are these for so many?" (John 6:9). Nevertheless, Jesus had the people recline on the grass, took the loaves and gave thanks, and then had the Apostles distribute the bread to all those present. When the fragments were gathered up after everyone had had enough to eat, there was enough left to fill twelve baskets (John 6:13).

Now there are skeptics who insist that nothing miraculous took place that day, that Jesus just inspired those in the crowd to share food that they had in their pockets. The absurdity of that theory is demonstrated by the desire of the crowd to carry Jesus off and "make him king" (John 6:15). Only a great miracle could have prompted such a reaction by the crowd.

The Bread of Life Discourse

This was further confirmed the following day on the other side of the Sea of Galilee, when many of the same crowd asked Jesus to perform another sign for them. Instead, the Lord delivered his famous "Bread of Life" discourse (cf. John 6:22-58), declaring over and over again that he was the Bread of Life and stating again and again that his flesh and blood were to be eaten.

"I am the bread of life," Jesus said. "Your ancestors ate the manna in the desert, but they died; this is the bread that comes down from heaven so that one may eat it and not die. I am the living bread that came down from heaven; whoever eats this bread will live forever; and the bread that I will give is my flesh for the life of the world" (6:48-51).

Some of those listening found his words too hard to take, and they walked away. It is the only time in Scripture that we read of disciples leaving Jesus. But did Christ soften his words? Did he say, "Wait a minute, friends, I didn't mean that literally"? No, he stated his message even more clearly:

Amen, amen, I say to you, unless you eat the flesh of the Son of Man and drink his blood, you do not have life within you. Whoever eats my flesh and drinks my blood has eternal life, and I will raise him up on the last day. For my flesh is true food, and my blood is true drink. Whoever eats my flesh and drinks my blood remains in me and I in him" (6:53-56).

When Jesus asked the Twelve if they also planned to leave him, Simon Peter replied: "Master, to whom shall we go? You have the words of eternal life. We have come to believe and are convinced that you are the Holy One of God" (6:67-69).

At the Last Supper on Holy Thursday, Jesus made his promise a reality when he consecrated bread and wine into his Body and Blood: "Then he took the bread, said the blessing, broke it, and gave it to them, saying, 'This is my body, which will be given for you; do this in memory of me.' And likewise the cup after they had eaten, saying, 'This cup is the new covenant in my blood, which will be shed for you'" (Luke 22:19-20).

Notice that Jesus didn't say, "This is a symbol of my body," but rather "This *is* my body." He didn't say, "This represents my blood," but rather "This cup *is* the new covenant in my blood, which will be shed for you."

Some years later, St. Paul, after criticizing the Corinthians for abuses at the celebration of the Eucharist, such as getting drunk or not sharing with those who were hungry, repeated the words of institution that Jesus had spoken at the Last Supper and also reaffirmed that the Eucharist was truly the Body and Blood of the Lord, and not just a symbol.

He said that "whoever eats the bread or drinks the cup of the Lord unworthily will have to answer for the body and blood of the Lord. A person should examine himself, and so eat the bread and drink the cup. For anyone who eats and drinks without discerning the body, eats and drinks judgment on himself" (1 Corinthians 11:27-29).

One could hardly expect to bring judgment on oneself for eating ordinary bread or drinking ordinary wine. But through the words of the priest, and by the process known to Catholics as transubstantiation, the bread and wine on the altar cease to exist and are replaced by the Body and Blood of Jesus Christ, the Son of God and second Person of the Blessed Trinity.

"O, what a friend we have in Jesus," says an old hymn. What a friend, indeed! A friend who knew that we would need all the spiritual help we could get to reach heaven, and who left us not just a symbol or reminder of him, but his actual Body and Blood. The one who was born in a town whose name means "house of bread" became the "Bread of Life." So every Catholic Church is another Bethlehem, another house of bread wherein dwells the Bread of Life.

The Eucharistic liturgy, says the *Catechism*, "is the work of the whole Christ, head and body. Our high priest celebrates it unceasingly in the heavenly liturgy, with the holy Mother of God, the apostles, all the saints, and the multitude of those who have already entered the kingdom" (n. 1187). It is the Church, the *Catechism* explains (n.1194) that, during the course of the year, " 'unfolds the whole mystery of Christ from his Incarnation and Nativity through his Ascension, to Pentecost and the expectation of the blessed hope of the coming of the Lord' " [*SC* 102.2).

Our Ticket to Heaven

Pope St. Pius X said that "Holy Communion is the shortest, surest way to heaven." So why do so many Catholics stay away from Mass and neglect the awesome privilege of receiving Jesus? If they had a winning lottery ticket, they would speedily cash it in. The Holy Eucharist is our spiritual lottery ticket to heaven. Let us not fail to "cash in that ticket" at least once a week on Sunday and to do so in a worthy manner by going to the sacrament of Penance and confessing any serious sins of which we are aware before receiving the Lord.

Another valuable spiritual practice is worship of the Lord through Eucharistic adoration. The more time spent before Christ in the Blessed Sacrament of the Eucharist, the holier we will become as individuals and as a Church, and that holiness will radiate out into and eventually transform a world mired in sin.

The Holy Eucharist is indeed "the source and summit of the Christian life," as the Second Vatican Council said (cf. *Lumen Gentium*, n. 11), and it must become the source and summit of our life as well. Let us meditate on these thoughts as we pray this decade of the Luminous Mysteries.

WORDS TO REMEMBER

* Transfiguration	* transubstantiation
* Holy Eucharist	* Last Supper
* Pharisees	* rosary

Chapter 20

The Sorrowful Mysteries of Christ's Life

> For God has not spurned or disdained
> the misery of this poor wretch,
> Did not turn away from me,
> but heard me when I cried out.
> — Psalm 22:25

The guards at the Auschwitz death camp were furious because a prisoner had escaped. So after lining up all the prisoners in the camp, they selected ten men to die for the man who had escaped. One of the ten, who said that he had a wife and children at home, begged to be spared, but the guards ignored him.

Then a prisoner stepped forward from the back of the line and offered to take the place of the man with a family. "Who are you?" a guard asked. "I am Fr. Maximilian Kolbe, a Catholic priest," the prisoner replied. The guard shrugged, sent the other man back into the group, and marched Fr. Kolbe and the other nine inmates to the extermination bunker.

The plan was to starve the prisoners slowly to death, and some died within a week. But Fr. Kolbe, who had been leading the prisoners in prayer from the time they entered the bunker, was still alive a week later. So the impatient guards injected him with poison, and his life came to an end on August 14, 1941.

Forty-one years later, Pope John Paul II canonized Maximilian Kolbe as a "martyr of charity," and the man whose life Fr. Kolbe had saved was there in Rome to witness the elevation of his benefactor to sainthood. The priest-martyr had followed in an extraordinary way the example of Christ, who had told the Apostles at the Last Supper: "No one has greater love than this, to lay down one's life for one's friends" (John 15:13).

Jesus never asks us to do anything that he did not do first, and no one can say that he does not know what it is like to suffer, as we will see in our examination of the Sorrowful Mysteries.

The Agony in the Garden

The Last Supper had been completed and it was nearing midnight as Jesus and the Apostles made their way out of the city of Jerusalem, across the Kidron valley, and up the Mount of Olives to the Garden of Gethsemane. "All of you will have your faith shaken," Jesus told them on the way, but Peter insisted that "mine will not be." Then Jesus said to him: "Amen, I say to you, this very night before the cock crows twice you will deny me three times." Peter vehemently replied, "Even though I should have to die with you, I will not deny you" (Mark 14:27, 29-31).

The garden was a grove of olive trees overlooking the city, and Jesus often went there to pray. He left eight of the Apostles (Judas was busy conspiring to betray the Lord) at the entrance to the garden and took Peter, James, and John along with him. "My soul is sorrowful even to death," he told them. "Remain here and keep watch with me" (Matthew 26:38).

Jesus walked a short distance away from the three, prostrated himself on the ground, and prayed, "My Father, if it is possible, let this cup pass from me; yet, not as I will, but as you will." As Jesus prayed, Peter, James, and John fell asleep. The Lord went over and woke them, saying, "So you could not keep watch with me for one hour? Watch and pray that you may not undergo the test. The spirit is willing, but the flesh is weak" (Matthew 26:39-41).

Jesus went back and prayed a second time that his Father might take away the cup of dreadful suffering from him, but stressed again the importance of doing the Father's will, not his own. As he prayed, his agony became so great that it caused his sweat to become like drops of blood falling to the ground. So the Father sent an angel to strengthen him (cf. Luke 22:43-44).

There is no specific mention of Satan being present in the Garden of Gethsemane, but it seems very likely, as the movie *The Passion of the Christ* suggests, that the Evil One was there trying to divert Jesus from his mission of redemption.

The third time that Christ woke his sleeping Apostles, telling them that "the hour is at hand when the Son of Man is to be handed over to sinners" (Matthew 26:45), a crowd of soldiers and guards, carrying lanterns and swords and clubs, rushed into the garden to arrest Jesus. Leading the mob was Judas, who had already arranged for a signal that would tell the soldiers which man to arrest in the darkened grove.

"Hail, Rabbi!" (Matthew 26:49), said Judas, kissing Jesus on the cheek. Jesus answered, "Friend, do what you have come for" (26:50). Christ was still reaching out to Judas, calling him "friend" as Judas was giving a signal to the soldiers. As the soldiers stepped forward to seize the Lord, Peter drew his sword and cut the ear off one of the slaves of the high priest.

"Put your sword back into its sheath," Jesus told Peter, "for all who take the sword will perish by the sword" (26:52). He said that he could call upon his Father to send thousands of angels to protect him, "but then how would the scriptures be fulfilled which say that it must come to pass in this way?" (26:54).

After healing the slave's ear, his last miracle before his Death, Jesus let the soldiers arrest and bind him and take him back to the city, while the Apostles fled into the night.

The Scourging at the Pillar

Before the Lord was brutally scourged, he had to undergo several "trials" in order to find him guilty of committing a crime for which he could be sentenced to death. The first interrogation took place before Annas, father-in-law of the high priest Caiaphas, who questioned Jesus about his teachings. "I have spoken publicly to the world," Jesus replied, and suggested that Annas ask those who had heard him speak "what I said to them. They know what I said" (John 18:20-21).

One of the Temple guards struck Jesus across the face and said, "Is this the way you answer the high priest?" Jesus replied, "If I have spoken wrongly, testify to the wrong; but if I have spoken rightly, why do you strike me?" (John 18:22-23). The guard made no reply, and Annas decided to send Jesus to Caiaphas for trial before the Sanhedrin later on in the early morning hours.

Meanwhile, Peter was outside in the courtyard of the high priest's house, waiting to see what the fate of Jesus would be. On three different occasions in a short space of time, Peter was asked if he were a disciple of Jesus, and three times Peter denied it, even cursing and swearing that "I do not know this man about whom you are talking" (Mark 14:71). He then heard the rooster crow twice and, remembering that Jesus had predicted his denials, Peter broke down and wept bitterly.

Perhaps around five o'clock on Friday morning, the full Sanhedrin was assembled by Caiaphas to put Jesus on trial. The high priest produced witnesses to testify against Christ, but their testimony was so confusing and contradictory, that even the enemies of Christ did not believe these witnesses.

Greatly concerned because he had gone to a lot of trouble to have Jesus arrested in the middle of the night, and seeing the case against him falling apart, Caiaphas disregarded the Sanhedrin's own laws and demanded that Jesus testify against himself. "I order you," said the high priest, "to tell us under oath before the living God whether you are the Messiah, the Son of God" (Matthew 26:63). Jesus, knowing that an affirmative answer would mean his death, declared, "I am" (Mark 14:62).

Caiaphas tore his garments and said, "What further need have we of witnesses? You have heard the blasphemy. What do you think?" (Mark 14:63-64). And they all condemned Jesus for claiming to be God and sentenced him to death. But the San-he-drin had no power to put anyone to death; that power belonged to the Roman governor, and so Jesus was marched across the city to the fortress of the governor, Pontius Pilate.

Trial Before Pilate

When Pilate asked why they had brought the prisoner to him, there was no mention of blasphemy since a charge of claiming to be God would have no meaning to the Roman official. So the enemies of our Lord accused him of "misleading our people; he opposes the payment of taxes to Caesar and maintains that he is the Messiah, a king" (Luke 23:2).

Pilate must have realized that these charges were spurious, but he decided to play it safe. So he brought Jesus into the prae-torium and wanted to know only one thing: "Are you the King of the Jews?" Jesus replied, "My kingdom does not belong to this world ... my kingdom is not here" (John 18:33, 36).

The Roman official believed Jesus and told the crowd, "I find this man not guilty" (Luke 23:4). But the mob insisted that Christ had been inciting the people ever since he came to Jerusalem from Galilee. When Pilate heard the mention of Galilee, he sent Jesus to Herod Antipas, who had jurisdiction over Galilee. However, after questioning Jesus and mocking him, Herod sent him back to Pilate.

"I have conducted my investigation in your presence," the Roman governor told the crowd, "and have not found this man guilty of the charges you have brought against him, nor did Herod, for he sent him back to us. So no capital crime has been committed by him. Therefore, I shall have him flogged and then release him" (Luke 23:14-16).

Though he had just declared Jesus an innocent man, Pilate thought he could pacify the crowd by having Jesus flogged, or scourged. This was a horrible form of torture, as graphically demonstrated in *The Passion of the Christ*, and victims frequently died from it. After his clothes were removed, Jesus was tied to a stone pillar and scourged with a whip that was tipped with balls of lead or pieces of bone that were designed to tear chunks of flesh from a human body and reduce a person to a bleeding mass of flesh.

The Crowning with Thorns

After the soldiers had finished scourging Christ, they threw a scarlet military cloak over his bruised and bleeding shoulders and then, weaving a crown out of rough thorns, placed it on his head and put a reed in his right hand. The soldiers knelt before Jesus, mocking him and saying, "Hail, King of the Jews!" (Matthew 27:29). They spit in his face and took the reed and struck him repeatedly on the head, causing him unbearable pain with the thorns in the crown.

It may have been Archbishop Fulton J. Sheen, the famous Catholic author and radio and television preacher of the last century, who said that Jesus' atonement for our sins was written in blood on his body during his Passion. The crown of thorns symbolizes all the sins of impure thoughts and lust, the marks of the scourging all the sins against chastity, the nail marks in the hands all the sins of theft and greed, the nail marks in the feet all the sins of running away from God and from those in need of our assistance.

How well did Isaiah prophesy the Passion of our Lord when he wrote hundreds of years earlier (Isaiah 53:4-5):

> Yet it was our infirmities that he bore,
>   our sufferings that he endured,
> While we thought of him as stricken,
>   as one smitten by God and afflicted.
> But he was pierced for our offenses,
>   crushed for our sins,
> Upon him was the chastisement that makes us whole,
>   by his stripes we were healed.

After trying to placate the angry crowd by having Jesus scourged, and by offering them a choice between releasing him or a dangerous murderer named Barabbas (they chose Barabbas), Pilate brought Christ out before the people and said, "Behold, the man!" He expected some sympathy for the blood-covered and horribly wounded man in front of them, but all he heard was "Crucify him, crucify him!" (John 19:5-6).

Pilate was still trying to release Jesus when he heard someone shout, "If you release him, you are not a Friend of Caesar. Everyone who makes himself a king opposes Caesar" (John 19:12). Not wanting word to get back to Rome that he had freed a foe of the Emperor, Pilate called for a basin of water, washed his hands in the sight of the crowd, and said, "I am innocent of this man's blood. Look to it yourselves" (Matthew 27:24). He then turned Jesus over to the soldiers to be crucified.

It is easy to criticize Pontius Pilate for sentencing to death a man he knew to be innocent because he was afraid of the crowd. But how many times in our own lives have we been afraid to do the right thing because of what others might think? There is a little of Pontius Pilate in all of us.

The Carrying of the Cross

Jesus was taken down to the basement of the Roman governor's fortress, the scarlet cloak was ripped from his body, opening up his wounds and causing them to bleed again, and his own clothes were put back on him. He was then given a very heavy cross to carry. It is not clear whether he had to carry the entire cross, or only the horizontal piece, but even the latter would have been a terrible burden on his wounded shoulders as he struggled through the streets toward the place of execution, a hill outside the city known as Golgotha, which meant "Place of the Skull" (Matthew 27:33).

(The Latin word for skull is *calvaria*, so the place of the crucifixion is also known as Calvary.)

It was not a long walk under ordinary circumstances from Pilate's residence to Golgotha, perhaps half a mile, but these were not ordinary circumstances. The man carrying the heavy cross had not slept in more than twenty-four hours, he had not had anything to eat or drink in more than twelve hours, and he had suffered violent damage to his body through a bloody sweat, beatings by soldiers, Scourging, and the Crowning with Thorns.

Tradition tells us that Jesus fell at least three times on the way to Calvary, causing more painful bruises and lacerations. The soldiers must have become concerned over whether he would be physically able to complete the journey because they forced a bystander named Simon of Cyrene to help Jesus carry the cross. He was the first of many persons down through history who would have the privilege of sharing the cross of Christ.

Following Jesus and the two criminals who were going to be executed with him was a large crowd that included many women who were lamenting his plight and crying over him. He turned to them at one point and said, "Daughters of Jerusalem, do not weep for me; weep instead for yourselves and for your children, for indeed, the days are coming when people will say, 'Blessed are the barren, the wombs that never bore and the breasts that never nursed.' At that time people will say to the mountains, 'Fall upon us!' and to the hills, 'Cover us!' for if these things are done when the wood is green what will happen when it is dry?'" (Luke 23:28-31).

Jesus knew the terrible fate that was to befall Jerusalem forty years later, when the Romans would level the city and kill all of its inhabitants either by crucifixion or starvation, and he was warning the women of the calamities to come. He was also warning the people that if the Romans treated him (the green wood), who was innocent, so badly, how would they treat those (the dry wood) who had condemned him to death? If he who had no sin underwent such suffering, Jesus was asking, what would be the fate on Judgment Day of those who were steeped in sin?

It was nearly noon when Jesus stumbled up the hill of Golgotha and the executioners began their cruel task. They first stripped him of his garments, causing more shocks to his body as his wounds were torn open and began to bleed again. His hands and feet were then fixed to the cross with nails, causing him excruciating pain. It seems certain that the nails were driven through his wrists instead of his palms, as many crucifixes show, because it is doubtful that nails in the palms would support the weight of a man hanging on a cross.

The Crucifixion and Death of Our Lord

Before the cross had been raised up between those of the two criminals, the soldiers had affixed a sign above Jesus' head with an inscription, in Hebrew, Latin, and Greek, that said "Jesus the Nazorean, the King of the Jews" (in Latin *Iesus Nazarenus*

Rex Iudaeorum, or INRI). The purpose of the inscription was to warn those passing by not to commit the same criminal offense for which the person on the cross was being executed.

The religious leaders who had instigated the plot to have Jesus killed were not happy with the sign, so they went to Pontius Pilate and told him, "Do not write 'The King of the Jews,' but that he said, 'I am the King of the Jews.' The Roman governor dismissed them with the reply, "What I have written, I have written" (John 19:21-22).

And so the one who had come to earth to die for our sins had been raised up between heaven and earth. Just as Moses had raised a bronze serpent on a pole so that those who looked upon it would recover from their poisonous snake bites (cf. Numbers 21:4-9), so those who looked at Jesus would recover from the poison of sin. The Son of Man must be lifted up, Jesus had said earlier in his public life, "so that everyone who believes in him may have eternal life" (John 3:15).

After the soldiers had crucified Jesus, they took his clothes and divided them into four pieces, a share for each soldier, but since his tunic was woven into one seamless piece and could not be divided, they cast lots for it. Lots were probably small stones or pieces of wood that were thrown or shaken like dice to determine the outcome of several choices. The action of the soldiers was a fulfillment of an Old Testament prophecy (cf. Psalm 22:19) that was recalled by John (19:24):

> "They divided my garments among them,
> and for my vesture they cast lots."

As Jesus hung on the cross, his body grew weaker and slumped downward, making it almost impossible for him to breathe and putting him at risk of suffocation. The only way for him to prevent this was to push down on the nail in his feet and pull on the nails in his wrists, and work his way slowly and painfully back up the rough wood of the cross until his arms were parallel with the crosspiece. When he was able to breathe again, he spoke for the first of seven times from the cross.

Some of the onlookers were mocking Jesus, shouting at him, "He saved others; he cannot save himself. So he is the king of Israel! Let him come down from the cross now, and we will believe in him" (Matthew 27:42). But instead of shouting back at them, or cursing them, Christ said, ["Father, forgive them, they know not what they do"] (Luke 23:34).

Imagine, asking forgiveness for those who had put him on the cross and were now sneering at him! No longer can we say that Jesus doesn't know what it's like for the innocent to suffer at the hands of the guilty. No longer can we say that God asks too much of us when he expects us to forgive those who have hurt us badly. Jesus gave us the example *par excellence* of offering up one's sufferings for others.

One of the criminals hanging next to Jesus joined in the jeering. "Are you not the Messiah?" he asked. "Save yourself and us." He wanted to be taken down. But his colleague on the right wanted to be taken up, and he rebuked him: "Have you no fear of God, for you are subject to the same condemnation? And indeed, we have been condemned justly, for the sentence we received corresponds to our crimes, but this man has done nothing criminal" (Luke 23:39-41).

The good thief had undergone a conversion experience in the presence of divinity, and he begged, "Jesus, remember me when you come into your kingdom." Recognizing the sincerity of the man's plea, Christ replied, "Amen, I say to you, today you will be with me in Paradise" (Luke 23:42-43). The good thief was a thief to the end, said Archbishop Fulton Sheen. His final act was to steal heaven.

The words of the Lord to the good thief, whom the Church gives the name Dismas, ought to be a great consolation to those hardened in sin. It is never too late to repent of one's sins and to throw oneself on the mercy of God.

The Women at the Cross

Only a few friends of Jesus were there at the foot of the cross on Good Friday. There were his mother, the Apostle John, Mary Magdalene, Mary, the wife of Clopas and the mother of James and Joses, and Salome, the mother of James and John. Looking at his mother and using again the word from Genesis 3:15 and John 2:4, the Lord said, "Woman, behold, your son." Then he said to John, the beloved disciple, "Behold, your mother" (John 19:26-27).

He did not use the words "Mother" or "John" because "woman" referred to Mary's universal motherhood, her spiritual motherhood to all of us, who are also her children, and "son" indicated that Jesus was not referring to John as the son of Zebedee but rather as the representative of the whole human race. "From that hour," says the Gospel, "the disciple took her into his home" (John 19:27).

As Jesus hung in agony on the cross, and darkness spread over the whole land, he cried out in a loud voice in Aramaic, "*Eloi, Eloi, lema sabachthani*," which means, "My God, my God, why have you forsaken me?" (Mark 15:34). In offering himself as a ransom for our sins, Jesus wanted to experience to the fullest the mental agony that encompasses all the loneliness and abandonment of those who have rejected God.

But Jesus was not giving in to despair. He was quoting the opening lines of Psalm 22, which ends with words of triumph:

> All the ends of the earth
> will worship and turn to the LORD;
> All the families of nations
> will bow low before you.
> For kingship belongs to the LORD,
> the ruler over the nations" (22:28-29).

In another effort to fulfill the words of Scripture, Jesus cried out, "I thirst" (John 19:28), and the soldiers put up to his lips a sponge soaked in a common wine that had turned to vinegar. When Jesus was first raised on the cross, he had rejected the offer of a wine that was probably a narcotic designed to lessen his pain (Mark 15:23); he did not want the pain that he was enduring for our sins to be deadened in the slightest. But now he would fulfill the words of Psalm 69:21-22:

> I looked for compassion, but there was none,
> for comforters, but found none.
> Instead they put gall in my food;
> for my thirst they gave me vinegar.

Jesus was experiencing a feverish physical thirst, but he was also expressing his thirst for souls, for people to turn away from sin and to follow him faithfully all the way to heaven. As God, Jesus knew those in the future who would reject him; he knew those for whom his terrible suffering would be in vain. This knowledge caused him immense mental agony, and he thirsted for the conversion of all sinners.

After taking the wine, Jesus said three very important words: "It is finished" (John 19:30). What Adam had lost at the tree in the Garden of Eden, Christ had won back on the tree of the cross. The great ransom had been paid, the work of redemption had been completed, all the prophecies and all the types of the Old

Testament has been fulfilled in him. The gates of heaven which Adam had closed, Jesus had now reopened.

But perhaps to show that he would determine the time of his death, Jesus struggled once more up the cross and spoke for the final time: "Father, into your hands I commend my spirit" (Luke 23:46). He then slumped forward and breathed his last. One of the soldiers who had witnessed this said, "Truly, this was the Son of God!" (Matthew 27:54).

The Death of Christ at three o'clock on Friday afternoon was accompanied by an eclipse of the sun, an earthquake, and the tearing from top to bottom of the veil in the Temple that had shielded the Holy of Holies from the sight of the people. No longer would the presence of God be hidden, but would be manifest in the new temple of Christ's body, the Church.

Since it was nearing sundown, and Jewish law forbade leaving bodies on the cross during the sabbath celebration the following day, the religious leaders asked Pilate that the legs of the three be broken and that they be taken down. The soldiers broke the legs of the two criminals, so they could no longer avoid suffocation by pushing down on the nails in their feet, but Jesus' legs they did not break because he was already dead.

Piercing the Heart of Christ

But one of the soldiers took a lance and thrust it into his side, causing blood and water to flow out, according to one eyewitness (John 19:34). The flow of blood and water indicated that the lance had pierced the heart of Christ and confirmed that he was dead.

The flow also symbolized the founding of the Church in the blood of the Eucharist and the water of Baptism, which the *Catechism* (n. 1225) calls "the sacraments of new life [cf. *Jn* 19:34; 1 *Jn* 5:6-8]. From then on, it is possible 'to be born of water and the Spirit' [cf. *Jn* 3:5] in order to enter the Kingdom of God."

After the death of Jesus, Joseph of Arimathea, a distinguished member of the Sanhedrin, but one who had not taken part in the vendetta against Jesus (Luke 23:51), obtained permission from Pilate to bury Christ in a new tomb near Golgotha. The body was wrapped in a linen cloth and placed in the tomb, and then a huge stone was rolled across the opening.

Meditating on the Sorrowful Mysteries gives us an insight first into the benevolent plan of God, who proved his love for us "in that while we were still sinners Christ died for us" (Romans

5:8). Second, we see that Jesus' whole life was inspired by "the desire to embrace his Father's plan of redeeming love" (cf. *Lk* 12:50; 22:15; *Mt* 16:21-23], "for his redemptive passion was the very reason for his Incarnation" (*Catechism*, n. 607).

In summary, says the *Catechism* (n. 614), "This sacrifice of Christ is unique; it completes and surpasses all other sacrifices" [cf. *Heb* 10:10]. First, it is a gift from God the Father himself, for the Father handed his Son over to sinners in order to reconcile us with himself. At the same time it is the offering of the Son of God made man, who in freedom and love offered his life to his Father through the Holy Spirit in reparation for our disobedience" [cf. *Jn* 10:17-18; 15:13; *Heb* 9:14; *1 Jn* 4:10].

WORDS TO REMEMBER

* Gethsemane   * Golgotha   * Calvary
* Scourging   * INRI   * Dismas
* Simon of Cyrene   * Redemption

Jesus appears to Mary Magdalene.

Chapter 21

The Glorious Mysteries of Christ's Life

They will sing of the ways of the LORD:
"How great is the glory of the LORD!"
— Psalm 138:5

There is a story about a little girl who was given a child's book about the Gospels. She had read many stories about Jesus and was enthralled with him. But one day she ran out of her room crying hysterically. "They killed him! They killed him!" she said to her mother.

Taking her weeping daughter into her arms, the mother calmed her down and then whispered to her: "I want you to go back and finish the story."

The followers of Jesus who had witnessed his brutal death on the cross must have felt the same as the little girl as they walked away from Calvary. Their demeanor was like that of the two disciples on the road to the village of Emmaus on that first Easter Sunday. They were downcast, they told the stranger who came up to them, because of "the things that happened to Jesus the Nazarene, who was a prophet mighty in deed and word before God and all the people, how our chief priests and rulers both handed him over to a sentence of death and crucified him" (Luke 24:19-20).

"Oh, how foolish you are!" said the stranger, who was really Jesus. "How slow of heart to believe all that the prophets spoke! Was it not necessary that the Messiah should suffer these things and enter into his glory?" (Luke 24:25-26). Jesus then explained to them all the Old Testament passages that referred to him, but it wasn't until they reached Emmaus, and Jesus broke bread, blessed it, and gave it to them that "their eyes were opened and they recognized him" (Luke 24:31).

So, too, today, it is at the Holy Sacrifice of the Mass, where the Scriptures are read and explained to us and where Jesus is made present on the altar in the breaking of the bread, that our eyes are opened and we are able to recognize him. For the rest of the story, we must look at the five Glorious Mysteries.

The Resurrection of Our Lord

Looking back from our vantage point, it seems odd that the disciples thought that Calvary was the end of the story. For Jesus on half a dozen occasions had predicted that he would rise from the dead. For example, on the way to Jerusalem one time, he took the Apostles aside and told them that "the Son of Man will be handed over to the chief priests and the scribes, and they will condemn him to death and hand him over to the Gentiles who will mock him, spit upon him, scourge him, and put him to death, but after three days he will rise" (Mark 10:33-34).

It is also curious that while the Apostles apparently had not been paying attention to the prediction of the Resurrection, the enemies of Christ had been listening. For the day after the crucifixion the chief priests and Pharisees went to Pontius Pilate and said, "Sir, we remember that this impostor while still alive said, 'After three days I will be raised up.' Give orders, then, that the grave be secured until the third day, lest his disciples come and steal him and say to the people, 'He has been raised from the dead.' This last imposture would be worse than the first" (Matthew 27:63-64).

Pilate told them to station their own guards at the tomb, and so they went and secured the burial place by sealing the stone across the opening and assigning men to guard the grave.

As the sun was coming up the following day, a group of women, including Mary Magdalene, Joanna, and Mary the mother of James, set out for the tomb to finish preparing Jesus' body for burial by anointing it with spices. Their main concern was who would roll the huge stone back for them, but when they reached the tomb, there was a great earthquake and an angel from heaven rolled back the stone and sat on it.

His appearance was dazzling and frightening, and the guards fell to the ground like dead men. "Do not be afraid!" the angel said to the women. "I know that you are seeking Jesus the crucified. He is not here, for he has been raised just as he said. Come and see the place where he lay. Then go quickly and tell his disciples, 'He has been raised from the dead, and he is going before you to Galilee; there you will see him' " (Matthew 28:5-7).

After the angel had departed, the guards reported to the chief priests and the Pharisees all that they had seen. After consulting with the elders, the chief priests gave a large sum of money to the soldiers and told them not to spread the story about the angel, but rather "to say, 'His disciples came by night and stole him while we were asleep.' And if this gets to the ears of the governor, we will satisfy [him] and keep you out of trouble" (Matthew 28:12-14). The soldiers did as they were instructed.

Meanwhile, Mary Magdalene had raced back to the city to tell the Apostles what she had witnessed, and she returned to the scene shortly afterwards with Peter and John. Although John reached the tomb first, he stepped aside to let Peter enter ahead of him. Both men observed the burial cloths, one where the body had lain, and the other that had covered the head of Jesus, rolled up in a separate place.

When John saw the burial cloths, he believed that Jesus had risen from the dead (John 20:8). He doesn't explain why he believed that, but we can surmise that perhaps the large shroud in which the body of Christ had been wrapped had not been disturbed, indicating that Jesus had passed through the cloth without unwrapping it.

After Peter and John left the tomb, Mary Magdalene stayed behind weeping. She saw a man standing nearby, but did not recognize him; she thought he was the gardener who took care of the grave. "Woman, why are you weeping?" the man asked. "Whom are you looking for?" Mary said to him, "Sir, if you carried him away, tell me where you laid him, and I will take him" (John 20:15). Jesus then spoke Mary's name, and she realized who he was and embraced him (cf. 20:17).

"Stop holding on to me," said Jesus, "for I have not yet ascended to the Father. But go to my brothers and tell them, 'I am going to my Father and your Father, to my God and your God.'"
(John 20:17). Mary, overjoyed at having seen Jesus alive, ran back to tell everyone that she had seen the Lord, but they did not believe her (Mark 16:11).

Appearance in the Upper Room

Later on that first Easter, the disciples from Emmaus reported to the Apostles that they had seen Jesus, and they were told that he had also appeared to Simon Peter. That evening, while the Apostles were discussing the amazing events of the day in the same Upper Room where the Last Supper had been held, suddenly Jesus came through the locked door, stood in their midst, and said, "Peace be with you" (Luke 24:36).

But the demeanor of the Apostles was anything but peaceful; they were terrified, they thought they were seeing a ghost. "Why are you troubled?" Jesus asked them. "And why do questions arise in your hearts? Look at my hands and my feet, that it is I myself. Touch me and see, because a ghost does not have flesh and bones as you can see I have" (Luke 24:38-39).

Jesus then asked them for something to eat, and they gave him a piece of baked fish, which he ate in front of them. He then said, " 'As the Father has sent me, so I send you.' And when he had said this, he breathed on them and said to them, 'Receive the holy Spirit. Whose sins you forgive are forgiven them, and whose sins you retain are retained' " (John 20:21-23).

The only other time in the Bible where God is said to have breathed on someone was when he breathed physical life into Adam (cf. Genesis 2:7). Now he was breathing spiritual life into the Apostles and giving them the power to forgive sins. Jesus then told his disciples to remain in Jerusalem "until you are clothed with power from on high" (Luke 24:49).

One of the Twelve, Thomas, was absent on Easter Sunday night and, when told of Jesus' appearance, said that he would not believe it unless he could put his finger into the nailmarks in Jesus' hands and his hand into the wound in his side. A week later, Thomas was present in the Upper Room when Jesus appeared for a second time.

Christ invited Thomas to put his finger into his hands and his hand into his side, saying to him, "do not be unbelieving, but believe." Thomas' only response was, "My Lord and my God!" To which Jesus said, "Have you come to believe because you have seen me? Blessed are those who have not seen and have believed" (John 20:27-29). Jesus may have been referring to those of us who believe in him without ever having seen him in person.

There are those who doubt that Jesus rose from the dead, but there are three very persuasive arguments in favor of his Resurrection. First, his tomb was empty on Sunday morning, and the attempt to explain this fact by saying that the Apostles stole the body while the guards were sleeping is not a credible explanation considering how afraid the disciples were.

Second, Jesus was seen by more than five hundred people in the forty days after his Resurrection (cf. 1 Corinthians 15:6).

To suggest that all of these persons were hallucinating because they wanted to believe that Jesus had risen is not a sound theory. Perhaps if he had been seen only by a few people, and they only saw him at night, the theory might have some plausibility. But over five hundred people in different places at different times? And how come five hundred allegedly crazy people all stopped being crazy exactly forty days after Easter?

Third, something spectacular must have happened to transform the Apostles from weak and frightened followers of Christ into strong and zealous missionaries who were willing to give their lives to spread his message to a hostile world. That something was Jesus' Resurrection from the dead and his promise that "I am the resurrection and the life; whoever believes in me, even if he dies, will live, and everyone who lives and believes in me will never die" (John 11:25-26).

The Ascension of Our Lord

Forty days after Easter, Jesus took the eleven Apostles to the town of Bethany, about two miles from Jerusalem, and gave them their great commission. He said that "all power in heaven and on earth has been given to me. Go, therefore, and make disciples of all nations, baptizing them in the name of the Father, and of the Son, and of the holy Spirit, teaching them to observe all that I have commanded you. And behold, I am with you always, until the end of the age" (Matthew 28:18-20).

Jesus' mission was to all nations, and he was passing along that universal mission to his chosen Apostles and their successors. Not only were they to bring members into his Church through a trinitarian baptism, but they were also commanded to teach all that Jesus had taught on such occasions as the Sermon on the Mount that Matthew has recounted in such detail.

When the Apostles asked the Lord when he was going to "restore the kingdom to Israel," he answered, "It is not for you to know the times or seasons that the Father has established by his own authority. But you will receive power when the holy Spirit comes upon you, and you will be my witnesses in Jerusalem, throughout Judea and Samaria, and to the ends of the earth" (Acts 1:6-8).

After having said this, Jesus was lifted up and a cloud took him from their sight. While they were still gazing intently at the sky, two angels suddenly stood beside them and said, "Men of Galilee, why are you standing there looking at the sky? This Jesus who has been taken up from you into heaven will return in the same way as you have seen him going into heaven" (Acts 1:11). The eleven disciples then returned to Jerusalem to await the coming of the Holy Spirit, through whom God's gift of love would be poured into their hearts (cf. *Catechism*, n. 733).

The Descent of the Holy Spirit on Pentecost

During the next ten days, the Apostles, along with the mother of Jesus, devoted themselves to prayer. It was during this time that a successor was chosen to fill the vacancy caused by the death of Judas. Speaking to about 120 followers of Christ, Peter announced that, although Judas "was numbered among us and was allotted a share in this ministry," he had betrayed the Lord and had taken his own life. "Therefore," said Peter, "it is necessary that one of the men who accompanied us the whole time the Lord Jesus came and went among us, beginning from the baptism of John until the day on which he was taken up from us, become with us a witness to his resurrection" (Acts 1:17, 21-22).

Two men were proposed to take the place of Judas, Joseph (also known as Barsabbas) and Matthias. The Apostles then prayed, "You, Lord, who know the hearts of all, show which one of these two you have chosen to take the place in this apostolic ministry from which Judas turned away to go to his own place" (Acts 1:24-25). Lots were distributed to them, and Matthias was selected as the twelfth Apostle.

On the tenth day after the Ascension, and the fiftieth day after the Resurrection, the Twelve were gathered in the Upper Room when "suddenly there came from the sky a noise like a strong driving wind, and it filled the entire house in which they were. Then there appeared to them tongues as of fire, which parted and came to rest on each one of them. And they were all filled with the holy Spirit and began to speak in different tongues, as the Spirit enabled them to proclaim" (Acts 2:2-4).

The sound was heard outside the house and soon a crowd had gathered. They were amazed because each person, no matter what part of the world he was from, heard the Apostles speaking in his own language. "Are not all these people who are speaking Galileans?" they asked. "Then how does each of us hear them in his own native language?" (Acts 2:7-8). Some scoffers suggested that the Apostles had had too much wine to drink.

While the crowd gathered on Pentecost was puzzling over what they had heard, Peter came out of the house and spoke to them. He told them that he and his colleagues were not drunk, for it was only nine o'clock in the morning, and then he delivered a powerful sermon that quoted from the Old Testament to prove that all that had happened to Jesus had been foretold.

"Jesus the Nazorean," said Peter, "was a man commended to you by God with mighty deeds, wonders, and signs, which God worked through him in your midst, as you yourselves know. This man, delivered up by the set plan and foreknowledge of God, you killed, using lawless men to crucify him. But God raised him up, releasing him from the throes of death, because it was impossible for him to be held by it" (Acts 2:22-24).

"Therefore," said Peter, "let the whole house of Israel know for certain that God has made him both Lord and Messiah, this Jesus whom you crucified" (Acts 2:36). Those listening to Peter were so moved by his words that they asked, "What are we to do?" Peter said to them, "Repent and be baptized, every one of you, in the name of Jesus Christ for the forgiveness of your sins; and you will receive the gift of the holy Spirit" (Acts 2:37-38).

Peter preached to them with many other arguments and exhorted them to "save yourselves from this corrupt generation" (Acts 2:40). His words were so persuasive that about three thousand persons asked to be baptized that day.

"On the day of Pentecost when the seven weeks of Easter had come to an end," says the *Catechism* (n. 731), "Christ's Passover is fulfilled in the outpouring of the Holy Spirit, manifested, given, and communicated as a divine person: of his fullness, Christ, the Lord, pours out the Spirit in abundance" [cf *Acts* 2:33-36]. This same Spirit poured out by Christ, the *Catechism* continues, "builds, animates, and sanctifies the Church. She is the sacrament of the Holy Trinity's communion with men" (n. 747).

Furthermore, the *Catechism* says, the Holy Spirit is " 'the principal agent of the whole of the Church's mission' [John Paul II, *RMiss* 21]. It is he who leads the Church on her missionary paths. 'This mission continues and, in the course of history, unfolds the mission of Christ....' " [*AG* 5].

The Assumption of Our Lady

Just as Jesus ascended into heaven, it was also fitting and proper that he should take his mother to heaven at the end of her earthly life. After all, who was more deserving of this honor than the great woman who said yes to God when she was asked to be the mother of the Savior? What better way for Jesus to fulfill the commandment to honor his mother than by preserving her body from corruption? We know that Jesus had the power to bring his mother back to life and into heaven, and what son would fail to do that for his mother if he could?

The Assumption of Mary is not specifically recorded in the Bible, but it is a revealed truth stemming from what we know of the sinless virgin's life. When the angel Gabriel addressed Mary as "favored one," or "full of grace," he was affirming that she was free from all taint of sin, including Original Sin, for how could she be God's favored one, or full of his divine life, if she were guilty of sin? This privilege we call her Immaculate Conception; it is closely bound to her Assumption, which the *Catechism* calls "a singular participation in her Son's Resurrection" (n. 966).

According to the first book of the Bible, the consequences of Original Sin include death and corruption of the body in the grave. "For you are dirt,/" God told Adam and Eve, "and to dirt you shall return" (Genesis 3:19). But if Mary did not have Original Sin, then her body would not be subject to decay after death. The Church has never officially pronounced whether the Blessed Mother died, but the virtually unanimous consensus of the Church's great saints and theologians is that she did die, but was immediately taken up to heaven, body and soul.

"And who, I ask, could believe that the ark of holiness, the dwelling place of the Word of God, the temple of the Holy Spirit, could be reduced to ruin?" said St. Robert Bellarmine. "My soul is filled with horror at the thought that this virginal flesh which had begotten God, had brought him into the world, had nourished and carried him, could have been turned into ashes or given over to be food for worms."

There is also a negative proof for her Assumption in that neither her tomb nor her remains were ever found. It was commonplace in the early Church to venerate the bones and the resting places of the saints, but there is no record of such veneration of the Virgin Mary. That is because there were no bodily remains to venerate, and the faithful knew that from the earliest days of the Church.

In defining this doctrine of the Church on November 1, 1950, Pope Pius XII declared that "it is to be a divinely revealed dogma:

that the Immaculate Mother of God, the ever Virgin Mary, having completed the course of her earthly life, was assumed body and soul into heavenly glory" (*Munificentissimus Deus*, n. 44).

The Crowning of Mary

The Coronation of Mary as queen of heaven and earth is also not specifically mentioned in the Bible, but her queenship makes good sense if we look at the role of the queen-mother in the Old Testament. The importance of the queen-mother is very clear in 1st and 2nd Kings. Virtually every time a new king is introduced, his mother's name is mentioned (e.g., 1 Kings 14:21, 15:2, 22:42). Many kings had multiple wives, making it difficult to choose one to be queen, so the king's mother was given the title and role.

Consider, for example, the role of Bathsheba, the wife of David and the mother of Solomon. When David was king and Bathsheba entered his presence, she bowed to the floor in homage to him and said, "May my lord, King David, live forever!" (1 Kings 1:31). But after David died and Solomon became king, Bathsheba went directly to him to ask a favor, and when she entered the room, Solomon "stood up to meet her and paid her homage. Then he sat down upon his throne, and a throne was provided for the king's mother, who sat at his right" (1 Kings 2:19).

She no longer pays homage to the king; he pays homage to her, and he seats her on his right, the position of authority. When Bathsheba told Solomon that she had a small favor to ask of him, the king said, "Ask it, my mother ... for I will not refuse you" (1 Kings 2:20).

Jesus did not use these same words when his mother told him at Cana that the wine had run out, but he deferred to her wishes and performed a miracle at her request, even though his hour had not yet come. He continues to defer to the wishes of his mother and queen in heaven.

As Vatican II's Dogmatic Constitution on the Church (*Lumen Gentium*) explained it:

Finally, preserved free from all guilt of original sin, the Immaculate Virgin was taken up body and soul into heavenly glory upon the completion of her earthly sojourn. She was exalted by the Lord as Queen of all, in order that she might be more thoroughly conformed to her Son, the Lord of lords (cf. Apoc. 19:16) and the conqueror of sin and death (n. 59).

<u>WORDS TO REMEMBER</u>

* Resurrection   * Ascension   * Pentecost
* Assumption   * dogma   * Holy Spirit

Peter (r) and John cure a beggar.

Chapter 22

The Early Church: St. Peter

> For God will hide me in his shelter
> in time of trouble,
> will conceal me in the cover of his tent;
> and set me high upon a rock.
>
> — Psalm 27:5

There is a legend about an incident involving St. Peter while the Christians were experiencing fierce persecution in Rome under the Emperor Nero some thirty years after the founding of the Church. So terrible was the persecution that Peter decided to leave the city to escape capture by the Roman authorities.

As he was fleeing Rome, the legend goes, he met up with Christ heading toward the city. "Where are you going," Peter asked the Lord, and Jesus replied, "I am going to Rome to be crucified all over again."

Embarrassed at the thought of abandoning the Lord a second time, Peter reversed direction and went back to Rome, where he continued evangelizing until he was eventually captured and martyred sometime between A.D. 64 and 67. The skeletal remains of Peter were found deep under the high altar of St. Peter's Basilica in Rome around the middle of the twentieth century.

While there is no historical evidence of the meeting between Christ and Peter on a road outside of Rome, it is a fact that Peter did establish a Catholic community there. He said in his first letter that he was writing from "Babylon" (5:13), which was the code name among the early Christians for Rome. And St. Irenaeus asserted in the second century that Matthew had written his Gospel "while Peter and Paul were evangelizing in Rome and laying the foundation of the Church."

It is understandable how the *Quo Vadis?* ("Where are you going?") legend might have arisen, since Peter is well-known for his triple denial of Christ in the early morning hours of Good Friday.

But a close look at Peter's role in the early Church, as recounted in chapters one to five, eight to twelve, and chapter fifteen of the Acts of the Apostles, shows his courageous leadership of the early Christians and confirms the trust that Jesus had placed in him by making him head of his Church.

Authority from Christ

As mentioned in previous chapters, Jesus gave Simon Peter alone full authority over the Church he was establishing to carry on the work of salvation in the world. He changed his name from Simon to Peter, which means "rock," and used the word "you" in specific reference to Peter seven times in Matthew 16:13-19. Peter was to be the strong foundation upon which Jesus would build his Church. He alone would possess "the keys to the kingdom of heaven" and have the authority to govern the Church of God. He would have the power on earth to bind and loose, that is, to absolve sins, to make laws and doctrinal pronouncements, and to promulgate disciplinary rules.

At the Last Supper, just before predicting that Peter would deny him three times, Jesus said, "Simon, Simon, behold Satan has demanded to sift all of you like wheat, but I have prayed that your own faith may not fail; and once you have turned back, you must strengthen your brothers" (Luke 22:31-32). Peter did indeed turn back from his abandonment of Christ and was able to strengthen the Apostles and disciples to withstand the harassment and persecution of the early Church.

Just as Jesus had once saved Peter from drowning in the sea (cf. Matthew 14:31), so now he was promising to save Peter and those entrusted to his care from the waves of sin and Satan. Peter was able to walk on water as long as he kept looking at Christ, but when he took his eyes off the Lord, he began to sink. A similar fate awaits us if we take our eyes off Jesus.

There is also the incident recorded only in John's Gospel (21:15-17) of the dialogue on the shore of the Sea of Tiberias between Jesus and Peter. Peter and six others had been out fishing all night, but had caught nothing. As they approached land, Jesus told them to cast their nets off the right side of the boat, and they hauled in a miraculous catch of fish.

After the Apostles had reached the shore and had eaten the breakfast that Jesus had prepared for them, the Lord asked Peter, "Simon, son of John, do you love me more than these?"

Peter replied, "Yes, Lord, you know that I love you," and Jesus said, "Feed my lambs." He asked the question a second time, and Peter responded with the same words, and Christ told him, "Tend my sheep."

When Jesus posed the question a third time (a not-so-subtle reminder of the Apostle's triple denial), Peter was distressed and said, "Lord, you know everything; you know that I love you." And the Lord told him, "Feed my sheep." Here again, Simon Peter was being given the mandate and the authority of a shepherd who would feed the flock of Christ with the solid food of truth and not the poison of error. Jesus had already promised that he would send the Holy Spirit, "the Spirit of truth" (John 14:17), to guide Peter and the Apostles to the truth.

The commissioning of Peter as the supreme shepherd of the Catholic Church was followed by a warning to him about the kind of death he would suffer. "When you were younger," Jesus told Peter, "you used to dress yourself and go where you wanted; but when you grow old, you will stretch out your hands, and someone else will dress you and lead you where you do not want to go." Jesus said this, according to John, to signify "by what kind of death he [Peter] would glorify God" (John 21:18-19). Tradition tells us that Peter died by crucifixion.

Authority in the Early Church

The leadership role of Peter in the early Church became apparent immediately, first when he presided over the selection of Matthias to replace Judas (cf. Acts 1:15-26). Second, when he delivered a powerful homily to the crowd assembled in Jerusalem on Pentecost. His call to "repent and be baptized, every one of you, in the name of Jesus Christ for the forgiveness of your sins" (Acts 2:38) was so persuasive that three thousand persons asked to be baptized that very day. And third, when Ananias and Sapphira fell dead at his feet after Peter scolded them for lying to the Holy Spirit in accepting the praise of the community for their generosity in selling some property, when in fact they were not deserving of praise. "Great fear came upon the whole church and upon all who heard of these things" (Acts 5:11).

In the days that followed Pentecost, many more were added to their number as the disciples "devoted themselves to the teaching of the apostles and to the communal life, to the breaking of the bread and to the prayers. Awe came upon everyone, and many wonders and signs were done through the apostles. All who believed were together and had all things in common; they would sell their property and possessions and divide them among all according to each one's need" (Acts 2:42-45).

The first recorded "wonder and sign" took place in the Temple area, where Peter and John had gone to pray in the middle of the afternoon, having already "broken bread" (celebrated Mass) in their homes. A man crippled from birth was begging at one of the gates of the Temple, and he asked the two Apostles for alms.

"I have neither silver nor gold," Peter told the beggar, "but what I do have I give you: in the name of Jesus Christ the Nazorean, [rise and] walk" (Acts 3:6). Peter took the man by the hand and helped him to his feet. The man's feet and ankles immediately grew strong, and he began to walk and jump around praising God. Soon a crowd had gathered, and they were astonished at what had happened to the beggar.

Seeing the crowd there, Peter explained that the man had not been healed through his and John's power, but rather through God's servant, Jesus, "whom you handed over and denied in Pilate's presence, when he had decided to release him. You denied the Holy and Righteous One and asked that a murderer be released to you. The author of life you put to death, but God raised him from the dead; of this we are witnesses. And by faith in his name, this man, whom you see and know, his name has made strong, and the faith that comes through it has given him this perfect health, in the presence of all of you" (Acts 3:13-16).

Peter told them that they and their leaders had "acted out of ignorance" in helping God to fulfill his plan "that his Messiah would suffer," but that the time had come for them to "repent, therefore, and be converted, that your sins may be wiped away, and that the Lord may grant you times of refreshment and send you the Messiah already appointed for you, Jesus" (3:17-20). His words convinced another five thousand to become believers.

The Opposition Begins

While Peter was still speaking, the chief priests and Temple guards, disturbed that he was teaching the people and proclaiming the Resurrection of Jesus, arrested him and John, along with the beggar, kept them in custody overnight, and brought them before the Sanhedrin the following day. "By what power or by what name have you done this?" (4:7), the Apostles were asked.

Peter, filled with the Holy Spirit, responded that they had acted "in the name of Jesus Christ the Nazorean whom you crucified, whom God raised from the dead; in his name this man stands before you healed. He is 'the stone rejected by you, the builders, which has become the cornerstone.' There is no salvation through anyone else, nor is there any other name under heaven given to the human race by which we are to be saved" (4:10-12).

Stunned at the boldness and eloquence of men whom they perceived to be uneducated fishermen, and seeing the man who had been cured standing there with them, the leaders of the Sanhedrin sent the Apostles away until they could decide what to do about them. They conceded that they could not deny the "remarkable sign" that was done through Peter and John, but they did not want their teachings to be spread any further among the people, so they called them back for a stern warning never to speak to anyone again in the name of Jesus.

But after hearing the warning, Peter and John said in reply, "Whether it is right in the sight of God for us to obey you rather than God, you be the judges. It is impossible for us not to speak about what we have seen and heard" (4:19-20). The Sanhedrin members threatened them further, but had to release them "on account of the people who were all praising God for what had happened" (4:21).

In a letter written some time later, Peter would emphasize that he could not deny what Jesus had done, particularly after seeing him transfigured on the mountain (cf. Luke 9:28-36). "We did not follow cleverly devised myths when we made known to you the power and coming of our Lord Jesus Christ, but we had been eyewitnesses of his majesty," Peter wrote. "For he received honor and glory from God the Father when that unique declaration came to him from the majestic glory, 'This is my Son, my beloved, with whom I am well pleased'" (2 Peter 1:16-17).

Peter went on to say that "we ourselves heard this voice come from heaven while we were with him on the holy mountain. Moreover, we possess the prophetic message that is altogether reliable. You will do well to be attentive to it, as to a lamp shining in a dark place, until day dawns and the morning star rises in your hearts" (1:18-19).

We today who belong to the Church first headed by Peter also possess the prophetic message that is altogether reliable, and we also would do well to be attentive to that message, since it will provide us with the light that we need to find our way through our sin-darkened world. Then we can look forward to hearing the Father say to us, "You are my beloved sons and daughters, with whom I am well pleased."

Rescued by an Angel

Following their first confrontation with the Sanhedrin, Peter and the Apostles continued to preach about Jesus and to perform miracles, which persuaded "great numbers of men and women" (Act 5:14) to join the new Church. The sick were carried out into the streets in the hope that "when Peter came by, at least his shadow might fall on one or another of them. A large number of people from the towns in the vicinity of Jerusalem also gathered, bringing the sick and those disturbed by unclean spirits, and they were all cured" (Acts 5:15-16).

This was all too much for the high priest, so he ordered his soldiers to seize the Apostles and put them in jail. But during the night, an angel of the Lord opened the cell doors, led them outside the jail, and told them, "Go and take your place in the temple area, and tell the people everything about this life" (5:20).

When the high priest convened the Sanhedrin the next morning and sent for the prisoners, he was told that, while the jail doors were securely locked and the guards were stationed outside the doors, the prisoners were not inside. Then someone reported to the high priest that the Apostles were seen preaching in the Temple area, so he sent the court officers to arrest them. The guards brought them back before the Sanhedrin, "but without force, because they were afraid of being stoned by the people" (Acts 5:26).

Once again the high priest ordered the Apostles to stop teaching in the name of Jesus, but Peter and the others replied: "We must obey God rather than men. The God of our ancestors raised Jesus, though you had him killed by hanging him on a tree. God exalted him at his right hand as leader and savior to grant Israel repentance and forgiveness of sins. We are witnesses of these things, as is the holy Spirit that God has given to those who obey him" (5:29-32).

These words infuriated the members of the Sanhedrin, and they wanted the Apostles put to death. But one of their number, a Pharisee named Gamaliel, after having the Apostles removed from the chamber, urged caution. He reminded his colleagues that the people had rallied around other men in the past, but when those men were killed, he said, their supporters disbanded.

Gamaliel advised the Sanhedrin to "have nothing to do with these men, and let them go. For if this endeavor or this activity is of human origin, it will destroy itself. But if it comes from God, you will not be able to destroy them; you may even find yourself fighting against God" (5:38-39). His advice was heeded, and the Apostles were released after being flogged and ordered again to stop speaking in the name of Jesus.

After leaving the presence of the Sanhedrin, Peter and the others rejoiced that "they had been found worthy to suffer dishonor for the sake of the name. And all day long, both at the temple and in their homes, they did not stop teaching and proclaiming the Messiah, Jesus" (5:41-42).

Lessons to Be Learned

Several lessons can be gleaned from this episode. First, our solemn and constant obligation to obey God rather than human beings. This precept is tested all the time in our society, particularly when believers are told not to impose their moral views on others. These critics, of course, are themselves imposing a moral view, namely, that of moral relativism.

The answer to these critics, while we are faithfully responding to Christ's call to discipleship, is to say that we have no power, that is, no police or military power, to force our moral views on anyone. We have only the power of persuasion to argue in favor of a just and moral society that honors Gospel values.

Second, we can take consolation in the words of Gamaliel and realize that our Catholic endeavor is of divine origin. This Church that Christ himself founded, and promised to be with all days, until the end of the world, can never be destroyed, although it can be weakened and marred by the sins of its members. Let us vow always to build up the Church, the Body of Christ, and never to say or do anything that would help to tear her down.

Third, we must continue to teach and proclaim Jesus as Messiah and Lord, even if it means physical pain or social ostracism, and rejoice if we are found worthy to suffer for the sake of his name. For as Jesus said, "Everyone who acknowledges me before others I will acknowledge before my heavenly Father. But whoever denies me before others, I will deny before my heavenly Father" (Matthew 10:32-33).

Stephen the First Martyr

When the Twelve discovered that providing for the needy members of the community was taking time away from proclaiming the word of God, they chose seven reputable men, who were filled with faith and the Holy Spirit, to take care of the needy. The most prominent of those who would become known as deacons was Stephen, a man "filled with grace and power" who worked "great wonders and signs among the people" (Acts 6:8).

While spreading the teachings of Christ, Stephen engaged in debates with opponents of the new Church and overpowered them with his wisdom and enthusiasm. These opponents accused Stephen of blasphemous words against Moses and God and so stirred up the people that he was arrested and put on trial before the Sanhedrin. All at the trial observed Stephen intently "and saw that his face was like the face of an angel" (6:15).

During the trial, Stephen delivered an eloquent summary of the history of salvation from the time of Abraham and finished with these strong words:

You stiff-necked people, uncircumcised in heart and ears, you always oppose the holy Spirit; you are just like your ancestors. Which of the prophets did your ancestors not persecute? They put to death those who foretold the coming of the righteous one, whose betrayers and murderers you have now become. You received the law as transmitted by angels, but you did not observe it" (7:51-53).

Stephen's words infuriated the Sanhedrin and, when he looked upward and said, "Behold, I see the heavens opened and the Son of Man standing at the right hand of God," they rushed upon him, dragged him outside the city, and stoned him to death. As he was dying, Stephen imitated Christ on the cross, first by calling, "Lord Jesus, receive my spirit," and then by crying out, "Lord, do not hold this sin against them" (7:56, 59-60).

Watching the cloaks of those who stoned Stephen to death, and consenting to his execution, was a young man named Saul, who would soon become one of the fiercest persecutors of the Church, dragging men and women out of their houses and handing them over for imprisonment. So intense was the persecution after the death of Stephen, that many Christians, but not the Apostles, fled into the countryside of Judea and Samaria.

Mission to the Gentiles

The persecution and harassment of the Church ceased temporarily after the conversion of Saul a few years later (see the next chapter for the details), and there was peace throughout all Judea, Samaria, and Galilee. During this time, while Peter was preaching and healing and even bringing a woman named Tabitha back to life (cf. Acts 9:36-41), a Roman centurion named Cornelius, who lived in Caesarea, experienced a vision in which an angel told him to summon Simon Peter to his house. Cornelius, a God-fearing man, sent his servants to get Peter in Joppa.

While the servants were on their way to Joppa, Peter had a vision of a large sheet being lowered from heaven in which was contained all the earth's animals, reptiles, and birds. A voice told Peter to "slaughter and eat," but the Apostle refused, saying that "never have I eaten anything profane and unclean." But the voice said, "What God has made clean, you are not to call profane" (10:13-15). This happened two more times, and then the sheet was taken up into the sky.

While he was puzzling over the meaning of the vision, the servants of Cornelius arrived, and Peter agreed to go with them to the centurion's house. Upon arrival there, Cornelius described his vision to Peter, and the Apostle realized that there was no longer any prohibition against associating with Gentiles. He preached to them about Jesus and, upon observing that the Holy Spirit had poured out his gifts on these Gentiles, for he "could hear them speaking in tongues and glorifying God" (10:46), Peter ordered that Cornelius and all in his house be "baptized in the name of Jesus Christ" (10:48).

Another Persecution Begins

While Paul and Barnabas were preaching in Antioch, where the disciples were first called Christians (cf. Acts 11:26), and were adding large numbers to the flock of Christ, King Herod initiated a persecution of the Church in Jerusalem. He had James, the brother of John, killed by the sword and also had Peter arrested. On the night before his trial, Peter, shackled by double chains and sleeping between two soldiers, was awakened by an angel and led through the prison gates out into the city without disturbing the guards (cf. 12:6-11).

Peter went to the house of Mary, the mother of Mark, and had to knock repeatedly on the door before those inside would believe that it was him and would let him in the house. Peter then went elsewhere and, when he was discovered missing from the jail the next day, Herod ordered a search. Not finding the leader of the Apostles, the king had the guards tried and executed, and then went to his palace in Caesarea (cf. 12:12-19).

Nor long after that, while Herod was attired in his royal robes and was addressing a crowd, they shouted, "This is the voice of a god, not of a man." At that moment, the angel of the Lord struck Herod down "because he did not ascribe the honor to God, and he was eaten by worms and breathed his last" (12:22-23).

The Council of Jerusalem

During those years, a debate raged among the followers of Christ over the question of whether Gentile converts had to follow the Mosaic law and be circumcised before becoming Christians. So the leaders of the early Church, guided by the Holy Spirit, convened a council in Jerusalem around the year 49 to decide the matter. After much debate, Peter stood up and said:

My brothers, you are well aware that from early days God made his choice among you that through my mouth the Gentiles would hear the word of the gospel and believe. And God, who knows the heart, bore witness by granting them the holy Spirit just as he did us. He made no distinction between us and them, for by faith he purified their hearts. Why, then, are you now putting God to the test by placing on the shoulders of the disciples a yoke that neither our ancestors nor we have been able to bear? On the contrary, we believe that we are saved through the grace of the Lord Jesus, in the same way as they (15:7-11).

At these words, "the whole assembly fell silent" (15:12). Thus was the supreme authority of Peter recognized in the early Church. The Apostles and presbyters then approved a letter to be sent to the whole Church, which said, among other things, that "it is the decision of the holy Spirit and of us not to place on you any burden beyond these necessities, namely, to abstain from meat sacrificed to idols, from blood, from meats of strangled animals, and from unlawful marriage. If you keep free of these, you will be doing what is right. Farewell." (15:28-29).

The decision of the Council of Jerusalem, which was inspired by the Holy Spirit, brought an end to the covenant of circumcision first promulgated by God in Genesis 17:11. From now on, Paul told the Galatians, "neither circumcision nor uncircumcision counts for anything, but only faith working through love" (Galatians 5:6). He told the Romans the same thing, saying that "God is one and will justify the circumcised on the basis of faith and the uncircumcised through faith" (Romans 3:30).

Paul also said that "true circumcision is not outward, in the flesh. Rather ... circumcision is of the heart, in the spirit, not the letter" (Romans 2:28-29). He declared that "circumcision means nothing, and uncircumcision means nothing; what matters is keeping God's commandments" (1 Corinthians 7:19). And he reminded the Gentiles that they were at one time "without Christ, alienated from the community of Israel and strangers to the covenants of promise, without hope and without God in the world. But now in Christ Jesus you who once were far off have become near by the blood of Christ" (Ephesians 2:12-13).

The Letters of Peter

After the Council of Jerusalem, Peter all but disappears from the pages of the New Testament, except for two letters that bear his name. He offers us much good advice in those letters, saying for example, that we are "living stones" that God wants to build into a "spiritual house" (1 Peter 2:5) and that we should rid ourselves "of all malice and all deceit, insincerity, envy, and all slander" (2:1).

The Apostle warns us to be "sober and vigilant. Your opponent the devil is prowling around like a roaring lion looking for [someone] to devour. Resist him, steadfast in faith, knowing that your fellow believers throughout the world undergo the same sufferings" (1 Peter 5:8-9). He adds, however, that "the God of all grace ... will himself restore, confirm, strengthen, and establish you after you have suffered a little" (5:10).

St. Peter also warns against "false teachers among you, who will introduce destructive heresies and even deny the Master who ransomed them, bringing swift destruction on themselves" (2 Peter 2:1). But despite what happens, he continues, "do not ignore this one fact, beloved, that with the Lord one day is like a thousand years and a thousand years like one day. The Lord does not delay his promise, as some regard 'delay,' but he is patient with you, not wishing that any should perish but that all should come to repentance" (3:8-9).

To help us escape "from the corruption that is in the world because of evil desire," says Peter, we must make "every effort to supplement your faith with virtue, virtue with knowledge, knowledge with self-control, self-control with endurance, endurance with devotion, devotion with mutual affection, mutual affection with love. If these are yours and increase in abundance, they will keep you from being idle or unfruitful in the knowledge of our Lord Jesus Christ .... For, in this way, entry into the eternal kingdom of our Lord and savior Jesus Christ will be richly provided for you" (2 Peter 1:4-11).

WORDS TO REMEMBER

* Christians   * Council of Jerusalem

Paul's vision of the Lord.

Chapter 23

The Early Church: St. Paul

> This I know: God is on my side.
> God, I praise your promise;
> in you I trust, I do not fear.
> What can mere mortals do to me?
> — Psalm 56:10-12

During the French Revolution at the end of the eighteenth century, many Catholic priests were imprisoned and killed. One of the most bloodthirsty foes of the Church, a man who had sworn that if any priest tried to enter his house he would not leave there alive, fell dangerously ill, and a priest was summoned to his bedside. The priest knew who the man was, and that he had a violent hatred for priests, but he went without hesitation to the man's house.

The man in bed was furious when the priest entered his room and he shouted for a gun. "I have strangled twelve such as you with my own hands," he said with a fierce hatred in his eyes. "You are wrong," the priest calmly replied. "You killed only eleven. The twelfth did not die. God kept him alive that he might save your soul. I am the twelfth."

Then the priest opened his cassock at the neck and showed the marks the man's hands had left when he had tried to strangle him. At this manifestation of courage and love, the revolutionist quieted down, expressed sorrow for his many sins, and received absolution from the priest.

There was a man in Damascus in the early years of the Catholic Church who undoubtedly experienced the same anxiety as the priest in France when the Lord told him to go to a house in the city and baptize a fierce persecutor of the Church named Saul. But Lord, said Ananias during his vision, "I have heard from many sources about this man, what evil things he has done to your holy ones in Jerusalem. And here he has authority from the chief priests to imprison all who call upon your name" (Acts 9:13-14).

But the Lord told Ananias to go, "for this man is a chosen instrument of mine to carry my name before Gentiles, kings, and Israelites, and I will show him what he will have to suffer for my name." So Ananias went to the house on Straight Street, laid his hands on the man from Tarsus, and said, "Saul, my brother, the Lord has sent me, Jesus who appeared to you on the way by which you came, that you may regain your sight and be filled with the holy Spirit" (9:15-17).

Something like scales fell from Saul's eyes and he regained his sight. He was then baptized by Ananias, ate food for the first time in three days, and regained his strength.

The Conversion of Saul

Ananias had good reason to fear Saul, for he was a man who had been "breathing murderous threats against the disciples of the Lord" (9:1) and who was on his way to Damascus to arrest and drag back to Jerusalem in chains any men or women who were followers of Christ. But as he neared the city, the persecutor was stunned by a flash of light from the sky. He fell to the ground and heard a voice saying to him, "Saul, Saul, why are you persecuting me?" Saul asked, "Who are you, sir?" The reply came, "I am Jesus, whom you are persecuting. Now get up and go into the city and you will be told what you must do" (9:4-6).

Notice that Jesus did not ask Saul why he was persecuting the early Christians, but rather why he was persecuting Jesus himself. This was another illustration of the principle that the Lord had enunciated in his parable about the final judgment at the end of the world, namely, that whatever one does to the least of the followers of Jesus, they do to him (cf. Matthew 25:40).

The men traveling with Saul heard the voice, but could see no one. They helped their blinded leader to his feet and led him by the hand into Damascus, where he fasted until the arrival of Ananias three days later. Meeting the Lord on the road to Damascus, Paul would write years later, had made him "a slave of Christ Jesus, called to be an apostle and set apart for the gospel of God" (Romans 1:1).

When questions arose later about whether Paul shared the same rank as the Twelve, he asked the Corinthians, "Am I not an apostle? Have I not seen Jesus our Lord?" (1 Corinthians 9:1).

He told the Galatians that he was "an apostle not from human beings nor through a human being but through Jesus Christ and God the Father who raised him from the dead" (Galatians 1:1).

From Saul to Paul

Who was this man who would go from persecutor to promoter of the Church, from Pharisee to apostle? Saul was born in the first decade of the first century in Tarsus, a center of culture and learning. His parents were Jews and citizens of Rome, and they sent their son to Jerusalem to study under a renowned teacher of the law named Gamaliel. This same Gamaliel would advise the Sanhedrin two decades later to have nothing to do with the Apostles, saying that if their religious movement was of human origin, it would destroy itself, but if it was of divine origin, "you will not be able to destroy them; you may even find yourselves fighting against God" (Acts 5:39).

A tentmaker by trade, Saul had a fiery and passionate personality. He became a zealous defender of Jewish beliefs, approved the stoning to death of Stephen (cf. Acts 7:58), rooted out and persecuted Christians wherever he found them, and asked the chief priest in Jerusalem for letters to the synagogues in Damascus so that he would have the authority there to seize any followers of Christ and bring them back in chains to Jerusalem. His conversion took place around A.D. 36.

Not long after his baptism, Saul began proclaiming Jesus as the Son of God in the synagogues of Damascus, astounding all who heard him. "Is not this the man who in Jerusalem ravaged those who call upon this name?" (Acts 9:21), they asked. But Saul confounded his opponents with his arguments proving that Jesus was the Messiah.

Saul left the city and spent three years in Arabia before returning to Damascus and devoting another three years to preaching the gospel of Christ. This time, however, some of his Jewish foes hatched a plot to kill him, and he escaped death at their hands by having his disciples lower him down the outer wall of the city in a basket. He then traveled to Jerusalem, where he spent fifteen days with Peter (Galatians 1:18).

Many of the Christians in Jerusalem were afraid of Paul and doubted the sincerity of his conversion. But Barnabas defended him against all charges and reported how Paul had spoken out boldly in the name of Jesus in Damascus. He preached boldly in

Jerusalem as well and aroused the hatred of Greek-speaking Jews known as Hellenists, who plotted to kill him. When the disciples learned of this plot, they sent Paul first to Caesarea and then on to Tarsus.

Paul's First Journey

Paul had been in Tarsus for several years when Barnabas came to get him and took him to Syrian Antioch, where they began evangelizing that community in which the followers of Christ were called Christians for the first time (cf. Acts 11:26). The two men then set off on a mission that took them first to Cyprus, where Paul converted a Roman proconsul by causing a false prophet named Elymas the magician to go blind after he had tried to keep the proconsul away from the faith (cf. 13:6-12).

They later traveled to Antioch in Pisidia, where Paul delivered a stirring homily that impressed not only many Jews and converts to Judaism, but also many Gentiles, who invited him to speak again on the following sabbath. However, Paul told protesting Jews that since they had rejected the word of God that was first spoken to them, "we now turn to the Gentiles" (13:46). This so infuriated many of the leading Jews that they expelled Paul and Barnabas from the city.

They enjoyed success in Iconium until attempts were made to attack and stone them, so they went on to Lystra, where Paul cured a man who had been crippled from birth. He was dismayed, however, when the excited crowds called him and Barnabas gods who had come down in human form. He and Barnabas shouted at them, "Men, why are you doing this? We are of the same nature as you, human beings. We proclaim to you good news that you should turn from these idols to the living God" (14:15).

But they were unable to stop the crowd from offering sacrifices to them and, when some Jews from Antioch and Iconium arrived and stirred up the people against them, Paul was stoned, dragged outside the city, and left for dead. When the disciples gathered around him, however, he got up and went back into the city. The next day, he and Barnabas began retracing their steps, arriving eventually back in Syrian Antioch.

There they learned of the controversy over whether Gentiles had to be circumcised under Mosaic law before becoming Christians, and they left for Jerusalem seeking an answer to that question, arriving in time to take part in the council there in A.D. 49. Following the council's decision not to burden Gentile converts with the circumcision requirement, Paul and Barnabas were sent back to Antioch, along with Judas and Silas. They brought with them a letter from the council saying that the only requirements for Gentile converts were "to abstain from meat sacrificed to idols, from blood, from meats of strangled animals, and from unlawful marriage" (Acts 15:29).

Paul vs. Peter

The controversy over whether Gentile converts had to observe the Mosaic dietary laws caused a dispute between Paul and Peter, who was also known as Cephas. It seems that Peter, while in Antioch, had been eating with Gentile Christians. But when some Jewish Christians, who were known as Judaizers and who wanted Gentiles to follow Jewish ceremonial laws, came to Antioch from Jerusalem, Peter drew back from the Gentiles and stopped eating with them.

This inconsistency caused Paul to oppose Peter "to his face because he clearly was wrong." He said that other Jews also "acted hypocritically along with him, with the result that even Barnabas was carried away by their hypocrisy. But when I saw that they were not on the right road in line with the truth of the gospel, I said to Cephas in front of all, 'If you, though a Jew, are living like a Gentile and not like a Jew, how can you compel the Gentiles to live like Jews?' " (Galatians 2:11, 13-14).

Modern-day Christians who oppose the idea of papal authority and infallibility often cite this incident as proof that popes can teach error and therefore cannot be infallible. But their argument has no merit. First of all, Peter was not making an infallible statement on a matter of faith and morals. Second, he was not teaching heresy, but rather engaging in behavior that Paul considered to be hypocrisy since Peter himself, at the Council of Jerusalem, had exercised his supreme authority in ruling that Gentiles could enter the Church without undergoing circumcision and observing Jewish dietary laws.

Third, this may not have been hypocrisy on Peter's part at all, but rather a temporary prudential action to keep from offending the visitors from Jerusalem and to head off a major confrontation between the Judaizers and the Gentiles. Perhaps Peter was just trying to keep the peace at a time in the early Church when there were strong proponents on each side of the question.

There is also some irony in Paul's criticism when we see that he engaged in similar "hypocrisy" himself when he had Timothy circumcised "on account of the Jews" in the region of Lystra and Iconium (cf. Acts 16:3). This also was probably more a prudential action than hypocrisy since Paul wanted to avoid needlessly upsetting the Jews of the area whom he was trying to bring into the Church. This action no more undermined Paul's authority to teach in the name of Jesus than Peter's action did to undermine his authority or that of his successors in the papacy.

Paul's Second Journey

After having separated from Barnabas because of a disagreement over whether Mark should accompany them (Paul said no because Mark had abandoned them during their first journey), Paul recruited Silas, and later Timothy and Luke, to accompany him throughout Asia Minor and into Europe. They were imprisoned in Philippi after Paul drove an evil spirit out of a slave girl who had earned a great deal of money for her owners by telling fortunes. The girl had followed Paul for several days, shouting, "These people are slaves of the Most High God, who proclaim to you a way of salvation" (Acts 16:17).

Annoyed because the girl had said that they were proclaiming *a* way of salvation when in fact they were proclaiming Jesus as the *only* way of salvation, Paul commanded the evil spirit to come out of her. The girl's owners, seeing that their source of income was gone, accused Paul and Silas of "advocating customs that are not lawful for us Romans to adopt or practice" (16:21). The magistrates of the city ordered the two disciples to be stripped and beaten and thrown into prison.

Around midnight, when Paul and Silas were praying and singing hymns to God as the other prisoners listened, a severe earthquake shook the jail, opened all the doors, and loosened the chains on the inmates. When the head jailer saw what had happened, he drew his sword to kill himself, thinking that all the prisoners had escaped.

"Do no harm to yourself; we are all here," Paul shouted to him. The man, trembling with fear, led them out of the jail and asked, "What must I do to be saved?" The disciples responded, "Believe in the Lord Jesus and you and your household will be saved." The jailer took them to his house, bathed their wounds, and then he and all his family were baptized (16:28, 30-31).

Note that Paul and Silas baptized all the members of the man's household, presumably including children and even infants. So at this juncture in the early Church, some twenty or so years after the Ascension of the Lord, baptism was not restricted to adults.

When the magistrates tried to release Paul and Silas secretly the next day, Paul refused, saying that they had been beaten publicly and imprisoned, even though they were Roman citizens, and that the magistrates should come to the jail and lead them out publicly. The magistrates were alarmed to learn that the prisoners were Roman citizens, so they came to the jail, led Paul and Silas out, and asked that they leave the city.

The apostles traveled next to Thessalonica, where they attracted many converts among Jews and Greeks alike, but an angry crowd forced them to leave that city and go on to Beroea. They were well received there and were enjoying success in evangelizing until some of their foes from Thessalonica arrived and stirred up the people in Beroea against them, so Paul went to Athens and delivered a major discourse to a large Gentile audience at the Areopagus.

Noting that the city was filled with statues and altars to various deities, even one inscribed "To an Unknown God," Paul praised the Athenians for their religiosity, but told them that they should be worshiping "the God who made the world and all that is in it, the Lord of heaven and earth ... he who gives to everyone life and breath and everything" (17:24-25).

He said that "God has overlooked the times of ignorance, but now he demands that all people everywhere repent because he has established a day on which he will 'judge the world with justice' through a man he has appointed, and he has provided confirmation for all by raising him from the dead" (17:30-31). Some of his listeners scoffed at the idea of resurrection from the dead, but some became believers and others said that they would like to hear more on the subject at another time.

When Paul reached Corinth and lashed out at some Jews who were reviling him for saying that Jesus was the Messiah, the Lord spoke to him in a vision that night. "Do not be afraid," he said to Paul. "Go on speaking, and do not be silent, for I am with you. No one will attack and harm you, for I have many people in this city" (Acts 18:9-10). Paul stayed in Corinth for eighteen months, befriending a husband and wife by the name of Aquila and Priscilla and spreading the word of God to all.

Paul's Third Journey

After having visited Ephesus, Jerusalem, and Syrian Antioch, Paul returned to Ephesus, where he "debated boldly with persuasive arguments about the kingdom of God" (Acts 19:8). So "extraordinary were the mighty deeds God accomplished at the hands of Paul," says Luke's account of the journey, "that when face cloths or aprons that touched his skin were applied to the sick, their diseases left them and the evil spirits came out of them" (19:11-12).

Among other things, Ephesus was noted for its temple of the goddess Artemis, which was one of the seven wonders of the ancient world, and there were in the city many silversmiths who earned their living making miniature silver shrines of the goddess. When they discovered that Paul's sermons were persuading people to abandon the worship of Artemis and to stop buying the miniature shrines, the silversmiths rioted. After the disturbance was over, Paul summoned his disciples and, after giving them words of encouragement, left for Macedonia and Greece.

While visiting Troas, where he broke bread with the disciples on the first day of the week, Paul spoke at great length because he was leaving the next day. It was nearly midnight when a young man in attendance, whose name was Eutychus, fell asleep while sitting on a windowsill and fell three stories to his death. Paul rushed down to Eutychus, threw himself on him, and said, "Don't be alarmed; there is life in him" (20:10). Assured that the young man would be well, Paul returned to the room upstairs, broke bread and ate, and continued talking until daybreak.

On his way back to Jerusalem, Paul delivered a farewell speech at Miletus to which the presbyters from the church in Ephesus had been summoned. Declaring that he did not know what the future held for him, except that "in one city after another the holy Spirit has been warning me that imprisonment and hardships await me" (20:23), the man from Tarsus said that none of his listeners would ever see his face again.

He urged them to keep watch over themselves and over the flock entrusted to them and warned that "after my departure savage wolves will come among you, and they will not spare the flock. And from your own group, men will come forward perverting the truth to draw the disciples away after them. So be vigilant and remember that for three years, night and day, I unceasingly admonished each of you with tears" (20:29-31).

During those years, the apostle said, "these very hands have served my needs and my companions. In every way I have shown you that by hard work of that sort we must help the weak, and keep in mind the words of the Lord Jesus who himself said, 'It is more blessed to give than to receive' " (Acts 20:34-35). This saying of Jesus is not recorded in the Gospels.

Arrival in Jerusalem

Upon reaching Jerusalem, Paul was welcomed back by the brothers there, and he reported to them in detail what God had accomplished among the Gentiles through his ministry. But when he was seen in the Temple a week later, Jews from Asia stirred up the crowd against him, and he was seized and beaten. Roman soldiers broke up the rioting and arrested Paul, but then allowed him to address the Jews of Jerusalem.

The crowd was not swayed by his recounting of how he had been converted on the road to Damascus, and they shouted that Paul should be killed. The Romans took him away and were about to have him whipped when Paul informed them that he was a citizen of Rome. So the soldiers freed him and brought him before the Sanhedrin to find out the reason for the accusations that had been made against him.

When Paul said that he was a Pharisee "on trial for hope in the resurrection of the dead" (23:6), a great uproar ensued between the Pharisees, who believed in resurrection, and the Sadducees, who did not. The Roman commander, afraid that Paul would be torn to pieces, ordered his troops to rescue him. That night, the Lord appeared to Paul and said, "Take courage. For just as you have borne witness to my cause in Jerusalem, so you must also bear witness in Rome" (23:11).

Trials in Caesarea

Learning of a plot to kill Paul, the Romans transferred him at night to Caesarea, where he asked that his case be heard by the governor, whose name was Felix. The apostle summarized his background and his beliefs at a trial before the governor and said that he was innocent of the charges against him. Over the next two years, while Paul remained in custody, Felix and his wife conversed with him often, but no decision about his fate had been made when Felix was replaced by Porcius Festus.

In a trial before Festus, Paul again defended himself, saying that "I have committed no crime either against the Jewish law or against the temple or against Caesar" (Acts 25:8). When Festus asked if he were willing to stand trial again in Jerusalem, Paul appealed to Caesar, and Festus said, "To Caesar you will go" (25:12). However, the governor then referred the case to King Agrippa and his wife Bernice, who were visiting Caesarea, and they arranged for Paul to defend himself once again.

After listening to Paul for some time, Agrippa said, "You will soon persuade me to play the Christian." Paul replied, "I would pray to God that sooner or later not only you but all who listen to me today might become as I am except for these chains." The king then left the audience hall and told his retinue, "This man is doing nothing [at all] that deserves death or imprisonment." He told Festus that "this man could have been set free if he had not appealed to Caesar" (26:28-32).

Arrival in Rome

Paul and some other prisoners boarded a ship bound for Rome, but the ship ran aground during a fierce storm and the passengers spent three months on the island of Malta, where Paul cured many sick persons. After reaching Rome in the spring of A.D. 61, Paul was placed under a mild form of house arrest, and for more than two years he was able to evangelize great numbers of people, mostly Gentiles, because many of the leading Jews of the city were not willing to listen to him. "He received all who came to him," says the final words of the Acts of the Apostles, "and with complete assurance and without hindrance he proclaimed the kingdom of God and taught about the Lord Jesus Christ" (28:30-31).

While Acts does not report on Paul's ultimate fate, there is a tradition that he suffered martyrdom by beheading around A.D. 67 during the reign of the Emperor Nero. How true were his words to Timothy: "I have competed well; I have finished the race; I have kept the faith. From now on the crown of righteousness awaits me" (2 Timothy 4:7-8).

That same crown of righteousness also awaits each one of us if we keep faith in Jesus Christ and finish the race that began with our baptism. St. Paul, pray that we may compete as well as you did and one day enjoy our reward in heaven with you.

Catholic Prayers

Sign of the Cross

In the name of the Father.
and of the Son,
and of the Holy Spirit. Amen.

In nomine Patris
et Filii,
et Spiritus Sancti. Amen.

The Lord's Prayer

Our Father, who art in heaven,
hallowed be thy name;
thy kingdom come,
thy will be done on earth
as it is in heaven.
Give us this day our daily bread,
and forgive us our trespasses
as we forgive those who
trespass against us,
and lead us not into temptation,
but deliver us from evil. Amen.

Pater noster, qui es in caelis,
sanctificetur nomen tuum;
adveniat regnum tuum;
fiat voluntas tua
sicut in caelo, et in terra.
Panem nostrum quotidianum
da nobis hodie,
et dimitte nobis debita nostra,
sicut et nos dimittimus
debitoribus nostris
et ne nos inducas in tentationem
sed libera nos a malo. Amen.

The Hail Mary

Hail Mary, full of grace,
the Lord is with thee,
blessed art thou among women,
and blessed is the fruit
of thy womb, Jesus.
Holy Mary, Mother of God,
pray for us sinners now and
at the hour of our death. Amen.

Ave Maria, gratia plena,
Dominus tecum,
benedicta tu in mulieribus
et benedictus fructus
ventris tui, Iesus.
Sancta Maria, Mater Dei,
ora pro nobis peccatoribus,
nunc et in hora mortis nostrae.
Amen.

Glory Be to the Father

Glory be to the Father,
and to the Son,
and to the Holy Spirit.
As it was in the beginning,
is now, and ever shall be,
world without end. Amen.

Gloria Patri, et Filio,
et Spiritui Sancto.
Sicut erat in principio,
et nunc, et semper,
et in saecula saeculorum.
Amen.

Hail Holy Queen

Hail, holy Queen, mother of mercy, our life, our sweetness, and our hope. To thee do we cry, poor banished children of Eve. To thee do we send up our sighs, mourning and weeping in this vale of tears. Turn then, most gracious advocate, thine eyes of mercy toward us and, after this our exile, show unto us the blessed fruit of thy womb, Jesus. O clement, O loving, O sweet Virgin Mary, pray for us, O holy Mother of God, that we may be made worthy of the promises of Christ. Amen.

Salve, Regina, matermisericordia, vita, dulcedo et spes nostra, salve. Ad te clamamus, exsules filii Evae. Ad te suspiramus, gementes et flentes in hac lacrimarum valle. Eia ergo, advocata nostra illos tuos misericordes oculos ad nos converte et Iesum, benedictum fructum ventris tui, nobis post hoc exilium ostende. O clemens, O pia, O dulcis Virgo Maria. Ora pro nobis, sancta Dei Genetrix. Ut digni efficiamur promissionibus Christi. Amen.

The Apostles' Creed

I believe in God, the Father almighty, creator of heaven and earth. I believe in Jesus Christ, his only Son, our Lord. He was conceived by the power of the Holy Spirit, born of the Virgin Mary, suffered under Pontius Pilate, was crucified, died, and was buried. He descended into hell. On the third day he rose again. He ascended into heaven and is seated at the right hand of the Father. He will come again to judge the living and the dead. I believe in the Holy Spirit, the holy catholic Church, the communion of saints, the forgiveness of sins, the resurrection of the body, and the life everlasting. Amen.

Credo in Deum, Patrem omnipotentem, Creatorem caeli et terrae; et in Iesum Christum, Filium eius unicum, Dominum nostrum, qui conceptus est de Spiritu Sancto, natus ex Maria Virgine, passus sub Pontio Pilato, crucifixus, mortuus, et sepultus. Descendit ad inferos; tertia die resurrexit a mortuis, ascendit ad caelos, sedet ad dexteram Dei, Patris omnipotentis inde venturus est judicare vivos et mortuos. Credo in Spiritum Sanctum, sanctam Ecclesiam Catholicam, sanctorum communionem, remissionem peccatorum, carnis resurrectionem vitam aeternam. Amen.

Glossary

Absolution: An element of the sacrament of Penance whereby a priest pardons someone's sins through power entrusted by the Church.

Almsgiving: Donations given to the poor out of penance or charity.

Analogy of Faith: The coherence of the truths of the faith among themselves and within the whole plan of Revelation.

Angel: A messenger from God who is a created and highly intelligent spirit; angels do not have bodies, but they can take on human form.

Annunciation: The visit of the angel Gabriel to the Virgin Mary to inform her that she was to be the Mother of God (cf. Luke 1:26-38).

Anointing with Oil: A sign that a person is dedicated to God and of the presence of the Holy Spirit; it is an important sacramental sign in Baptism, Confirmation, Holy Orders, and Anointing of the Sick.

Apocrypha: Seven inspired books found in Catholic Bibles (Judith, Tobit, Wisdom, Ecclesiasticus or Sirach, Baruch, and 1 and 2 Maccabees) that some Christians do not consider inspired by God.

Archangel: The only three specifically mentioned in the Bible are Raphael (Tobit 12:11-21), Gabriel (Luke 1:11-20 and 26-38), and Michael (Revelation 12:7-9).

Ark of the Covenant: A small chest covered with gold inside and out that held the two stone tablets with the Commandments written on them, a jar of manna, the staff of Aaron that had flowered, and a copy of the book of the covenant; the ark vanished in 587 B.C. during the Babylonian destruction of the Temple in Jerusalem.

Ascension: The entry of Jesus in his humanity into heaven forty days after he rose from the dead.

Assumption: The dogma that the Blessed Mother was taken up to heaven body and soul at the end of her earthly life.

Beatitudes: Eight blessings given by Jesus that are a blueprint for virtuous living and true happiness (cf. Matthew 5:1-12).

Betrothal: The legal or true marriage of a couple under Jewish law.

Bible: A collection of 73 books (46 in the Old Testament and 27 in the New) that contains the truth of God's revelation.

Birthright: The position of honor in the family given to a first-born son, which accorded him double the share of his father's possessions.

Blasphemy: Any speech, thought, or action involving contempt for God, the Church, or things dedicated to God. Jesus was found guilty of blasphemy because he claimed to be God.

Born again: The act of spiritual rebirth through Baptism with water and the indwelling of the Holy Spirit.

Canaan: The Promised Land across the Jordan River to which God had led the people of Israel; the old name for Palestine.

Canon of Scripture: The Church's complete and official list of the sacred books of the Bible.

Capital Sins: The seven deadly sins (pride, covetousness, envy, anger, gluttony, lust, and sloth) that are at the root of all sins and vices.

Christ: A Greek translation (*Christos*) of the Hebrew word *Messiah*; this title of Jesus means "anointed one."

Circumcision: The rite prescribed by God in Genesis 17:11, which involved cutting off the foreskin of a male as a sign of God's covenant with the people of Israel; it prefigured the rite of Christian initiation in Baptism and was abolished by the Council of Jerusalem in A.D. 49.

Concupiscence: The human inclination toward sin resulting from disordered appetites and desires that stem from original sin.

Confession: Telling one's sins to a priest; another name for the sacrament of Penance/Reconciliation.

Contrition: Sincere sorrow for sin; one of the key elements of the sacrament of Penance/Reconciliation.

Covenant: A solemn agreement between God and human beings involving mutual commitments or guarantees; examples are God's covenants with Noah, Abraham, and Moses, and Jesus' everlasting covenant with humanity that was sealed by his blood shed on the cross.

Dead Sea Scrolls: A collection of 850 manuscripts, written mostly in Hebrew, that was discovered between 1947 and 1956 near the Dead Sea at a place called Qumran. About one-fourth of the manuscripts are from the Old Testament, but none are from the New Testament.

Deposit of Faith: The heritage of faith contained in Sacred Scripture and Tradition, handed on in the Church from the time of the Apostles, from which the Magisterium draws all that it proposes for belief as being divinely revealed.

Divine Pedagogy: God's gradual communication to man by stages of supernatural Revelation that is to culminate in the person and mission of the Incarnate Word, Jesus Christ.

Dogma/Doctrine: The revealed truths and teachings of Christ that are proclaimed by the Church's magisterium (teaching office) and which the faithful are required to believe.

Economy of Salvation: God's revelation and communication of himself to the world in time, particularly in the person and work of Jesus Christ, for the sake of the salvation of all humanity.

Faith: The theological virtue by which we believe in God and accept as true all that he has revealed to us because he cannot deceive us.

Gifts of the Holy Spirit: Imparted at Confirmation, the gifts are wisdom, understanding, knowledge, counsel or right judgment, fortitude or courage, piety or reverence, and fear of the Lord or wonder and awe in God's presence.

Gnostic Gospels: Documents discovered in 1945-1946 in the Egyptian village of Nag Hammadi that were written some 100 to 300 years after Jesus and that portray him not as the God-man of Christianity, but rather as a guru or spiritual master.

Golgotha: A hill outside the city of Jerusalem whose name means "place of the skull" and on which Jesus was executed on Good Friday.

Guardian Angels: Special angels assigned by God to watch over and guide each human being from birth to death (cf. Matthew 18:10).

Grace: A gift of God that gives us a share in his divine life.

Hebrews: The name of the Israelite people descended from Abraham; later called Jews from the province of Judah after the Exile.

Holy Eucharist: The Body, Blood, Soul, and Divinity of Jesus under the appearances of bread and wine; also known as Holy Communion.

Holy of Holies: The innermost sanctuary of the Temple where the Ark of the Covenant was kept and where God was believed to dwell.

Holy Spirit: The third divine Person of the Blessed Trinity, also called the Paraclete, Advocate, and "Spirit of truth," who descended on the Apostles on Pentecost and is at work with the Father and the Son from the beginning to the completion of the plan for our salvation.

"I AM": The name and title of God that he made known to Moses (cf. Exodus 3:14-15) and that Jesus applied to himself (cf. John 8:58).

Immaculate Conception: The dogma defined infallibly in 1854 that says Mary was preserved from original sin, by virtue of the merits of Jesus, from the moment of her conception in the womb of her mother.

Immanuel/Emmanuel: The name given to Jesus which means "God is with us" (cf. Isaiah 7:14 and Matthew 1:23).

Incarnation: When Jesus, the second Person of the Blessed Trinity, came down from heaven and took on human flesh and a human nature to bring about our salvation.

Inerrancy: The attribute of the books of Sacred Scripture whereby they firmly, faithfully, and without error teach the truth which God, for the sake of our salvation, wished to have confided to us through the Bible.

INRI: The inscription fixed above Jesus' head on the cross; in Latin *Iesus Nazarenus Rex Iudaeorum* or "Jesus of Nazareth, King of the Jews."

Inspiration: That special influence that the Holy Spirit exerted on the human authors of the Bible that enabled them to express the truths God wanted expressed while using their own human faculties. Scripture must also be read and interpreted in the light of that same Spirit.

Israel: The name that God first gave to Jacob and then to the chosen Jewish people with whom he established his covenant.

Judaizers: Jewish converts to Christianity who wanted Gentile converts to observe Jewish laws regarding food and circumcision.

Judges: Military leaders provided by God to protect the Israelites from their enemies; examples include Gideon and Samson.

Levirate Law: A law requiring a man to marry his brother's widow if the brother died before they had children (cf. Deuteronomy 25:5).

Literary Forms: The style of writing used by the human authors of the Bible that was best suited at the time they wrote for conveying the truths that God wished to have conveyed; examples include history, biography, poetry, songs, parables, proverbs, allegories, and letters.

Magi: The wise men from the East who followed a star to Bethlehem to pay homage to the newborn Savior.

Magisterium: The living, teaching office of the Church, whose task is to give the faithful an authentic interpretation of the word of God, whether in its written form (Scripture) or in the form of Tradition.

Magnificat: Mary's hymn of praise proclaming the greatness of God (cf. Luke 1:46-55).

Manna: Special bread-like wafers that God sent from heaven to feed the Israelites in the desert; a foreshadowing of the Holy Eucharist.

Melchizedek: The king of Salem, priest of God, and type of Christ as priest of God and king. He offered a sacrifice of bread and wine to celebrate Abram's victory in battle; his offering prefigured the offering of bread and wine by Jesus at the Last Supper and by the priest at Mass.

Messiah: A Hebrew word meaning "anointed" that when translated into Greek (*Christos*) becomes "Christ," the anointed one.

Miracles: Signs or wonders outside nature that can only be explained by the power of God; e.g., healing the sick, raising the dead.

Oil of Catechumens: Oil ordinarily blessed by a bishop and used at Baptism to symbolize a share in the priestly, prophetic, and kingly mission of Christ.

Oil of Chrism: A mixture of olive oil and balsam consecrated by a bishop. It is used at the Baptism of infants, placed on the forehead of a candidate for Confirmation to seal him with the Holy Spirit and strengthen his faith, and used on a candidate for Holy Orders to show his deeper configuration and special consecration to Christ.

Oil of the Sick: Oil ordinarily blessed by a bishop and used by a priest in the Anointing of the Sick to heal spiritually, and sometimes physically, those who are seriously ill or in danger of death.

Onanism: The contraceptive practice of withdrawal during marital relations to prevent conception of a child (cf. Genesis 38:8-10).

Original Sin: The sin by which Adam and Eve, at the instigation of Satan, chose to disobey God and lost the grace of original holiness and justice; their sin brought evil and death into the world, left every human being with a fallen nature, and made necessary the redeeming death of Jesus on the cross.

Parables: Stories or images or comparisons used to teach a spiritual or moral lesson; examples include the Good Shepherd, the Good Samaritan, the Prodigal Son, and the Rich Man and Lazarus.

Paschal Mystery: Christ's work of redemption accomplished principally by his Passion, Death, Resurrection, and Ascension. The paschal mystery is celebrated and made present in the liturgy of the Church, and its saving effects are communicated through the Sacraments, especially the Eucharist.

Passover: The time when God struck down every first-born in Egypt, but passed over the houses of the Israelites who had smeared the blood of a lamb on the doorposts of their houses.

Pentecost: The fiftieth day after Easter when the Holy Spirit descended on the Apostles and gave them the gifts they needed to spread the message of Christ throughout the world.

Pharisees: Religious leaders of Israel, many of whom opposed Jesus out of jealousy or fear that he would bring down the wrath of Rome on their city.

Precepts of the Church: Positive laws decreed by the Church to help the faithful grow in love of God and neighbor (see page 92).

Presentation of Jesus: The dedication of Jesus to God by Mary and Joseph in the Temple in accord with the law of Moses (cf. Luke 2:22-39).

Protoevangelium: The proto- or "first" gospel announced in Genesis 3:15, when God promised to send a Messiah or Redeemer to overcome sin and death.

Providence: The protecting and guiding love of God over all creation as it journeys toward its ultimate perfection.

Purgatory: The state of final purification after death and before entrance into heaven for those who died in God's friendship without being thoroughly cleansed from temporal punishment attached to forgiven sin.

Redemption: The entire life, Passion, Death, Resurrection, and Ascension of Jesus. His whole life is a mystery of redemption.

Resurrection: The bodily rising of Jesus from the dead on Easter which prefigures the bodily resurrection of all the righteous on the last day.

Revelation: God's communication of himself, by which he makes known the mystery of his divine plan, which is realized by deeds and words over time, and most fully by sending us his own divine Son, Jesus Christ.

Rosary: Prayer in honor of the Blessed Virgin Mary which repeats the Our Father, Hail Mary, and Glory Be to the Father while meditating on events in the life of Jesus and his mother.

Sabbath: The day of the week set aside to give worship and praise to God. Christians replaced the Jewish Sabbath on Saturday with the Lord's Day on Sunday.

Sacraments: Seven efficacious signs of grace, instituted by Christ and entrusted to his Church, by which divine life is dispensed to us.

Sadducees: A group of religious leaders at the time of Jesus who disagreed with the Pharisees on such matters as resurrection from the dead, but who joined with them in opposing Jesus.

Samaritans: Residents of the province of Samaria and enemies of the Jews who had broken away from the Temple in Jerusalem four centuries before Christ and built their own temple on Mt. Gerizim.

Sanhedrin: The 71-member national-religious court of Israel before whom Jesus was tried and sentenced to death.

Satisfaction: The penance (prayers or good works) assigned by the priest in Confession and performed by a penitent to atone for his sins.

Senses of Scripture: Four ways or means (literal, allegorical, moral, and anagogical) of helping us to understand what is contained in the Bible in all its richness.

Septuagint: A pre-Christian Greek translation of the 46 Old Testament books that was later adopted by Greek-speaking Christians.

Servant Songs: Passages from chapters 42, 49, 50, 52, and 53 of the Book of Isaiah that foretell the sufferings of Jesus.

Sodomy: Unnatural sexual acts between persons of the same sex that were condemned by God when he destroyed the cities of Sodom and Gomorrah (cf. Genesis 19:1-29) and by St. Paul (cf. Romans 1:24-27).

Son of Man: Title used by Jesus for himself (cf. Mark 14:62) that was first used by Daniel (7:13) and that indicates Christ's messianic mission of bringing salvation to the world.

Torah: A Hebrew word meaning "law" that refers to the first five books of the Bible (Genesis, Exodus, Leviticus, Numbers, Deuteronomy).

Tradition: The transmission of the teachings of Christ and the Apostles, whether expressed in writing or orally, through customs or liturgy, that have been passed down by the Church over the centuries.

Transfiguration: The glorification of Jesus on the mountain in the sight of Peter, James, and John (cf. Luke 9:28-36).

Transubstantiation: The theological term that describes the unique change of the entire substance of the bread into the body of Christ and the entire substance of the wine into the blood of Christ, even though the appearances of bread and wine remain, when the priest pronounces the words of Jesus at Mass ("This is my body .... This is the cup of my blood").

Trinity: The mystery of one God in three divine Persons — God the Father, God the Son, and God the Holy Spirit — that was revealed to us by Jesus, the second Person of the Blessed Trinity.

Typology: The discernment of persons, events, and things in the Old Testament which prefigure or foreshadow persons, events, and things in the New Testament, which is what St. Augustine meant when he said that the New Testament lies hidden in the Old, and the Old Testament is unveiled in the New.

Visitation: Mary's visit to her elderly relative, Elizabeth, who was pregnant with John the Baptist (cf. Luke 1:39-56).

Bibliography

Anderson, Joan Wester. *Where Angels Walk*

Baker, Kenneth, S.J. *Inside the Bible*

Catechism of the Catholic Church
Compendium of the Catechism of the Catholic Church
Currie, David B. *Rapture*

Daniel-Rops, Henri. *Daily Life in the Time of Jesus*
Documents of Vatican II, The. Walter M. Abbott, S.J., Editor
Duggan, Rev. Michael. *The Consuming Fire*

Ellis, Peter F., C.SS.R. *The Men and Message of the Old Testament*

Fuentes, Antonio. *A Guide to the Bible*

General Directory for Catechesis
Goodier, Most Rev. Alban. *The Public Life of Our Lord Jesus Christ*
Graham, Henry G. *Where We Got the Bible*
Gray, Tim. *Mission of the Messiah*
Gruden's Complete Concordance

Hahn, Scott, and Cavins, Jeff. *Our Father's Plan* (Video)

Jenkins, Philip. *Hidden Gospels*
Jerome Biblical Commentary, The
John Paul II, Pope. Mother of the Redeemer (*Redemptoris Mater*)
_____. Redeemer of Man (*Redemptor Hominis*)
_____. Rosary of the Virgin Mary (*Rosarium Virginis Mariae*)
_____. The Splendor of Truth (*Veritatis Splendor*)
_____. *The Theology of the Body*

Kellmeyer, Steve. *Bible Basics*

Leo XIII, Pope. On the Study of Sacred Scripture *(Providentissimus Deus)*

Madrid, Patrick. *Pope Fiction*
_____. *Where Is* That *in the Bible?*
McBride, Alfred, O.Praem. *The Second Coming of Jesus*
_____. *Teen Guide to the Bible*
McKenzie, John L., S.J. *Dictionary of the Bible*
_____. *The Two-Edged Sword*

National Directory for Catechesis
Navarre Bible New Testament, The
New American Bible, The
New Testament, The (From the Original Greek), Joseph Lilly, Editor
New World Dictionary Concordance to the New American Bible

Paul VI, Pope. On Human Life (*Humanae Vitae*)
Pius XII, Pope. Promotion of Biblical Studies (*Divino Afflante Spiritu*)
_____. On the Origins of the Human Race (*Humani Generis*)
Pontifical Biblical Commission. *The Historicity of the Gospels*
_____. *The Interpretation of the Bible in the Church*
_____. *The Jewish People and Their Sacred Scriptures in the Christian Bible*

Ray, Stephen K. *St. John's Gospel*
_____. *Upon This Rock*
Ricciotti, Giuseppe. *The Life of Christ*

Sacred Congregation for Divine Worship. *Christian Faith and Demonology*
Shea, Mark P. *Making Senses Out of Scripture*
Sheed, Frank. *To Know Christ Jesus*
Sheen, Fulton J. *Life of Christ*
Steinmueller, Msgr. John. *The Sword of the Spirit*

Thigpen, Paul. *The Rapture Trap*

Walsh, John Evangelist. *The Bones of St. Peter*

Other Books in This Series

Catholicism & Reason and Leader's/Teacher's Manual
Catholicism & Life and Leader's/Teacher's Manual
Catholicism & Society and Leader's/Teacher's Manual
Catholicism & Ethics and Leader's/Teacher's Manual

These books may be ordered by calling toll-free (877-730-8877), by visiting our website at www.crpublications.com, or by writing to the address below:

C.R. Publications Inc.
345 Prospect St.
Norwood, MA 02062

Index

Aaron, 85, 86, 87, 89, 98-99, 100
Abel and Cain, 23, 48
Abram/Abraham, 25, 51-54, 55-56
Adam and Eve, 23, 32, 40, 42-43, 45-46, 99, 181, 240, 250
Amos, 30, 154
Angels, 32, 54, 55, 59, 63, 71-82, 88, 111, 113, 179, 182, 210,
    212, 213, 220, 244, 247, 250, 258, 261
Annunciation, 210-211
Anointing, 131-132, 135; of the sick, 206
Ark of the Covenant, 97, 106-107, 135, 141, 142
Assumption of Mary, 223, 249-251
Augustine, St., 16, 17, 201, 213

Babel, Tower of, 24, 49-50, 249
Barak, 110-111
Barnabas, 267, 268, 269, 270
Beatitudes, 91-92, 201-202
Benjamin, 68-69, 116
Blessed Virgin Mary, 23, 32, 47, 52, 56, 77, 122, 157; Annunciation, 210-
    211; Assumption, 249-251; birth of Jesus, 213-215; at Calvary, 239;
    crowning as Queen of Heaven, 251; ever-Virgin, 212-213; finding Je-
    sus in Temple, 216-218; "New Eve," 210-211, 223, 251; presenta-tion of
    Jesus in Temple, 215-216; seven sorrows of, 216; visitation to Eliza-
    beth, 211-212; wedding at Cana, 222-224
Bronze serpent, 101, 238

Caiaphas, 187-188, 197, 233-234
Cana, wedding at, 222-224
Capital sins, 45
Catechism of the Catholic Church, 14, 16, 40, 50, 54, 72, 77, 157,
    204-205, 217, 221, 222, 223, 226
Catholic Church, 35, 92, 143, 203
Circumcision, 25, 53, 215, 262-263, 268-269
Confession of sins, 102, 156, 205, 246
Council of Jerusalem, 53, 262-263, 268-269
Covenant, 24, 25, 27, 49, 53, 90-91, 96-97, 109, 136, 165-166
Creation, 41-43

Daniel, 31, 179-180, 197
David, 29, 97, 133-138, 251
Deborah, 110-111

Eleazar, 122-123, 177
Elijah, 150-153, 184, 226, 250

Elisha, 152, 153-154
Elizabeth, 76, 122, 210, 211, 220
Esau, 25-26, 57-59, 63-64
Esther, 119-120
Exodus, the, 87-88
Ezekiel, 31, 161, 166-170
Ezra, 172-173

Gabriel the Archangel, 76-77, 210
Gamaliel, 258-259, 267
Gideon, 111-112
Gifts of Holy Spirit, 132, 144-145
Golden calf, 27, 98-99
Guardian angels, 73, 80

Hannah, 129-130
Hell, 204
Herod the Great, 32, 185, 214, 216
Herodias, 186-187, 222
Holy Eucharist, 27, 124, 205, 227-230, 241
Holy Spirit, 16, 35, 97, 203, 211, 221, 242, 248-249, 262, 263, 278-279
Homosexuality, 54
Hosea, 30-31, 154-155

"I AM," 85, 197, 198
Immaculate Conception, 47, 211, 223, 250
Immanuel/Emmanuel, 157, 212
Incarnation, 210
Isaac, 25-26, 55, 56-59
Isaiah, 31, 156-159, 212, 220, 225, 235

Jacob (Israel), 25-26, 57-60, 61-65, 68-70, 116
Jeremiah, 31, 59, 147, 161, 162-166, 214
Jesus, 23, 24, 25, 27, 29, 31, 40, 41, 42, 45, 47, 52, 55, 56, 77, 107,
    110, 116, 117, 135, 138, 144, 153, 155, 162, 231, 259, 271, 273;
    agony in garden, 232-233; angels in his life, 79-81; Ascension into
    heaven, 247-248; awareness of his divine mission, 217-218; bap-
    tism in Jordan, 220-222; on baptism, 124, 205, 247; Beatitudes,
    91-92, 201; birth in Bethlehem, 213-215; Bread of Life, 206, 228;
    on bronze serpent, 101, 238; "brothers and sisters," 212-213;
    Cana miracle, 222-224; carrying of cross, 236-237; claim to be
    God, 196-198; commandments, 93, 200; conversion of Saul, 266;
    covenant in blood, 96-97, 229; crowning with thorns, 235-236;
    crucifixion, 237-241; on Elijah, 152; finding in the Temple, 216-
    218; good man or God, 197-198; Good Shepherd, 168, 204; hard
    sayings, 200-201; on hell, 204; on Holy Eucharist, 205, 227-230;

human testimony about him, 195-196; on hypocrisy, 62; "I AM," 85, 234; on Jeremiah, 164-165; on Judas, 190-191, 232-233; on judging others, 167; on Judgment Day, 204; on the kingdom, 224-226; the Lamb of God, 221; on marriage, 44, 206; and Mary Magdalene, 126-127, 245; his miracles, 198-199, 228; his moral code, 33, 200; and Nicodemus, 124; his parables, 224-225; Passover meal, 87; on Penance/Reconciliation, 102, 205, 246; and Peter, 254-255; and Pilate, 189-190, 234-235; prefigured by Moses, 83; presentation in Temple, 215-216; promise of our resurrection, 169, 204; prophecies about him, 198; his Resurrection, 244-247; and Samaritan woman, 196; his scourging, 235; his Second Coming, 80; Sermon on the Mount, 200; Sermon on the Plain, 201-202; and Solomon, 142; Son of Man, 180, 238, 244; source of life, 204-205; his sufferings, 158-159, 232-241; summary of his life, 32-35, 194-207; take up your cross, 123; on the Temple, 143; temptations by Satan, 181-182; and Thomas, 125-126, 199, 246; his Transfiguration, 226-227; trial before Sanhedrin, 187-188, 233-234; truths he taught, 203-204
John the Apostle, 82, 226, 232, 239, 245, 256, 257
John the Baptist, 33, 76, 186-187, 195, 211, 220-222
John Paul II, Pope, 43, 56, 164, 183, 218, 219-220, 231
Joseph (of Egypt), 26, 65-70, 116
Joseph, St., 210, 212, 215
Joshua, 28, 90, 101, 103, 106-109
Judas Iscariot, 182, 190-192, 232-233, 248
Judges, 28, 110-114
Judith, 120-122

Kings of Israel, 131, 135, 138, 146

Last Supper, 96-97
Leo XIII, Pope, 14, 15, 77-78

Maccabees, the, 174-178
Magi, the, 32, 156, 186, 214
Magnificat, the, 211-212
Mary Magdalene, 126-127, 239, 241, 244, 245
Mass, Holy Sacrifice of, 87, 97
Melchizedek, 52, 135
Micah, 31, 155-156
Michael the Archangel, 77-78
Moses, 27-28, 83-93, 96-104, 144, 226, 238

Nathan, 135, 136-137, 138
Nehemiah, 172, 173-174
Nicodemus, 124-125, 205
Noah, 23-24, 48-49

Original Sin, 23, 40, 45-48, 99, 250

Passover, the, 27, 86-88
Paul, St., 7, 179, 181, 183, 202, 207, 215, 234, 253, 260, 265-274
Paul VI, Pope, 183, 251
Penance, Sacrament of, 102, 156, 205, 246
Pentecost, 248-249
Peter, St., 8, 24, 35, 81, 183, 191, 195, 203, 205, 226, 229, 232-233, 245, 248, 249, 253-264, 269-270
Pilate, Pontius, 188-190, 202, 226, 234-235, 236, 238, 241, 244
Pius XII, Pope, 9, 14-15, 39-40, 159, 250-251
Precepts of the Church, 92
Prophets, the, 150-159, 161-170
Purgatory, 178-179

Raphael the Archangel, 75-76
Resurrection of the body, 227
Reuben, 65, 68-69
Rosary, the, 219-220
Ruth, 118-119

Sacraments, the, 204-205
Samaritan woman, the, 196
Samson, 113-114, 220
Samuel, 29, 129-134, 220
Sanhedrin, the, 187-188, 256-257, 257-258, 260, 273
Satan, 23, 33, 45-46, 77, 81, 181-183, 223, 225, 232, 254, 263
Saul, King, 29, 131-135
Servant Songs, 158-159
Simeon, 215-216
Sin, 23, 40, 45-48
Solomon, King, 29, 137, 138, 139-143, 144, 251
Stephen, St., 260

Temple, the, 142-143, 169-170, 172-176, 185
Ten Commandments, 27, 91
Thomas, St., 125-126, 199, 246
Tobiah and Tobit, 74-76, 117-118
Transfiguration, 27, 99, 226-227, 257
Trinity, Blessed, 10, 203, 221

Vatican Council II, 7, 8, 9, 11, 12, 16-17, 230
Visitation, the, 211-213

Zechariah, 76, 220